Take Back
Your Government

Take Back
Your Government

A Citizen's Guide to Grassroots Change

Morgan Carroll

FULCRUM
GOLDEN, COLORADO

Library of Congress Cataloging-in-Publication Data
Carroll, Morgan.
  Take back your government : a citizen's guide to grassroots change / Morgan Carroll.
     p. cm.
  Includes bibliographical references and index.
  ISBN 978-1-55591-445-5 (pbk.)
1. Public administration--United States--States- -Citizen participation--Handbooks, manuals, etc. 2. State governments--United States--Citizen participation--Handbooks, manuals, etc. 3. Legislation--United States--States--Handbooks, manuals, etc. 4. Political participation--United States--States--Handbooks, manuals, etc. I. Title.
  JK2443.C38 2012
  322.40973--dc23
                                2011042044

Printed in the United States
0 9 8 7 6 5 4 3 2 1

Design by Jack Lenzo

Fulcrum Publishing
4690 Table Mountain Dr., Ste. 100
Golden, CO 80403
800-992-2908 • 303-277-1623
www.fulcrumbooks.com

Contents

Part One: Why You *Must* Get Involved

Part Two: Advocacy for Beginners

Part Three: Intermediate Advocacy

Part Four: Beyond Legislation

Part One

Why You Must Get Involved

Chapter 1
You Can Do This

*The most common way people give up their power
is by thinking they don't have any.*
—Alice Walker

Government in a free **democracy** is us—all of us. It reflects the goals and values of those who participate and the absence of the goals and values of those who don't. When we are dissatisfied with any aspect of how government works, it's easy to disengage and give up, but doing so only ensures we'll be governed by narrow, well-funded special interests rather than broad public interests.

Everybody cares about something or someone. Everyone has some idea of what they would like to see improved in their community. Anyone can make a difference, but many people don't realize it or don't know how to go about it.

We elect people to represent our interests, but our elected officials cannot adequately represent *you* unless they hear from you. Without your input, representation is, at best, a guess and, at worst, a personal agenda.

If you have ever wanted the best education for your children,

a good-paying job with dignity, affordable access to higher education, fair access to the courts, to retire comfortably, to get affordable high-quality healthcare, to see increased efficiency in government spending and services, paved roads, reduced traffic jams, family farms and ranches to thrive, to grow a successful business, to protect your rights, safer communities, to increase prosperity and reduce poverty, every child to have an equal and great opportunity to succeed, to protect our environmental resources, to see scientific advances, then you're qualified to speak up. If you believe society can and should be improved in any way, then you should be involved.

If you don't participate in your government, then the only remaining participants in the system are **legislators** and **lobbyists**. A legislator is a representative we elect to make our laws, and a lobbyist is a person who specializes in advocacy, paid to promote the interests of an organization or interest group, usually by influencing legislators on particular issues. Even if you add up all lobbyists and their organizations, not all people, interests, or issues are represented. In fact, there are gaping holes where significant segments of the population or critical issues go unrepresented entirely.

In most states, lobbyists dramatically outnumber legislators, and in some

3

states, elected officials are restricted by **term limits**, but lobbyists are not. This has shifted the institutional power to unelected lobbyists and staff and away from representatives elected by the people. Lobbyists, as you'll see, exert a significant amount of power over legislators and the lawmaking process.

When there's a vacuum of public input, lobbyists usually fill it. But when there's public input, the people usually win.

While it is clearly the responsibility of your elected officials to filter what they

hear from lobbyists and to prioritize input they get from their districts, silence from **constituents** (that's you!) increases the odds that the **lobby corps** will prevail. This is not the version of democracy that our Founding Fathers envisioned.

That's where you come in. *You* are the only real **check and balance** to the power of the lobby corps or **special interests** at the capitol. Democracy only works when citizens participate, engage, and become informed voters. Yet voting is only one of many citizens' rights and responsibilities. The truth is that legislators don't hear from very many constituents on most bills. Out of 800 bills, only 20 of them might get constituent input.

But there's good news: it's easier to participate than you may think. *You can make and change law now. You don't need to be elected or have a law degree. You don't need money, nor do you need experience. You can learn as you go. You can choose how much time you want to dedicate and how many issues you wish to pursue. Everybody can participate, and any participation improves the system as a whole.*

During my time serving at the Colorado state Capitol, I've watched ordinary men and women make and change law for the better in Colorado. I've also watched important bills die for lack of public participation and horrible bills pass for lack of public scrutiny. You truly are the most powerful player in our entire democratic process.

Sometimes the best dose of common sense for elected officials are the words of wisdom from the real experts—you. Everyone is an expert on something, whether your expertise is the result of your education, your work, or your life.

If you care about anything, get involved. Your participation changes priorities, votes, and outcomes. Your participation changes law, culture, society, and reality for the better.

History is made by those who show up.
—Prime Minister Benjamin Disraeli

Chapter 2
You Need to Do This

...that government of the people, by the people,
for the people, shall not perish from this earth.
—Abraham Lincoln

The **right to petition** your government for redress is found in the **First Amendment** of the US Constitution. The **framers** of our constitution intended for *you* to have the right, and indeed the responsibility, to participate in your own government. So where do lobbyists fit in?

The United States is set up to function as a **representative democracy** and a **republic**, as opposed to a monarchy (hereditary rule) or a **dictatorship**. The key difference is whether or not you have or exercise the right to participate in your own government.

Apathy and representative democracy are antithetical to one another. In order for your elected officials to represent you, they need to hear from you. If you have ever found yourself exasperated by the actions or inaction of government but have not taken the time to call, write, or e-mail your elected officials, ask yourself why not. Because if you don't, lobbyists will.

A **lobbyist** advocates in the legislative process, promoting the interests of an organization or interest group. There are five types of lobbyists:

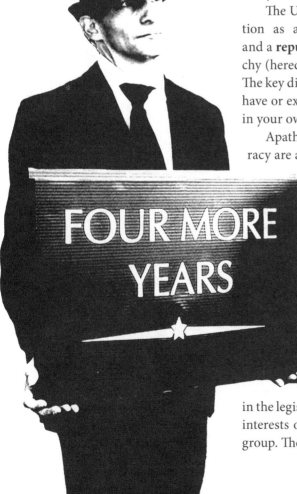

- **Professional captive lobbyist**—A person paid to promote the agenda and policy interests of one organization
- **Contract lobbyist**—A person paid to promote the agenda and policy interests of multiple organizations, which can sometimes conflict
- **Government lobbyist or legislative liaison**—A person paid to promote the interests of different departments or levels of government to other levels of government
- **Volunteer lobbyist**—A person who advocates on behalf of a specific group but is not paid to do so
- **Citizen lobbyist**—A person who exercises his or her rights and responsibilities in a representative democracy to advocate for his or her own policy interests and vision of how to improve a community

So what's wrong with relying on paid lobbyists? While they can sometimes have relevant and accurate information to contribute to the process, there are a few problems with deferring to professional paid lobbyists to represent your interests.

Affordability. Not all people or groups can afford to hire a lobbyist to represent their interests. In fact, most people can't. Therefore, the paid lobby corps disproportionately represents the interests of wealthy industries or individuals. The average salary of a

5

lobbyist is $100,000, but the pay can range from $50,000 to more than $1 million per year.

Disagreement. Chances are high that you will disagree with some or even most of the ideas for which lobbyists advocate. Even if you're part of a professional trade association or an issue group that hires a lobbyist, you may be surprised at what they are pursuing—in your name.

Holes in priorities. Not all interests or segments of society have paid advocacy. For example, there really isn't a homeowners' lobby, a patients' lobby, a tenants' lobby, or a students' lobby in most states. Many interests go utterly unrepresented. There is a very high probability that some or all of what you care about will not be represented unless you speak up.

Skewed priorities. Because it is expensive to hire a lobbyist, there are certain groups and interests that are proportionately overrepresented by the paid lobby corps. There is an incredible amount of lobbyists representing insurance companies, the pharmaceutical industry, developers, oil and gas, and the financial services sector. Chain corporate interests are visibly present, whereas small and local business are less so. Consumers, employees, average families, low-to-middle-income people, or those living on the margins have almost no representation through the lobby corps at all.

The presence and influence of paid lobbyists has been increasing. While more than one person has probably considered attempts to ban them, the reality is that they have a First Amendment right to do what they do. According to the Center for Responsive Politics, the number of lobbyists has increased from 10,404 in 1998 to 12,951 in 2010. The amount of money spent on lobbyists has also gone up from $1.44 billion in 1998 to $3.51 billion in 2010.

Top Spenders on Lobbying (by Organization) 1998–2011
Reproduced with permission from the Center for Responsive Politics

US Chamber of Commerce	$755,875,680
American Medical Association	$247,647,500
General Electric	$245,660,000
AARP	$202,752,064
Pharmaceutical Research & Manufacturers of America	$199,713,920
American Hospital Association	$198,887,055
Blue Cross/Blue Shield	$164,875,795
Northrop Grumman	$161,865,253
Exxon Mobil	$159,702,742
National Association of Realtors	$158,997,380
Verizon Communications	$153,709,841
Edison Electric Institute	$150,775,999
Business Roundtable	$145,404,000
Boeing Co.	$143,474,310
Lockheed Martin	$138,430,053
Southern Co.	$122,010,694
AT&T Inc.	$121,599,336
General Motors	$119,959,170
PG&E Corp.	$118,520,000
Pfizer Inc.	$111,157,268

Top Spenders on Lobbying (by Industry) 1998–2011

Pharmaceuticals/Health Products	$2,145,641,331
Insurance	$1,540,185,356
Electric Utilities	$1,451,888,787
Business Associations	$1,205,257,671
Computers/Internet	$1,171,271,871
Oil & Gas	$1,114,552,107
Misc. Manufacturing & Distributing	$979,883,531
Education	$976,696,415
Hospitals/Nursing Homes	$922,059,253
Civil Servants/Public Officials	$887,960,846
Real Estate	$868,526,833
TV/Movies/Music	$848,543,297
Securities & Investment	$823,743,174
Health Professionals	$817,954,884
Air Transport	$774,506,906
Misc. Issues	$693,426,834
Automotive	$649,430,697
Telephone Utilities	$635,693,666
Telecom Services & Equipment	$618,694,295
Defense Aerospace	$561,365,151

The good news is that when citizens get involved, they often can and do win. The bad news is that when the public doesn't get involved, the majority of paid lobby interests tend to get their way. If you do nothing, the top spenders dominate the representation.

According to the Center for Public Integrity, lobbyists outnumber legislators 5 to 1 nationally. The state with the highest ratio of lobbyists to legislators is New York (24:1), followed by Florida and Illinois (12:1). The states with the lowest ratio of lobbyists are Maine, New Hampshire, Rhode Island, Pennsylvania, and North Dakota (1:1). Colorado has a ratio of 6:1.

At first blush it may appear that the reason lobbyists have so much influence is simply because they are wealthy and give a lot of money to candidates, but it is more complicated than a simple **quid pro quo** of cash for votes—which is, of course, illegal.

In order to understand why you are so important in the system, it is helpful to illustrate how, in my experience, lobbyists affect legislators.

Lobbyist Roles That Exert Influence

- **The Mentor.** Trying to learn the ropes immediately after election can be a daunting task. Term limits have meant a higher turnover of elected officials, but lobbyists aren't term limited. While there is training available for new legislators, there will always be a steep learning curve. Lobbyists are wise to this, and helping new legislators learn the ropes can be one of their methods of influence.
- **The Information Resource.** No one elected to any office can know everything about everything. Lobbyists will offer to "explain" the bill, the problem, or how something works and will, of course, explain it in such a way that benefits their client, while often trying to present information as neutral.

- **The Drafter.** Some legislators don't know what bills they want to carry or how to draft them. And while there's a professional drafting office, lobbyists have learned how to fill a vacuum of ideas or solutions by identifying bills their clients want carried and "shopping" for a legislator to carry them. Legislators will sometimes give permission for lobbyists to draft the bill with the drafter. If a legislator carries a lobbyist's bill, they have the promise of someone else doing most of the work in drafting and passing the bill. If a legislator carries their own bill, he or she is usually on their own and faces greater uphill challenges to its passage.
- **The Ally.** When a legislator does have his or her own ideas and is passionate about seeking reforms, a lobbyist might have a client who agrees with the legislator and might be willing to support a measure. A good lobbyist will often search for a legislator they can help with one of their bills, which helps store some goodwill for when they will be opposing others in the future.
- **The Gossip.** The currency of the professional lobby corps is information. Because many spend all of their time at the capitol, they network with others, overhear conversations, and can pass on tips to help the people they support or to undermine those they oppose. Lobbyists can exert subtle influence by being the bearer not just of news, but also of gossip, which may pertain to other legislators or other bills.
- **The Friend.** Some lobbyists rely more on the strength of their relationships with legislators than the strength of their facts or the virtues of their client or policy. This can create some strange votes. People who spend a lot of time together become more alike over time, which is why legislators can get out of touch. If you spend all of your time with the same people, you are more likely to develop a shared worldview.

You Need to Do This 7

Many lobbyists rely on dinners, receptions, gifts, and personal outings to build rapport with legislators. Studies show that most people (in any profession) don't think these gifts affect *them,* but they do think it affects *others.*[*] It's not that a ten-dollar meal directly buys a person's conscience, but research supports the proposition that all human beings are more *receptive* to a given message over a meal. They may seem small taken individually, but these gifting practices add up to staggering expenditures, and if they didn't have any impact, why would lobbyists do it?

- **The Flatterer.** It's true that you catch more flies with honey than vinegar, and a good lobbyist will have spent time studying each legislator's background, hobbies, interests, and skills. Flattery is a time-tested form of persuasion that often works. And let's face it, there's a healthy presence of egos to flatter.

- **The Bully.** Veiled threats are rare and delicate business. Legislators may find some lobbyists suggesting that certain votes would not be good for their reelection or could cost an endorsement. I had one lobbyist tell a reporter that if I didn't reverse my position of refusing to take lobbyist cards—which requires I leave the floor in the middle of voting to speak with lobbyists—that I would never see another dime from anyone and wouldn't get reelected.

In addition to playing all or some of these roles, lobbyists are also able to exert influence because of a variety of imbalances.

- **Staffing shortages.** For example, Colorado legislators have only one part-time aide for less than half of the year to help serve 77,000–143,000 constituents (depending on whether they are in the House or the Senate). Lobbyists, on the other hand, typically serve one to ten clients and have full-time support staff.

- **Volume differences.** Legislators in Colorado typically read and handle about 800 bills per session. Lobbyists typically work on one to five bills per session. (This varies greatly by state. Colorado limits by rule the number of bills each legislator can introduce to five bills. Some states have higher limits or no limits at all. I've heard that states that don't have Colorado's five-bill limit can see as many as 5,000 bills per session.)

- **Time differences.** Many state legislators work other jobs outside the legislature, whereas most lobbyists have a single full-time job—lobbying. Legislators split their time between research, promoting bills, reading bills, considering amendments, participating in town hall meetings, serving constituents' needs, attending community events, and providing community outreach. Lobbyists generally split their time between advocating for their few bills and interacting with their client(s).

These time and staffing shortages create a power imbalance, even if unintentional, between a legislator and a lobbyist. Lobbyists can exert influence by offering to do things that save a legislator time, such as "summarizing" the bill or helping with constituent needs.

So, you can see why it would be easy for someone to be disillusioned

Barbara Bush is both a wife and a mother to a former president. You probably already knew that. but did you know her maiden name was Pierce? Barbara is a distant cousin of Franklin Pierce. the fourteenth president of the United States. So that makes Barbara Bush the only person who is a mother. wife. and. cousin to a former president.

Did You Know...?

*[*] M. A. Steinman, M. G. Shlipak, and S. J. McPhee, "Of principles and pens: Attitudes and practices of medicine housestaff toward pharmaceutical industry promotions," *The American Journal of Medicine* 110, no. 7 (May 2001) 551–557; and F. S. Sierles et al., "Medical students' exposure to and attitudes about drug company interactions: A national survey," *JAMA* 294, no. 9 (2005):1032–42.

and give up on the whole process, right? It can be enough to make a lot of people angry—and who can blame them?

When I was first elected to the Colorado House in 2004, no one told me about lobbyists. I had reached out to my district, obsessed over my policy priorities, and thought I was elected to try to pursue those reforms. I was overwhelmed by the number of lobbyists who wanted to meet with me and wanted me to carry "their" bills.

During **floor debates** (second reading of the bill), lobbyists would send in their business cards, followed by a long-honored tradition of the elected official dutifully getting up out of his or her chair and leaving in the middle of debating and voting to go get lobbied on something. Now imagine hundreds of lobbyists doing this to each legislator every day. This practice has meant that a majority of legislators may not even be present during this crucial phase, and the long arm of the lobby can be felt all the way through voting. Colleagues would miss votes and critical amendments, or they'd cast their vote one way only to realize (sometimes) they had meant to vote the other way. It doesn't take a purist to realize that this isn't the way to make sound law that impacts millions of people.

Originally, like all of my other colleagues (of both parties), I would leave the floor and try to go speak to these lobbyists. I quickly learned I couldn't do it. Within two weeks, I made a policy for myself that I would not leave the floor during votes or debate to talk to a lobbyist. Doing proper floor work commanded all of my attention. After all, if I wouldn't leave during a vote for a constituent, why would I do it for a lobbyist?

I asked our sergeants at arms to add a permanent sign in the lobby outside of the chambers: NO LOBBYIST CARDS. —M. CARROLL.

What I didn't realize was what kind of hysteria that would create. The lobby corps was collectively outraged. They said I was arrogant for refusing to meet with them during votes and questioned how I would ever expect to get anything done at the capitol. They approached me. They approached my leadership. My leadership approached me. Colleagues asked me to reconsider. I thought about it again and came to the same conclusion. No cards.

Given the scandal I created the first year, I had lots of inquiring minds wanting to know if I'd reverse my position by the second year. I didn't. And I was told I would be unable to raise any money and would never get reelected. I didn't know if they were right or not, but I decided I would rather lose an election than give in on this point. It became more than a pragmatic need for me to focus on legislation; to me, it became highly symbolic of the power struggle between elected officials and lobbyists and, more importantly, between the public and special interests generally. Which side ultimately wins is up to you.

Their predictions (or threats) were unrealized, and I was reelected in 2006 by an even greater margin (62 percent) by my district as they learned about my stance with lobbyists, and again in 2008 for the Colorado State Senate with 69 percent of the vote. My stance is still the same—no lobbyist cards.

But the battle over refusing lobbyist cards was by no means the only evidence of their collective power **under the dome**. In an effort to give injured workers a right to choose

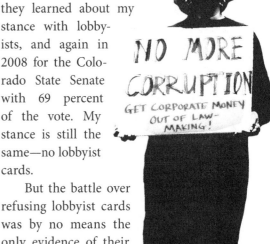

or change their physician (a right given to people on private health insurance, Medicaid, Medicare, and even to your pets), I quickly learned how powerful the lobby was. While 87 percent of people outside the capitol think choosing a physician is a basic human right, the proposition became one of the most controversial bills at the capitol, triggering millions of dollars in spending in opposition and at least 240 lobbyists working against the measure.

It worked something like this: The insurance lobby mobilized because they feared a loss of control that might impact their profits. They mobilized the business lobby by telling them this would raise rates (though rates actually went down), and the self-insured lobby mobilized the higher-education lobby and school district lobby and told them they would have to take teachers out of the classroom if you gave injured workers their choice of doctors. The insurance lobby went to the nonprofits and told them that they would face rate increases that would jeopardize their core mission if injured workers could choose doctors. The business community told leadership that if they did not defeat this bill, they wouldn't be in a good position to work with them on other matters. The insurance lobby hired high-profile former elected officials on both sides of the aisle to add a little extra star power to the defeat effort.

Injured workers had no lobby. They didn't even know about the bill. So they lost.

After this defeat, it took us three years to get minimal reforms passed granting a limited right to choose and change physicians. But it happened. It happened because ordinary citizens got involved—that was the difference.

Over the three-year effort and with increased press coverage, hundreds of injured workers heard about the effort, contacted me, testified, wrote letters, made phone calls, and educated their legislators throughout the state about how their care and treatment was harmed by the inability to have any say in the selection of their physician. They met Ron, who was sent back to work for two years with a broken back because the workers comp insurance doctor failed to do an MRI. They met Lester, a business owner whose leg was amputated as a result of a work injury and fought his insurance company for years for a prosthetic. They met Vivian, who would not be in a wheelchair if she had been given proper medical care in the first place.

As an **idealist** and **populist**, passionate about the importance of a functioning democracy, I was heartbroken over much of what I saw and almost didn't run again. But instead, I decided that this was even more reason to return—to fight for reforms. After all, if I folded, they'd win by default.

My response was to run **legislation** for lobbying reform—giving the public access to know who every lobbyist is, who they work for, how much they're paid, and who's working for or against each bill in the legislature. I also joined an effort to add several other ethics and conflict-of-interest reforms to help Colorado lead in best practices in lobbying activities. My bigger response has been to proselytize about the need for and power of public input, the need for people to reclaim their government, and the need for government to be a "we" instead of an "it" if we are to honor the heritage of our American democracy.

So while it's easy to become disappointed, cynical, or apathetic, that response simply ensures the victory for special interests with lobbyists and, more critically, the weakening of our democracy. There are two reasons this should catapult you into action rather than retreat.

First, when citizens participate, they often win, even when outnumbered and outspent by lobbyists. No one ever gets their way 100 percent of the time, but in my experience at the Colorado General Assembly, when people engage, they can often defeat even the most powerful paid lobby.

Second, if you don't participate, we hand our democracy over to paid special interest groups who, without your input, get their way most of the time. If you fold, they win by default.

So how can you become a citizen lobbyist? It's easy. In the chapters ahead, you'll find everything you need to be an effective advocate and make government work for *you*, not special interests. The only way to fail is to not try.

Why does your participation work?

You're different. Generally, when a member of the public testifies, calls, or writes, it gets noticed. We don't get any general public input on the majority of bills. When we do, it gets cataloged and included in notes for bills. Your contact may be the only one an official gets. Your representative may be undecided, or persuaded by what you say. Your contact may make the difference in how your representative votes.

You're authentic. When someone takes time out of their busy day, without pay, to talk about an issue, it's usually because of a genuine interest and a real need for change. The fact that you aren't manipulating the system to serve a particular interest group, and that you aren't paid to say what you do, will give your input more weight.

The *real* expert is you. Because of your life experiences, your work, your education, and your training, you're the real expert. You can often share real-world stories that reveal the importance of the issue.

You have common sense. Sometimes debates can become obscure and fly off the rails. The power of a citizen lobbyist is often to cut to the chase and expose what really matters (and what's absurd), and bring some much-needed common sense to the discussion.

You care. Because you're not simply being paid to regurgitate talking points, your presence says you care. Your passion says you care. Legislators are people too and are most moved by real people telling real stories and reminding them why they're all there.

You vote. You have the power to help hire and fire your elected officials. If your representatives know you vote and know you're active (i.e., you'll tell others), they'll respect the need to carefully consider your input or face the consequences.

One person can make a difference and everyone should try.
—John H. Kennedy

Part Two

Advocacy for Beginners

Chapter 3
Asking for Help— Constituent Services

[It is] the people, to whom all authority belongs.
—Thomas Jefferson

Your elected officials work for you— and if they don't, you should fire them. If you aren't entirely sure who can help you with what, start by contacting an elected official who represents you, and they can either help you or direct you to someone who can.

Issues an Elected Official Can Help You With

- **Dealing with agencies or departments** (unemployment, licensing, permitting). This can be addressing waiting lists, denials, quality of customer service, or identifying rules or procedures that don't makes sense or are unduly cumbersome.
- **Cutting through red tape** (correcting errors, long delays). Sometimes it's helpful to go straight to the top. If you find yourself spinning your wheels trying to get an answer, a decision, or a result, your legislator can often contact a director-level person and ask them to look into it and cut through any red tape.
- **Reaching out to other elected officials** (helping connect you). Take advantage of the networking done by your elected officials. While your issue may be at another level of government (city, county, federal, school board, special district, homeowner association), your elected official can often reach out on your behalf to help you get prompt attention from other elected officials.

- **Identifying community resources**. Because legislators work with many different community groups, they may be aware of community resources that can be very helpful. This can include foreclosure and mortgage restructuring, advocacy organizations, nonprofits, debt-counseling organizations, and social justice or rights-based organizations.
- **Creating or changing the law**. Finally, your journey may point to the fact that there is a problem with a current law. You can ask your legislator to make or change the law to avoid or remedy the problem. This will be the detailed subject of other chapters.
- **And much more**. When in doubt, call anyway.

Areas a Legislator *Can't* Help With

- **Offering legal advice**. Your legislator cannot give you legal advice, and you shouldn't construe the information they give you as legal advice. If you need legal advice, contact an attorney. You may be referred to private resources or pro bono or low-income assistance if this is what you need.
- **Discussing pending litigation**. Your legislator cannot help you with pending litigation. Your experiences can be helpful to them to understand how to better write the law in the future, but they cannot weigh in for you in a case pending before the courts.

Did You Know...?

The first African American elected to a state legislature was Alexander Lucius Twilight in 1836 for the Vermont legislature.

Act as if what you do makes a difference. It does.
—William James

GET STARTED

☐ **Find out who represents you.** To find out who represents you, visit Project Vote Smart (www.votesmart.org) or the website of your state legislature (see appendix A). It's always best to begin with the elected official who actually represents you, even if he or she doesn't share your political party affiliation.

☐ **Identify yourself.** You should provide your name, the fact that you live in the elected official's district, your phone number, and your e-mail address. (You'd be surprised how often someone contacting us forgets to do this, making follow-up impossible.) Also, it's common for constituents who live in the official's district to be given priority.

☐ **Determine the best method of contact.** This may depend on how comfortable you are, but e-mail is generally best when you have facts and details that your official needs in order to know how to proceed. This allows your legislator to print out a copy and reread it as needed. It also facilitates forwarding to the right person to help. Phone calls are best when you have a fairly quick question that can elicit a fairly quick answer.

☐ **State the problem you would like to see fixed.** When contacting people, it's useful to have ready a concise statement of the problem so people helping with constituent services can start thinking right away about how to best help.

☐ **Suggest a solution, if you have one.** You don't have to have a solution in mind, but if you do, suggest it—it can facilitate brainstorming and problem solving.

☐ **Determine the complexity of the problem.** If it's fairly complex, consider preparing a summary timeline of key events or a very short written narrative. Because of a high volume of work, shorter and simpler requests get processed first, so try to distill your question or need into a concise statement, and allow your elected officials to follow up if they need clarifying information or details.

☐ **Summarize prior attempts to fix the problem.** Provide a quick summary of what the prior attempts were and who made them so that earlier dead ends aren't pursued again. This information can also help illustrate where some process reforms might be warranted so future constituents don't have to encounter the same problems.

☐ **Wait for a response.** How long you should wait depends on whether your legislature is in session or not, since staffing levels may vary dramatically during these distinct times. If it is in session, you should get a response within forty-eight hours that at least acknowledges receipt of your inquiry. Allow up to two weeks if it is out of session.

☐ **If you get no response, follow up.** You should make at least a second attempt. With spam filters on e-mail and high turnover among volunteers and interns, it's possible your query was missed. But if two attempts have failed, you should reach out to a different elected official and try to get help there. Your second attempt can either be someone else in your district or someone you know who has a reputation for being an advocate in your area of concern.

☐ **Be patient and gracious.** You'll have the greatest impact and likelihood for success if you're concise and polite and share your own suggestions. While there may be very good reason to be frustrated or angry, it tends to measurably reduce (rightly or wrongly) the impact and credibility of the constituent. Your elected officials and their staff are, after all, people just like you.

☐ **Don't overdo it.** If you're asking for specific constituent help (rather than weighing in on a bill), it is better to contact one office at a time. If an elected official sees an e-mail blast to everyone, they may assume someone else has it covered and the chances are increased that it'll be missed.

☐ **Say thank you.** Politics, like anything else in life, ultimately comes down to people. While certainly not required, a thank-you goes a long way to making the people in an office want to work even harder for you, and it'll help build a rapport and relationship between you and your elected official in the event you have future needs, suggestions, or input on how you think he or she should vote.

By raising problems and wrinkles in the system, not only is there a good chance that your elected official can help you with a problem or concern, but you are also making the system better for everyone. Chances are, if you're having a problem, someone else is too, and it may point to the need for greater systemic reforms or the need to improve community education on avoiding certain pitfalls. *Your information will be kept confidential* unless you request to submit something as written **testimony** and want it to be public.

Chapter 4
Monitoring Legislation

*A basic tenet of a healthy democracy
is open dialogue and transparency.*
—Peter Fenn

In the age of the Internet, it's easier than ever to monitor legislation and voting records. So why do you need to know how to do this?

You'll want to know how to monitor legislation in your state because you may want to help write it or amend it. You may care about the idea or policy and want to help advance it, stop it, or change it. You'll find that the overwhelming majority of legislation introduced in the states is never reported in the press, so even highly informed people never know the bulk of what policies are being introduced. Your ability to monitor legislation is also critical voter self-defense so you're not at the mercy of negative political campaign ads or the mainstream press to get your information about the voting record or policy priorities of your elected officials. Further, whether a particular bill is good, bad, or mixed is best determined by your own critical judgment and not someone else's spin or agenda.

In order to monitor legislation, you'll need to know when your state's legislature is in session (see appendix B). There can be no action on bills when they're not in session, and most states' legislatures are part-time, which means they don't convene year-round.

Once the legislature is in session, most states post this information on their website (see appendix A), where one can typically get the following information on every bill:

- the entire text of the bill
- a summary
- the sponsors
- a fiscal analysis
- committee assignments
- recorded votes taken on the bill
- a Status Sheet revealing where the bill is in the legislative process

You can also typically get an updated daily calendar online (see appendix A) for the House and Senate to find out when the next action may be taken on a bill. The purpose of monitoring a bill is so that you can have the input and impact you want at a time when it can still be effective.

Finding a bill. In order to find a specific bill, you'll generally need to know at least one piece of information about it—for example, the bill number, the sponsor, the title or subject matter, or the committee to which it has been assigned. Use the website provided for your state in the appendix to begin your search inquiry. If you don't have access to the Internet or have problems finding the bill you're looking for, there's also general contact information for the legislative **chambers** in the appendix.

If you don't know which bill you're looking for but are just generally interested in seeing what's going on, most states have an entire table of contents or summary status sheet where you can

in ways that can change your stance from support to opposition, or vice versa. In order to avoid arguments on talking points or ideology, it's extremely helpful to read the actual language of the bill. While it can be opaque at times due to legalese, you as a citizen are most empowered when you don't need to rely on someone else to tell you what the bill says.

Accountability of votes. You can monitor bills in order to track how your

QUESTIONS TO ASK ABOUT A BILL

☐ What is the purpose of the bill? What are the problems it's trying to solve? Is there a problem?

☐ Is there evidence to support that the proposed policy in the bill may in fact solve or at least help the purported problem? Is there a better way to solve it?

☐ Are the terms defined in a way that makes sense?

☐ Are there contradictions in the bill?

☐ How does the bill incentivize or deter behavior?

☐ What are the possible unintended consequences of the bill? Can they be averted with different language or a different approach?

☐ Is the bill ideological? Or is it evidence based?

☐ Is the bill a good-faith attempt to engage public policy? Or is it a political "gotcha," meant to make a good slogan for political talking points or partisan campaigns?

☐ Are there unrelated or extraneous provisions of the bill or any poison pills buried in the bill?

☐ Is the bill serving a narrow special interest, or is it a broad community interest?

☐ What are the principles of justice or fairness underpinning the bill?

peruse a brief chart of all introduced legislation. Skim the chart for topics or possible bills of interest. You can learn a lot by seeing the big picture of how many bills are introduced, trends on topics, trends by legislators, and the relative proportion of trivial versus substantive legislation.

Content of the bill. If you're monitoring a bill for its content on policy, you'll want to download it at *each stage.* A bill can radically change at each step

elected officials vote. Consider sending a thank-you note if you agree with their vote. This is important feedback for them so they can best represent you. If you disagree with their vote, consider sending a note along the lines of "I'm disappointed with your vote." In either case, include a short statement of why you agree or disagree. If you disagree, let them know what you would have preferred to see done and *offer to make yourself available as a resource in the future* on certain topics. While it probably goes without saying, an ad hominem attack has never persuaded anyone to change their vote and hurts your credibility as an advocate. Even if you're right, you and your message are likely to be discredited if you're rude.

Timing and advocacy. You may be monitoring a bill so you can see where it is in the process so you can determine when and how to best advocate.

It can be tricky to ensure that the feedback you submit is received and considered *before* a vote. Your most effective windows (when) for input and most receptive contacts (to whom) during these windows will be:

- **immediately after introduction (when)—to the caucus leadership (to whom)** of both parties to try to encourage support or defeat of the measure. If you support the measure, you want to urge leadership to ensure that the

bill receives a full, fair public hearing. (Colorado guarantees a full public hearing on every piece of introduced legislation, but most states don't.)

- **immediately after assignment to a committee (when)—to the chair of the committee and the committee members (to whom).** Pay particular attention to getting input to your elected officials and letting them know you're a constituent and a voter. Call or write *before* the committee meets if possible to try to persuade the elected official before they've made up their mind or before the professional lobby corps has worked the committee.

- **during testimony in the committee (when)—to committee members (to whom).** While Colorado guarantees the right for citizen testimony on every bill, many states don't. Therefore, ask the **chair** (or the chair's staff) what the policy is on public testimony. Also, see the appendix for a summary of public testimony rights in each of the states. If there will be public testimony, try to testify because you will have the most impact in person. Check with the chair on rules regarding length of testimony and any unique procedures. Consider watching or listening to public hearings to build your comfort level. Your elected officials will benefit from hearing from *you*.

- **prior to a floor vote (when)—to the chamber casting the vote, especially your elected official (to whom).** If a bill passes out of committee, your next critical timing for advocacy input is before it goes to a vote on the floor. You, as a citizen, can both persuade votes and also help count votes. You can keep track of the responses you get from each contact as to whether the official will support a bill, oppose a bill, seek to amend a bill, or has yet to take a position on the bill. Start with those who have not yet decided, then reinforce those who agree with you.

Then reach out to those who disagree with you, find out their reasons, and respond with any information you have that addresses their assumptions, reasons, or conclusions with which you disagree.

- **prior to action by the governor (when)—to the governor (to whom)** or his or her policy team. You want to call or write to urge signing or **veto** of the measure before the deadline hits. In order to know what deadline applies to the governor's actions on legislation before him or her, consult the appendix.

Tools for monitoring. Depending on the state you live in, you can monitor the legislative process by attending in person, listening to live-stream Web broadcast, or obtaining recordings of public proceedings on CD.

Even if you weigh in on one bill once in the process once per year, you'll be doing more than most people do in a lifetime. If fact, if everyone weighed in on at least one bill once per year, it would revolutionize American democracy and dwarf the role and influence of professional lobbyists.

Clearly, people are busy and cannot monitor all bills all the time. Many people hope that after elections their officials will make good decisions even in the absence of their input, while others forfeit their right to participate on the assumption that it won't make a difference. It will. You won't get your way all the time (none of us do). But you *will* have your interests reflected almost none of the time if you stay silent.

*Politics ought to be the part-time profession of every citizen
who would protect the rights and privileges of free men.*
—Dwight D. Eisenhower

Chapter 5
How to Read a Bill

We're a nation of laws, but the good thing about America,
is that laws reside in the people and
people can change the laws.
—Rick Warren

Legislators are often asked why bills are written in legalese. Such specialized language can be very off-putting and can turn even the most important and exciting issues into dry cures for insomnia. The fact is that legislation is quite literally writing laws, so words and phrases have precise legal meaning and impact. But you don't need a law degree in order to read or write legislation. This is an empowering realization that opens up the legislative process to everyone.

When people are first elected into office, reading, writing, and understanding legalese can be one of the greatest learning curves they face. Lawyers are admittedly at an initial advantage here, and legislators can be unwittingly gullible to misinformation or excessive lobbyist influence if they haven't read or don't understand how to read the bills they're voting on. Like every other skill, though, it improves with practice.

This chapter is intended to give you an overview on the anatomy of a bill and tips on understanding what the bill really means.

Bill number. Legislation is typically assigned a bill number, which will appear on the front page at the time of introduction. A bill number will usually be preceded by the words *House Bill* or *Senate Bill*, possibly abbreviated as *HB* or *SB*. This tells you which is the originating chamber of the legislation. Most states begin numbering sequentially after the chamber designation. Once you know the bill number, you can track every aspect of the process pertaining to the bill.

Sponsors. You'll generally see a list of names on the front page. The first name listed is the **prime sponsor** (the author and primary mover of the bill). The subsequent names listed are **cosponsors** (cosponsorship indicates early support of a bill from other members).

Title. Most bills will also have a title on the front page. In states with a legal single subject requirement, the entire bill must legally pertain to the single topic in the formal title. So the formal title is the frame for the **single subject** matter of the bill. Amendments that don't fit the original title will be rejected as not fitting the single subject. Most bills also have what's referred to as a short title, which primarily exists to help the public quickly search basic subjects of different bills.

Legislative declaration. Occasionally bills will include a **legislative declaration** at the beginning of the measure. A legislative declaration is *not* law but may be included to help shed light on the purpose of the bill or to give direction to the courts that may be interpreting these laws in the future.

Enactment clause. "Be It Enacted by the legislature or General Assembly in the State of _____." This is a standard clause that gives legal effect to the content of the bill if passed.

Sections. You'll often see bills broken down by sections (for example, Section 1, 2, 3, or abbreviated as Sec. 1, 2, 3). This part of the drafting

structure tells you that you're about to get into a different area within the bill. Any definitions of terms in a bill are usually listed in Section 1. The subsequent section numbers change when they're amending a different section of statute or have a different purpose. The interim sections usually form the meat of a bill—what's required, allowed, or prohibited under the proposed law. That section is typically followed by a section delineating any exceptions. The end of the bill usually includes an appropriations clause, if applicable. The last section of most bills is usually the effective date of the legislation should it pass.

Definitions section. If any new or previously undefined terms are being used in the bill, you'll often find a definitions section. Terms are usually in alphabetical order.

New versus old law. A piece of legislation will typically start by replicating the current language in the **statute** and then identify changes to the existing law by showing a strikethrough of any current language that's being removed. For example:

Proposed deletions of current language in the law will usually look like this. New language will often appear either in CAPITAL LETTERS or with an underline, depending on the state, to denote added language to the state statute. This can take a while to read, but you'll get used to it. There is an example of legislation at the end of this chapter for practice.

Civil or criminal. The rights or prohibitions spelled out in most laws are either given as a part of **civil law** or **criminal law**. The enforcement mechanism and consequences vary for each type. Some laws can be both. For example, both civil fraud and criminal fraud are prohibited by most states.

Who. Each bill pertains to someone. Laws generally grant rights or responsibilities to people, businesses, or other government actors. When reviewing a bill, determine to whom it applies.

What. Each bill will generally describe required, authorized, or prohibited behavior. When reviewing a bill, determine what conduct is required, authorized, or prohibited.

Qualifications or eligibility. When reviewing a bill, determine if there are any preconditions that apply in order to trigger the rights or responsibilities in the bill.

Exceptions. When reviewing a bill, determine who is exempt and under what circumstances. Exceptions can be important to properly define or limit the scope of the bill. But they can also be a red flag for special-interest exemptions achieved by lobbying organizations on behalf of their clients.

How. Depending on the complexity of the bill, there may need to be an explanation of how a process works. This should be a road map telling someone how to do something. For example, it could describe the process for applying for a driver's license.

Appropriations clause—$. In most states, a bill that costs money requires an appropriations clause to identify the source of funds that pay for something. When reviewing a bill, you will want to identify how much it costs and how it will be funded.

Enforcement clause. Even though there are thousands of different laws, there are really only a few different ways laws are enforced. Police and prosecutors typically enforce criminal laws (although there are some regulatory crimes). Civil laws are enforced either through regulatory agencies by **administrative law** or by citizens through **private rights of action.** Violation detection occurs either through audits, inspections, or citizen report or complaint. Every **right** should come with a **remedy** or an **enforcement mechanism** or it's an empty right.

May versus *shall.* These small word choices have big consequences in law. Whether something is permissive or mandatory can make a huge difference. One of the best ways to gut a bill or a responsibility is to change a *shall* to a *may.* Also note that *may* has two meanings. The first meaning is "is permitted to." This often means that there are suggested guidelines or behavior but they aren't necessarily required. This can cause one to question why the law should be passed at all—if it's merely a suggestion, a law is likely not required. However, there's a second meaning to *may*: "is authorized to." Some behavior may require specific authorization. For example, a person may practice medicine if he or she has accomplished A, B, and C. This also has the inverse meaning that a person may not practice medicine if they have not accomplished A, B, and C. In other words, it's actually a prohibition.

Notwithstanding. You'll often see this term in bills like so: "notwithstanding other provisions of law X, Y, and Z." This can be confusing. Does this mean it overrides the other conflicting sections, or that it is overridden by any provision to the contrary? When you see this phrase, it means that it overrides any other sections of statute, even if they appear to conflict. If you're trying to preserve other sections of law that could occasionally conflict with some interpretation of your bill, one will generally see the phrasing "unless otherwise provided by law."

Statutory citation. One of the more intimidating aspects in the beginning can be interpreting the statutory cross-references in bills. For example, C.R.S. § 24-80-905 is a Colorado statutory citation that provides that the columbine is the state flower of Colorado. Let's break this down. *C.R.S.* stands for the "Colorado Revised Statutes." States have different initials specific to their own code. The § symbol means "section." Now, to understand the numbers, think of the organization of the laws in terms of an outline. The numbers mean the following: Title 24—Article 80—Section 905. Titles are the broadest topics. Articles are like subtopics beneath that, and sections are subtopics beneath that. Basically, each paragraph or concept is supposed to be assigned a unique number to help you find it. The

more complicated the law, the more subsections you're likely to find, so you may see something like C.R.S. § 5-2-201(1)(a)(II). And at the end of the day, if this is too tedious, don't worry too much about it. You don't have to know it to make an impact on the process.

Effective date. Any new law will include an effective date indicating when the new law would take effect, if passed. An effective date farther into the future may be used if the public or certain departments need time to prepare for compliance. An immediate effective date may be used to close a **loophole** or to respond to an urgent need.

Bill summaries. Many bills include a bill summary, which more closely resembles plain English. You may also receive information from various organizations that include their version of a bill summary. This can be helpful, but you should know that those summaries are not the law, and a summary can be incomplete, inaccurate, or even, at times, misleading. So if you have the time to read the bill for yourself, it's a good idea to do so.

Overall, my best suggestion is to just practice. Download prior bills online to try your eye at reading and understanding them. Consider buying a legal dictionary to look up any phrases that don't make sense to you. It's also helpful to write down your questions on the bill as you're reading it. You may catch something that the sponsor or no one else does.

If you can read a bill as a citizen, you're a very serious force to be reckoned

SAMPLE ACT

AN ACT

NOTE: This bill has been prepared for the signature of the appropriate legislative officers and the Governor. To determine whether the Governor has signed the bill or taken other action on it, please consult the legislative status sheet, the legislative history, or the Session Laws.

HOUSE BILL 06-1149

BY REPRESENTATIVE(S) Carroll M., Weissmann, Buescher, Carroll T., Garcia, Green, Larson, Paccione, Penry, Romanoff, Todd, Witwer, Coleman, and Frangas; also **SENATOR(S) Tupa**, Bacon, Grossman, and Shaffer.

CONCERNING DISCLOSURE OF ADDITIONAL INFORMATION TO BE SUBMITTED BY PROFESSIONAL LOBBYISTS IN CONNECTION WITH THEIR DISCLOSURE STATEMENTS FILED WITH THE SECRETARY OF STATE UNDER THE "COLORADO SUNSHINE ACT OF 1972," AND MAKING AN APPROPRIATION THEREFOR.

Be it enacted by the General Assembly of the State of Colorado:

SECTION 1. 24-6-301, Colorado Revised Statutes, is amended BY THE ADDITION OF A NEW SUBSECTION to read:

24-6-301. **Definitions**—legislative declaration. As used in this part 3, unless the context otherwise requires:

(5.5) "PRINCIPAL" MEANS ANY PERSON WHO EMPLOYS A LOBBYIST. IF AN ASSOCIATION, CORPORATION, LIMITED LIABILITY COMPANY, PARTNERSHIP, OR ANY OTHER ORGANIZATION OR GROUP OF PERSONS OR FORM OF BUSINESS ENTITY ENGAGES A LOBBYIST, A PERSON SERVING AS AN OFFICER, EMPLOYEE, MEMBER, SHAREHOLDER, OR PARTNER OF THE ASSOCIATION, CORPORATION, LIMITED LIABILITY COMPANY, PARTNERSHIP, OR OTHER ORGANIZATION OR GROUP OF PERSONS OR FORM OF BUSINESS ENTITY SHALL NOT BE CONSIDERED A PRINCIPAL.

SECTION 2. 24-6-301 (1.9) (a) (X), Colorado Revised Statutes, is amended, and the said 24-6-301 (1.9) (a) is further amended BY THE ADDITION OF THE FOLLOWING NEW SUBPARAGRAPHS, to read:

24-6-301. **Definitions**—legislative declaration. As used in this part 3, unless the context otherwise requires:

(1.9) (a) "Disclosure statement" means a written statement that contains:

(X) The nature of the legislation, standards, rules, or rates for which the disclosing person is receiving contributions or making expenditures for lobbying and, where known, the specific legislation, standards, rules, or rates. IN THE CASE OF SPECIFIC LEGISLATION, DISCLOSURE SHALL INCLUDE, DURING A REGULAR OR SPECIAL SESSION OF THE GENERAL ASSEMBLY, THE BILL NUMBER OF THE LEGISLATION, AND WHETHER THE DISCLOSING PERSON'S PRINCIPAL IS SUPPORTING, OPPOSING, AMENDING, OR MONITORING THE LEGISLATION IDENTIFIED AS OF THE TIME A DISCLOSURE STATEMENT IS REQUIRED TO BE FILED PURSUANT TO SECTION 24-6-302 (3), AFTER THE DISCLOSING PERSON IS RETAINED TO ADVOCATE OR MONITOR IN CONNECTION WITH THE LEGISLATION. THE DISCLOSURE STATEMENT SHALL SPECIFY THAT THE DISCLOSING PERSON'S REPRESENTATION IS ACCURATE AS OF THE DATE OF DISCLOSURE ONLY AND THAT SUCH REPRESENTATION IS NOT BINDING ON THE DISCLOSING PERSON AFTER SUCH DATE AND IS SUBJECT TO CHANGE SUBSEQUENT TO SUCH DATE AND PRIOR TO THE TIME THE NEXT DISCLOSURE STATEMENT IS DUE. IF A DISCLOSURE STATEMENT FROM A DISCLOSING PERSON DURING A REGULAR OR SPECIAL SESSION OF THE GENERAL ASSEMBLY FAILS TO SHOW ANY BILL NUMBERS OR NATURE OF THE LEGISLATION, AS APPLICABLE, THE DISCLOSING PERSON SHALL BE REQUIRED TO MAKE AN AFFIRMATIVE STATEMENT THAT HE OR SHE WAS NOT RETAINED IN CONNECTION WITH ANY LEGISLATION. NOTHING IN THIS SUBPARAGRAPH (X) SHALL REQUIRE ANY ADDITIONAL DISCLOSURE ON THE PART OF A DISCLOSING PERSON BEFORE THE NEXT APPLICABLE REPORTING DEADLINE PURSUANT TO SECTION 24-6-302 (3). FOR PURPOSES OF THIS SUBPARAGRAPH (X),

"LEGISLATION" MEANS THE PROCESS OF MAKING OR ENACTING LAW IN WRITTEN FORM IN THE FORM OF CODES, STATUTES, OR RULES.

(XI) IF THE DISCLOSING PERSON'S PRINCIPAL IS AN INDIVIDUAL, THE NAME AND ADDRESS OF THE INDIVIDUAL AND A DESCRIPTION OF THE BUSINESS ACTIVITY IN WHICH THE INDIVIDUAL IS ENGAGED. IF THE DISCLOSING PERSON'S PRINCIPAL IS A BUSINESS ENTITY, A DESCRIPTION OF THE BUSINESS ENTITY IN WHICH THE PRINCIPAL IS ENGAGED AND THE NAME OR NAMES OF THE ENTITY'S CHIEF EXECUTIVE OFFICER OR PARTNERS, AS APPLICABLE. IF THE DISCLOSING PERSON'S PRINCIPAL IS AN INDUSTRY, TRADE, ORGANIZATION OR GROUP OF PERSONS, OR PROFESSIONAL ASSOCIATION, A DESCRIPTION OF THE INDUSTRY, TRADE, ORGANIZATION OR GROUP

OF PERSONS, OR PROFESSION THAT THE DISCLOSING PERSON REPRESENTS.

(XII) A STATEMENT DETAILING ANY DIRECT BUSINESS ASSOCIATION OF THE DISCLOSING PERSON IN ANY PENDING LEGISLATION, MEASURE, OR QUESTION. FOR PURPOSES OF THIS SUBPARAGRAPH (XIII), A "DIRECT BUSINESS ASSOCIATION" MEANS THAT, IN CONNECTION WITH A PENDING BILL, MEASURE, OR QUESTION, THE PASSAGE OR FAILURE OF THE BILL, MEASURE, OR QUESTION WILL RESULT IN THE DISCLOSING PERSON DERIVING A DIRECT FINANCIAL OR PECUNIARY BENEFIT THAT IS GREATER THAN ANY SUCH BENEFIT DERIVED BY OR SHARED BY OTHER PERSONS IN THE DISCLOSING PERSON'S PROFESSION, OCCUPATION, OR INDUSTRY. A DISCLOSING PERSON SHALL NOT BE DEEMED TO HAVE A DIRECT PERSONAL RELATIONSHIP IN A PENDING BILL, MEASURE, OR QUESTION WHERE SUCH INTEREST ARISES FROM A BILL, MEASURE, OR QUESTION THAT AFFECTS THE ENTIRE MEMBERSHIP OF A CLASS TO WHICH THE DISCLOSING PERSON BELONGS.

SECTION 3. Appropriation. In addition to any other appropriation, there is hereby appropriated, out of any moneys in the department of state cash fund created in section 24-21-104 (3) (b), Colorado Revised Statutes, not otherwise appropriated, to the department of state, for the fiscal year beginning July 1, 2006, the sum of thirty-six thousand four hundred dollars ($36,400), or so much thereof as may be necessary, for the implementation of this act.

SECTION 4. Effective date. This act shall take effect July 1, 2006.

SECTION 5. Safety clause. The general assembly hereby finds, determines, and declares that this act is necessary for the immediate preservation of the public peace, health, and safety.

Andrew Romanoff
SPEAKER OF THE HOUSE
OF REPRESENTATIVES

Joan Fitz-Gerald
PRESIDENT OF
THE SENATE

Marilyn Eddins
CHIEF CLERK OF THE HOUSE
OF REPRESENTATIVES

Karen Goldman
SECRETARY OF
THE SENATE

APPROVED_____

_____

Bill Owens
GOVERNOR OF THE STATE OF COLORADO

with. You can defend your legitimate questions or concerns against misinformation, sloppy or skewed reporting, spin, campaign rhetoric, or inadequate platitudes. You can help drive policy changes. In short, you're a very powerful citizen if you learn how to do this. And you should insist, at minimum, that your elected officials commit to reading every piece of legislation before they take a position or vote on a bill.

A popular government without popular information or the means of acquiring it is but a prologue to Farce or Tragedy or perhaps both. Knowledge will forever govern ignorance, and a people who mean to be their own Governors must arm themselves with the power knowledge gives.
—James Madison

Chapter 6
Registering Your Support or Opposition

If you have a plan, we want to hear it.
Tell your community leaders, your local officials,
your governor, and your team in Washington.
Believe me, your ideas count.
An individual can make a difference.
—George H. W. Bush

Now that you know how to find, read, and understand bills that are introduced, it's time to weigh in on the bills you're interested in. Before you contact your elected officials, it's helpful to get clear in your own mind what your position is and what you'd like your elected official to do and why.

PREPARE YOUR POSITION

☐ **Make your position clear in your outreach.** You might be surprised how often people contact legislators without any clear statement of what they're asking them to do. This undermines the efficacy of outreach or advocacy, even with a receptive legislator. Your position on a bill will generally be one of the following:

- You have questions and would like more information about the bill.
- You support the measure and would like them to vote yes.
- You oppose the measure and would like them to vote no.
- You like parts but dislike other parts and would like to see the bill amended in a certain way.

☐ **Identify a few reasons to support your position.** Your reasons may be based on your education, your vocation, your research, or your personal experiences.

☐ **Share any facts you relied on to reach your conclusion and the sources for those facts.**

☐ **Acknowledge one or two points from the other point of view and proceed to explain why your points are more persuasive.** This not only shows you've thought of the other side, but it also might provide your elected official with more ammunition.

☐ **State some of the consequences if the legislator doesn't adopt the position you are requesting.**

☐ **Prepare two versions of your position.** The first version can be your raw, stream-of-consciousness, cathartic version. The second version should be designed to maximize your impact, knowing your audience.

Now that your position is prepared, you're ready to register it.

Methods of Registering Your Position

- Call your elected officials.
- E-mail your elected officials.
- Write a letter to your elected officials.
- Circulate a petition and present it to your elected officials.
- Start your own blog or comment on someone else's.
- Write a Letter to the Editor.
- Call in to a talk–radio show.
- Make use of social media like Facebook, Twitter, and LinkedIn.
- Testify at a public hearing.
- Attend town hall meetings and register your input in person.
- Schedule a meeting with your elected official to discuss in person.
- Reach out to any issue organizations to which you belong.

Depending on how strongly you feel about the issue, you may want to consider all of the above methods.

It can also be helpful to know what *not* to do when registering your positions or reaching out. This may seem obvious, but trust me, I'm including it here for a reason. Many people make these blunders and undermine their own efficacy.

What *Not* to Do When Registering Your Position

- **Don't threaten a public official.** Not only will this undermine your credibility and the persuasiveness of the message you wish to deliver, but in many jurisdictions this is a crime. Also, there can be restraining orders issued for threatening a public official (or anyone, for that matter). Clearly, physical threats are a no-no. But what about other threats, such as, "If you do/don't do X, I won't vote for you and will tell everyone I know not to vote for you"? While perfectly legal, these aren't a particularly effective way to persuade a legislator.
- **Don't tell the legislator you think they're stupid, even if you think they are.** Legislators, after all, are human, and most people don't respond well to personal insults. I know this sounds like common sense, but we really do get e-mails like, "You must be the dumbest person ever if you vote yes/no." Your message will get lost even if you have a very compelling point. Personal attacks are not an effective way to shape public policy or to persuade people to do what you want.

How to Register Your Position More Effectively

- **Keep it positive.** While it may feel cathartic to release political frustration when you make contact, it tends to cloud the power of the actual points you're making. Be careful about attributing motives that may not exist. In other words, an e-mail simply stating "I'm sure you're just running this bill because X gave to your campaign" or "I know you're beholden to Y special interest group" isn't really appropriate.

You can think those things—and you may even be right—but your ultimate message will not get through and persuade if you do.

- **Be mindful of overdoing it.** There is such a thing as "too much." If a legislator gets more than one call, e-mail, or letter from you per week, burnout can set in, where your concerns are at risk of moving to the bottom of the to-do pile, while the needs of other people who haven't contacted him or her will rise to the top. Calling a legislator at home or on their cell phone four times during Mother's Day is not the best way to make your point.

- **Customize and personalize.** It's helpful to customize form letters so yours will stand out and not get lost. If you're writing unprompted by any other organization or group, your letter will inherently be unique. But if you're writing at the urging of an organization, there's a risk of a high volume of cookie-cutter letters or e-mails reaching your elected officials. Consider changing a few sentences and adding a personal statement about why the issue is important to you. If possible, personalize your letters for the particular recipient. If you send an e-mail blast out to all elected officials, the chances are that no one will respond. Why? If an elected official sees everyone who's included, they may conclude you're not their constituent and someone else will respond. Send e-mails one at a time or make the recipient list blind so all recipients can't see who else is getting

it. Also, if you know even one unique thing about the elected official, including it helps catch his or her attention.

- **Avoid hyperbole.** Passion has a way of impacting how we write about what we care about. Be careful about using statements such as "this is the best/worst bill ever in the history of the world." This can create an impression in the reader's mind that you're overstating your case, and they'll read the rest of what you have to say with that filter. You want to sound reasonable and well informed.

- **Don't be too political.** It's more effective to stick to issues and your reasoning than to get into party rhetoric or campaign ideologies. While everyone elected is typically from a political party, you don't want to pigeonhole the elected official, because your goal is to persuade him or her to your policy position regardless of your **party affiliation** or theirs.

In the end, (1) make sure that your name and contact information are clear, and (2) offer to make yourself available as an ongoing resource on the issues you care about (whether or not you agree on everything). Remember, the single most effective method for outreach is a personal relationship. Make a point to meet and introduce yourself to your legislators. This will help put a little added weight on your feedback in the future. If you make a good first impression as a reasonable and credible source of information, you may find that you have ongoing impact on a variety of issues.

People often say that, in a democracy, decisions are made by a majority of the people. Of course, that is not true. Decisions are made by a majority of those who make themselves heard and who vote—a very different thing.
—Walter H. Judd

Chapter 7
Know Your Elected Officials

*The only title in our democracy superior
to that of President is the title of citizen.*
—Louis Brandeis

If you know who your state legislators are, you're in a distinct minority of people in the United States. While you're free to contact any elected official, it is *your* elected officials who should help you with constituent matters and who need to know what you think and how you'd like them to vote.

Knowing who your officials are will depend upon your address. Every state has legislative districts that are drawn following the US census to try to achieve equal population (one person, one vote) and preserve communities of

PATRIOTIC LEAGUE

interest. Therefore, your districts and your elected officials can change.

I highly recommend that you bookmark the website for Project Vote Smart, www.votesmart.org. You can enter your address on the home page prompt and it'll tell you who your elected officials are. Your best search results will be retrieved if you can enter your ZIP-plus-four code. Print out and keep this list, as it will be your road map to ensuring your government works for you. Another great feature of Project Vote Smart is the hyperlinks that direct you to the contact information for the elected officials in your districts.

Depending on the state you live in, you can also get this information by consulting your county clerk and recorder office or state secretary of state. Additionally, many state legislatures have information on their websites to help you find and contact your elected officials based on the district number or your address (see appendix A).

Once you've gone through the effort to find your elected officials, I strongly recommend that you enter their information into your contacts, your phone, and your e-mail programs. It can also be helpful to enter the contact information of all the other legislators in your state because you may find you want to advocate to committee chairs, committee members, or an entire chamber to voice your opinion.

Now that you know who they are and where to contact them, it's useful to know something about them. This will help you cater your outreach to their unique proclivities, interests, and idiosyncrasies. While you don't *have* to do that, it's a great way to customize your message for greatest impact.

Find the individual websites (assuming each has one) for your elected officials and bookmark them. Read them over for what you can learn about bills they've run in the past. You

you'll be informed, meet your elected officials, and have maximum impact.

Try to identify any areas you have in common (even if you're very different in **political ideology**), and see if you can ascertain what motivates this person. This will help you determine your best approach for persuasion. It's something we as legislators have to do every day, because none of us can pass a bill without a majority vote in each chamber and a governor's signature. If you're good at reading people, this will come naturally. I learned the importance of different types of persuasion the hard way.

can often find a biography page, where you can learn more about what makes your elected officials tick. These sites can tell you a lot if you review photos, blogs, and the content they post. You can also learn something by how often they update (or don't update) their website.

A good website should include information about how to sign up for electronic newsletter updates and when and where town hall meetings are being held. You'll often find links to your legislators' Facebook and Twitter pages as well as other **social media outlets**. You should avail yourself of all those avenues to maximize the chances that

For three years I tried to pass a law to give injured workers in Colorado some ability to choose or change their physicians. The goal was to ensure a good doctor-patient relationship and to ensure some independence of the physicians from the insurance company. For the first two years, I collected mountains of data, charts about what each state in the country did, and their respective premium rates. The data showed that the majority of states allow some patient choice, that the public overwhelmingly supports patient choice, and that the premiums in choice states were not higher than non-choice states. But it wasn't until my third year in pursuing this effort that it passed. So, what changed? In part, the insurance and business lobby were probably sick of dealing with my bills, but the other thing that changed was *me*. I spent more time trying to understand how different people work. Ultimately, my style is very data driven, and I made the mistake of assuming that everyone else worked that way as well.

Legislators, like everyone else, are multifaceted people, but most people have a primary motivation or style that they respond to the most. I've found that my colleagues generally have a primary motivation in one of the following areas:

- **Facts and data.** This person will want documentation of both the problem and your proposed solution. What are the other states doing? What has worked and what hasn't, as supported by empirical data? Be prepared to collect and cite your sources, but know that this will not move everyone equally.
- **Constituent connection.** Some legislators will be most moved by even one contact by a constituent in their district unless they just morally disagree with what he or she wants. You want that constituent to be you.
- **Emotional personal story.** More legislators than you might imagine are ultimately moved by *emotional* stories that reveal the nature of the problem and the importance of the solution. One powerful story will do more here than a mountain of statistics. Share your story, or find the right person to share theirs.
- **"If it ain't broke, don't fix it" mentality.** Every legislator has a different

threshold for how significant they believe a problem has to be before a legislative intervention is appropriate. Be ready for this.

- **Personal connection.** Some legislators are moved most based on *who* is approaching them. Is it a friend, relative, coworker, supporter, volunteer? You want this to be you or someone you know.
- **A strong lobby.** Some legislators will be moved based on which lobbyists or special interest groups are working for or against a bill. It would be unusual for the legislator to admit this, and it may be subconscious, but it's a possible reality nonetheless.
- **Political loyalty.** Some legislators will vote primarily how the leadership in their party asks them to vote. Likewise, some legislators vote based on how their friends or enemies vote.

As you can see, not all motivations are equal in an ideal world, but you're likely to run into each of them sooner or later. It's a mistake to assume all elected officials operate by one mode or the other. In a cynical society, some people may assume that lobbyists or political favors motivate all legislators, but if you make a one-size-fits-all assumption, you'll be wrong in many cases and you might even hurt your cause.

For example, if you approach a facts-and-stats legislator or the emotional-personal-story legislator with discussion about who is lobbying what or their political friendships, you'll lose them—not only on the immediate issue, but possibly for good.

Given that you may not always know what type your legislator is, it's usually safest to approach him or her based on facts and statistics and compelling personal stories, and if you come into direct knowledge about other potential styles of motivation, you can always modify. Almost no one will be

offended if you present information based on straight-up facts and reasons.

I have found that speaking in the first person helps. You want to talk about what you believe and why, rather than directly telling someone else what they ought to think or believe.

Finally, network and ask others. Chances are if you don't know your legislator personally, someone does. Knowledge is power when you're trying to decide who you need to persuade and how to best do so.

We all have some idealized version of the justice of the issues we pursue. In a perfect world, you would customize your persuasion efforts to the justice and moral frame of the legislator. For example, most people in Colorado know I see myself as a civil libertarian who is very concerned with the little guy. If someone wants my vote, they generally try to frame their argument in those terms.

You may also find some legislators have a frame based on cost and efficiency, so be prepared to explain how their choices increase or decrease costs and the relative efficiencies of their choices. You get the point.

While knowing the personality and motivation of your elected officials may not guarantee you will persuade him or her, it does *maximize* the probability that you will. Knowing who your elected officials are will give you key insights on how to approach the remainder of your strategy.

Surely anyone who has ever been elected to public office
understands that one commodity above all others,
namely the trust and confidence of the people,
is fundamental in maintaining a free
and open political system.
—Hubert H. Humphrey

Chapter 8

How to Testify
at a Legislative Hearing

Never doubt that a small group of thoughtful,
committed citizens can change the world.
Indeed, it is the only thing that ever has.
—Margaret Mead

Testifying is easy! **Testimony** serves a tremendously important function in the legislative process, but most citizens will never testify before a legislative body. There are a few reasons for that. It may be as simple as not knowing that such a process exists or that one *can* testify, or perhaps one assumes that testifying is something other people do. Testimony is simply public comments offered at a legislative hearing that become part of the record and reason for supporting or opposing a bill and can include fact-finding or investigative efforts. Ultimately, testimony can persuade legislators to vote how you want them to.

This process varies a bit in each state, so refer to appendix C for applicable rules in your state.

Citizens of Colorado are lucky. The state constitution guarantees a public hearing on every bill that's introduced and creates a constitutional right for citizens to testify for or against any bill. (This was referred to as the GAVEL [Give A Vote to Every Legislator] amendment, which was passed through the initiative process in 1988.) Reformers were tired of bills being killed by powerful committee chairs without the benefit of a public hearing. The former rules committee would ensure that even if a bill *did* pass out of a committee, it wouldn't necessarily get a vote on the floor unless the Speaker of the House or the president of the Senate wanted it to get to the floor. Since the passage of GAVEL, every bill gets a public hearing, whether the chair or party leadership wants one or not, and any member of the public can testify on any bill. This has been a positive change for democracy in the State of Colorado.

In many other states, getting a public hearing is neither automatic nor constitutionally guaranteed. Advocates may need to (1) persuade a chairperson to schedule a bill for hearing, or (2) persuade the majority party leadership to schedule a bill for a hearing. Also in some states, even if a bill passes out of committee, advocates may need to count votes on a rules committee to get a measure scheduled for a floor vote.

However, once a bill is scheduled for a hearing, virtually all states will make a calendar publicly available, usually online. This will help you know when and where a bill is scheduled for hearing. Chances are your bill won't be the only one on the calendar, so block out some extra time. You may want to confirm the order of bills with the chair of the committee to better estimate when you should arrive.

Once you know what committee the bill is going to, you'll want to look up which legislators are on the committee. Those legislators will be the audience for your testimony. Knowing the committee makeup will also help you count votes. **Vote counting** is the process of reaching out to each legislator who has a vote and asking them how they plan to vote. If you're seeking passage of a bill, you want to count to a majority of members of the committee as an affirmative vote. If you're seeking defeat of a measure, you count for a majority of no votes. In most states, a bill or amendment will die on a tie vote.

You can count votes by setting up personal meetings, sending e-mails or letters, or making phone calls. Ideally, before counting you would send a **fact sheet** to each voting member summarizing how you'd like them to vote and why. Some legislators commit their votes before a hearing either to a lobbyist or a fellow legislator. While some legislators may know how they're voting before a hearing, some don't, and it's not unheard of for someone to change their mind after listening to testimony.

Even so, your chances are best when you reach out early and in advance of the hearing to try to persuade the legislator of the merits of your voting preference. It's also a good idea to check with the chairperson or committee staffer on any unique protocols for testifying in your state. You may want to watch a few proceedings before you testify just to build your comfort level and confidence.

*As citizens of this democracy,
you are the rulers and the ruled,
the lawgivers and the law-abiding,
the beginning and the end.*
—Adlai Stevenson

TESTIFY
AT A LEGISLATIVE
HEARING

☐ **Look for a sign-in sheet and sign it.** Wait until you're called by the chair to testify.

☐ **Recognize the chair and the committee.** "Thank you, Madam/Mister Chair and members of the _____ committee for hearing my testimony today."

☐ **Introduce yourself and who, if anyone, you represent.** If you live in a committee member's district, add that to your introduction. "I'm a constituent of Representative/Senator _____."

☐ **State your position on the bill.** "I'm here to testify in support/opposition to Bill # _____."

☐ **Give a sentence or two of personal context that helps add some weight or credibility to your testimony.** "I have personal experience with _____"; "I have the following professional credentials: _____;" "I have the following academic credentials: _____." In other words, state why you know or care about the bill.

☐ **Give about three reasons for your position and any brief facts that support your reasons.** "I support/oppose this bill because _____, _____, and _____.

☐ **Prepare your testimony to be about three to five minutes long (unless directed otherwise).**

☐ **Don't read your testimony verbatim.** Doing so weakens your impact. Even if you want to write your testimony out verbatim to help you prepare, you should speak without it when testifying and try to make eye contact with each of the members. Make an outline of your talking points so you can refer to it as you speak.

☐ **Bring handouts.** You can provide a copy of your fact sheet, any key articles, or important photographs. Try to bring enough for the whole committee plus one extra to give to the committee staffer to add as part of the public record. These can be a helpful mnemonic device that helps reinforce your testimony and give legislators something to revisit later.

☐ **Go through the chair.** This means that the chair needs to recognize you or a member of the committee prior to your speaking. The purpose of this is to create an audio record of who is speaking and to ensure only one person is talking at a time.

☐ **Answer questions.** After you finish your testimony, committee members may have questions for you. If so, the chair will call on the committee member, then they will ask with their question—but don't answer immediately. The chair will turn to you and recognize you by name to indicate it's your turn to respond. Then you proceed with "Thank you Madam/Mister Chair and Representative/Senator _____for your question" and answer the question.

☐ **It's okay to say you don't know.** No one expects you to be an expert on all things. Don't feel cornered into speculating or making up an answer. If you don't know, just say so.

☐ **Dress comfortably.** But avoid jeans, hats, partisan political apparel, T-shirts, tank tops, bare shoulders, or anything considered skimpy.

☐ **Conclude your testimony.** Tell them how you'd like them to vote and thank the committee for their time.

☐ **If you can, stick around for the vote.** Your presence while the members vote is an important accountability function.

☐ **Follow up.** Send a thank-you-for-your-vote note to those who voted the way you wanted. Likewise, for those who didn't vote the way you wanted, it can be very effective to write a note like, "I'm disappointed in your vote, but don't hesitate to contact me in the future on this issue," or, "Perhaps I can get you some additional information and you might reconsider?"

Aside from the chair announcing who is speaking, the process is actually less formal than you might think. It's not like being in a courtroom and no one is there to "cross-examine" you. You really don't have to have any previous experience; the chair will be glad to walk you through the process. Remember, if you don't show up to testify, there's a high probability that there will only be paid lobbyists at the table, which can deeply skew a committee's impression of the public sentiment or public good.

Meet Richard Mijares

Richard isn't your usual voice at the capitol, but you wouldn't know why just by looking at him. After all, he's successfully employed with a solid work history (complete with promotions), owns a house, is registered to vote, pays his taxes, does volunteer work, and has a truck, a dog, and two cats. He's articulate, well read, analytical, and polite.

Richard served seventeen years in prison for a crime he committed when he was a juvenile. The crime was very serious: murder. Seventeen-year-old Richard was charged as an adult, and he served his time as a juvenile in the adult prison population. Richard knows what he did was wrong and takes full responsibility for his actions. More than anything, he wishes he could go back and handle things differently, for so many reasons. His original sentence was thirty-six years, reduced to twenty-six, and he served seventeen years in prison followed by three years on parole.

Across the country there's a debate raging in criminal justice circles about whether or how to differentiate between juveniles and adults in matters of crime and punishment. Do we believe juveniles are as culpable as adults? Does the age of the offender make any difference from the victim's perspective? Do we believe that people can change? Do we believe in redemption?

Richard had showed no outward warning signs that might have predicted such a serious crime; he had neither prior criminal record nor any problem conduct in school. Still, Richard couldn't tell his story at the time, and he didn't tell his attorney. When the judge asked for his statement, he said nothing. He was without friends or support and had no one to tell. Even if he did, Richard couldn't talk about it because he was so filled with shame.

But there *was* a story, and in 2005 he shared it publicly for the first time, with lawmakers. He had never participated in the legislative process before. Richard didn't testify for himself—there was no way he would ever benefit from the reforms he was pursuing. He testified hoping he might help other people and offer insight.

Richard learned there were other kids like him. We'd lock them up for life, throw away the key, and never review them for the possibility of parole—no matter what. This meant that there was no hope for those kids.

Even if they claimed personal responsibility for their crimes or underwent a major change or transformation, it would never make a difference in the eyes of the law. For juveniles serving life without the possibility of parole, there was no chance for redemption or second chances. It was one thing to have a parole hearing and decide against a juvenile because the offender was still dangerous to society; it was quite another to never even review a person for parole.

Here's what Richard told the committee. Richard's abuse began early. He grew up knowing he was unwanted, and violence and fear was a way of life for him. His father would beat him for such small infractions as dropping a sock out of the laundry basket. His father would corner him and kick him in the shins until they were bloody. Richard was afraid to go home after school. When his father arrived home after work, Richard would run and hide. He knew that if he cried out, the punishment would only be worse. He was taught to accept the abuse without question. He "learned" it was his fault, and he deserved to be punished. He was taught it was okay to lash out and hurt someone if you are angry or frustrated.

By the time Richard was fourteen, suicide was part of his daily thoughts. He was angry, isolated, desperate, and depressed, and he couldn't see a way out. His sense of fair and normal was distorted. He wanted to die. A few years later, he got in an argument with his mother and decided he wanted to kill himself. He left the argument, went and got a gun, and sat in a chair—talking to himself, trying to convince himself to put a bullet in his brain. His mother came down the stairs, still arguing, and he pointed the gun at her and pulled the trigger. She died instantly. Richard tried to suppress what he had done. He shut down. Nothing would ever be the same.

Richard spent his time in prison soul searching and thinking about what he'd done, what he would do differently, and what kind of person he wanted to be. This wasn't easy. He was young, and some predatory prisoners thought he was "cute." Within two weeks of arriving, he was stabbed by one of these adult inmates while a guard watched and did nothing. The type of "education" he was likely to receive in adult prison wasn't really conducive to becoming a better person. Surviving as a juvenile in an adult prison population, filled with corrupting influences and dangerous people, is tough. And surviving prison and learning the right lessons to become a high-functioning person outside of prison are not necessarily one in the same.

Richard learned that kids in Colorado can be charged as adults without any hearing or proceeding conducted by an independent fact finder to determine if they should be charged as juveniles or adults. This is hugely important because the rights, responsibilities, treatment, and consequences are very different depending on whether one is charged as a juvenile or adult. The entire rationale is different: the juvenile justice code is written on the premise that young people *might* be able to reform, are less developed, and are therefore less culpable than an adult who commits the same crime. Richard would serve his sentence and then have the chance to make a new life for himself. Other juvenile offenders serving life without parole would never get that chance.

During his time in prison, Richard read a lot and began to advocate for some people within the Department of Corrections (DOC) and for policy changes. He felt that education was a critical part of self-improvement and being able to better contribute to society on the outside. He learned that the DOC policy did not give credit for education against earned time. Richard worked a variety of angles and was able to get some changes to that policy, but not to the extent that he wanted. He started acting as a representative or advocate for other inmates in situations when some internal procedures seemed unfair.

Transitioning from prison to a halfway house was a big step for Richard. Other house inmates could check out for a few hours to visit their family; Richard had no place to go and no one to see. He used his time to attend events such as a Criminal Justice Awareness Day fair. As he began to meet and spend more time with organizations dedicated to juvenile justice reform, he learned about a bill that was before the legislature. Richard decided to testify.

In his testimony, he invited lawmakers to explore why we treat juveniles and adults differently under the law and whether we believe in second chances or redemption. He was testifying in support of a bill that would have allowed a judge to review juvenile LWOPs (life without parole) after serving a majority of their life sentence. Richard asked us not to give up on all the youth in prison. He didn't want them thrown away without the opportunity for reform. The bill (HB 05-1109) was heavily amended to create a legislative oversight project on juveniles serving life sentences, and it received bipartisan support. The governor vetoed the bill. The following year, two legislators introduced another version that allowed an inmate originally convicted as a juvenile to be considered for the possibility for parole after serving *forty* years, and it was signed by the governor. Yet, even with its passage, the bill still meant that the first review opportunity for a juvenile offender would happen between the ages of fifty-four and fifty-seven, and the kids who were already serving life sentences would still never get a review.

The committee had a lot of questions for Richard. What would he do differently? Had his parents faced criminal charges for the abuse they inflicted? How could this have been prevented? Where were human services when he was a child? Did he ever ask for or get any help prior to that fateful day? What would he say to other kids facing serious abuse? He answered all of the committee's questions. That day, a statistic became a person. Richard was willing to open himself up to public scrutiny in the hope that we might learn something that would make better public policy.

Richard is now living a completely new life—one of his own making. He'll never be able to forget what he did, and he makes no excuses, but he had a choice—throw the rest of his life away or choose to start a new one. He chose to start over and do the very best he could, and for him that includes helping others and speaking out on their behalf. Since his first day of testimony at the capitol, he has continued to pursue reforms through a variety of different channels. He's really just getting started and hopes to have much more to contribute to society before all is said and done. Richard's advice to you: take every opportunity you can to network and learn from other people. Those conversations lead to new people, new resources, and new ideas. Perhaps the greatest lesson is that we can all learn *something* from *everyone*.

Chapter 9
The Legislative Calendar

*Liberty cannot be preserved without a general knowledge
among the people, who have a right...and a desire to know.*
—John Adams

Most states now have their **legislative calendars** online. There's typically one calendar for the **House** and one for the **Senate**. These calendars change every day in session, so it's worth bookmarking them so you can quickly note any changes. Reading a legislative calendar isn't always straightforward and can be a bit frustrating.

Sometimes a calendar item is a firm event, and sometimes it simply serves as notice that the measure can be brought up anytime on or after the listed date. The states have different rules about how much notice must be given before action can be taken on a scheduled item. So, which is it and how can you tell?

Committee work on the calendar. If a bill or topic is scheduled to be heard in a committee for a specific day, it's usually held on that day. Most scheduled committee items happen as scheduled. However, the actual time can be difficult to predict. Bills may be scheduled "upon adjournment," which means when the legislature is dismissed from floor work. That could be at 9:15 AM, 10:30 AM, or noon, for example. Bills may be scheduled for an

afternoon docket, say at 1:30 PM, but there may be several bills on the calendar. The chairperson has the prerogative to change the order in which the bills are heard as there may be strategic reasons to do so. For example, a chairperson may consider changing timing to better align with media interests, disabled witnesses who physically can't wait for hours, a time conflict in which a legislator needs to be in two places at once, or as a favor to the bill sponsor, and so forth. If your bill is number three on the list, it can be difficult to know when to show up.

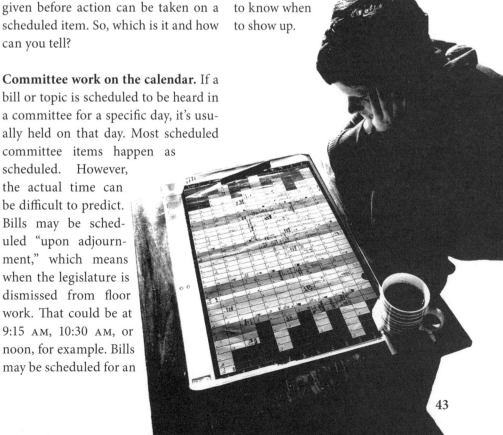

TIP: Start with the calendar, but it's a good idea to confirm with the chair whether a bill will still be heard and in what order before you take the time to go down and listen or testify.

Floorwork on the calendar. Floorwork is less precise. **Floorwork** is when the entire House or Senate meets to debate and vote on a bill after it has passed committee. A bill that's defeated in committee will never be scheduled for the floor. Just because a bill appears on the calendar doesn't mean it'll necessarily be debated or voted upon on the floor that day. The day a measure appears on the calendar really means "We could hear this bill anytime today or later." In some states, it can even mean "never."

The **majority leader** runs the schedule for the floor in both chambers and decides what bills to hear when. There may be rules that he or she must operate within, but to the extent there is discretion is up to the majority leader.

TIP: Start with the calendar, but ask either the legislative sponsor of the bill or the majority leader to be sure when a bill will actually come up on the floor.

The calendar is critical to your advocacy—it's how you plan your strategy, depending on which stage in the process you choose to engage. The best and most persuasive efforts won't matter if you're too late and the vote has already taken place.

Better use has been made of association and this powerful instrument of action has been applied for more varied aims in America than anywhere else in the world.
—Alexis de Tocqueville

Chapter 10

How a Bill Becomes Law and How You Can Impact Each Phase

The life of a republic lies certainly in the energy, virtue, and intelligence of its citizens.
—Andrew Johnson

1. Pre-introduction. This is a preliminary drafting stage where the initial version of the language is prepared by legal staff. The bill doesn't yet have a number and is still confidential and treated as a work product. Therefore, you can get a copy only if the sponsor consents to share it with you.

How you can advocate: Depending on how involved you are, you may be able to help write, amend, or shape a piece of legislation prior to its introduction.

2. Introduction of a bill. This is sometimes referred to as **first reading** of a bill. This is a process whereby the **Speaker of the House** or **president of the Senate** "reads the bill across the desk." This is the moment where a bill shifts from being confidential to a public document. At this juncture, it's assigned a bill number and the Speaker or president assign it to one or more committees. Bills are generally assigned to committees based on subject matter expertise.

How you can advocate: If you know a bill you're interested in will fare more favorably in one committee over another, you can try to persuade the Speaker or president to make a favorable assignment.

3. Assignment to a committee. Once the bill is assigned to a committee, the chairperson has discretion over when (or if, in some states) to schedule the bill for a hearing, within the rules. In many states, there's no requirement that a bill ever get a hearing.

How you can advocate: If you live in a state where a bill may never get a hearing, you have some advocacy work here to try to persuade the chair to schedule a hearing for a bill you support (or conversely, to not schedule a hearing for a bill you oppose.)

4. Committee hearing. Once a bill is scheduled for a hearing, the chairperson will often establish ground rules for testimony—for example, the order and length of testimony. The legislative sponsor and his or her allies typically do the primary work to bring in supportive witnesses. Opposition witnesses come from lobbyists or the public. The bill must receive a majority vote to pass out of committee, and most states provide that a bill "dies on a tie" vote. The committee can offer amendments to the bill at this phase.

How you can advocate: You can reach out to the legislators who have a vote on the committee, including the chair, in advance of the hearing to maximize input. This is a critical phase because the paid lobbyists are working hard during this time to **count their votes** and try to get commitments from legislators to vote the way they want before the hearing. You can provide fact sheets, media outreach, and petitions, seek personal meetings, write e-mails or letters, make phone calls, and give live testimony to have an impact at this phase.

5. Appropriations committee. If the measure has a financial impact to the state, it's typically assigned to the appropriations committee, where an appropriations clause can be added.

How you can advocate: If you support a measure that has a cost, you'll need to help find a funding source or a way to pay for it. This can be accomplished by taking funds from other areas or through helping to rewrite the bill to eliminate the fiscal cost. This is particularly key if you're in a balanced-budget state.

6. Second reading. The second reading of a bill is the phase during which it's referred to the entire House or Senate for debate, discussion, or amendment. These procedures are run by a presiding chair. The majority political party typically gets to decide who "is in the chair" for the day for floor work. As for amendments, well, there's a whole separate chapter on offensive and defensive strategies to making amendments. Passage at this stage is generally by **voice vote**, which has a few implications. A voice vote is imprecise, so it's a good idea to know your vote count in the entire House or Senate before proceeding to second reading. It takes a majority vote or voice ruling by the chair for legislation to pass at this phase.

How you can advocate: If there is someone who disagrees with your position in the chair but you would have your votes, then a **division** can be called. A division is a body count of votes—people stand up and are counted if they support the bill, and then later those who oppose do the same. While you can't provide testimony at this phase, you can provide fact sheets, media outreach, and petitions, seek personal meetings, write e-mails or letters, or make phone calls to try to influence the vote.

7. Third reading. The third reading of a bill is the final individually recorded vote. Debate and amendments are much more narrowly restricted at this stage, and it's usually a rather perfunctory formality of recording the final vote. The bill requires a majority to pass.

How you can advocate: Most legislators have made up their mind by this time, but focus your efforts on the swing votes—those who haven't made up their mind. Also, you can advocate for timing for a bill to go more quickly or slowly depending on whether or not you think you have your votes.

8. Same song, other chamber. If the bill began in the House, it'll now go through a parallel process, steps 1–7, in the Senate. If it began in the Senate, it will move to the House and do the same.

9. Reconciling different language in the House and Senate. If the second chamber makes changes to the

Did You Know...?

In 2008, 71 percent of voting-age citizens in the United States were registered to vote, with 63.6 percent actually voting—yet 89.6 percent of people self-reported that they voted that year!

language in the bill that were not in the language in the first chamber, then there are a few options:

- The first chamber can **concur**, or agree, with the changes made in the second chamber, which requires majority vote to concur and then readopt the bill.
- The first chamber can **reject** the amendments made in the second chamber and ask that a **conference committee** be formed. The Speaker of the House and president of the Senate then appoint a small group of people to a conference committee, where they try to come up with compromise language that both chambers can support. It takes a majority vote in the conference committee to adopt new language, and if adopted, it goes back to each chamber for adoption of the conference committee report and readoption of the bill. It takes a majority vote in both chambers to make this happen. If there's not a majority vote on agreed-upon language and readoption, then the bill dies.
- The first chamber can **adhere** to their original position, which then forces the second chamber to **recede** (in which case the bill passes in its original form) or also adhere, in which case the bill dies.

How you can advocate: If you have a strong opinion about which version of the bill is better, you can advocate at this point by pursuing concurrence, conference committee, or adherence. This is pretty advanced-level stuff, so don't

worry if this seems a bit much for now. You can also advocate by trying to get legislators who are supportive of your position appointed to the conference committee.

10. The governor. After a bill passes both the House and Senate with the same language, it goes to the governor, where he or she can:

- **sign the bill.** When the governor signs a bill, it becomes a law.
- **let it become law without signature.** If the governor isn't wild about the bill but doesn't really want to veto it, he or she can just wait it out. A bill will automatically become a law, even without the governor's signature, after the expiration of a certain time frame, usually ten days.
- **veto the bill.** If the governor vetoes a bill, it dies and does not become law unless there's a two-thirds majority vote to override the veto. This can only occur if the legislature is still in session. If the legislature isn't in session, the bill dies. A veto statement to explain the reason for the veto may accompany this decision.

How you can advocate: If there's a measure you want to see become law, then it's worthwhile to write the governor to urge his or her signature of the bill. If there's a measure you oppose that has nonetheless made it through the rest of the process, you may want to urge the governor to use his or her veto authority to defeat the bill.

Let us never forget that government is ourselves and not an alien power over us. The ultimate rulers of our democracy are not a president and senators and congressmen and government officials, but the voters of this country.
—Franklin D. Roosevelt

Chapter 11
Meeting Your Legislators

The effect of [a representative democracy is] to refine and enlarge the public views, by passing them through the medium of a chosen body of citizens, whose wisdom may best discern the true interest of the nation.
—James Madison

Before I ran for office, I had never met my legislators. To be honest, it never occurred to me to try. I didn't know them and assumed they would only meet with people they already knew or who were more "important" than me. I always had strong engagement on issues but assumed that politics was an insider's game, and I was not an insider. My assumption was that "other people" had those meetings, not people like me. I was wrong.

It's now clear to me that the people who get meetings and appointments are simply those who *ask* for them. You may not be able to control when the meeting occurs or how long the legislator will be able to meet with you, but you really can control the decision to meet your legislators and be on a first-name basis.

If your legislator has met you before, it helps increase the chances that he or she will recognize and respond to your e-mails, letters, and phone calls. It also increases the weight and credibility afforded to your future and subsequent input (unless you made a horrible impression). It increases the likelihood that he or she will help you with your reform interests and will keep your issue preferences in mind when voting. If possible, it's better to meet your legislator before you have a specific project or issue you would like them to adopt. Meeting your elected officials face-to-face is the best accountability mechanism out there, especially if they know they're likely to see you again.

To be clear, legislators can and do help everyone who reaches out,

not just those they know. But they're regular people who, consciously or unconsciously, are likely to give more attention and effort to those they have met.

Ways to Meet Your Legislators

- **Ask for a meeting.** Ideally, you should do this when they're not in legislative session—they'll have more time to talk with you and will be less distracted. If they're in session, you might be able to expect five to fifteen minutes of their time. Out of session, you might be able to expect fifteen minutes to an hour, depending on their schedule. Make sure to tell your legislator that you're his or her constituent.
- **Attend town hall meetings.** This is a great way to keep informed and learn more about key policy issues and community events. It's also a good way to introduce yourself, either before or after the event. Your elected officials will appreciate the fact that you were there, and it increases the odds they will recognize you when you meet again.
- **Attend community or public events.** Legislators will often be at community events when their schedule permits. Introduce yourself. Share a card, if you have one, as that provides a physical reminder of the meeting to the legislator and ensures they have your contact information.
- **Intern or volunteer.** Nearly every legislator is understaffed. If you have any time to volunteer to work in his or her office, you will be forever appreciated. It will give you an opportunity to work together and learn from each other.

Generally, I'd recommend at least one get-to-know-you meeting *before* you have any specific requests to make. A first meeting can be most effective in the long term if you don't have anything in particular you're asking for, but just getting to know each other briefly. However, that may not always be realistic. In-person meetings are also effective when there's a specific vote you want on a bill or if you would like them to introduce legislation on a specific matter. Meetings can also be helpful if you're aware of a particularly good report or resource, and you're able to cover the highlights.

While there are many ways to reach out and have an impact on your legislator, the most effective way is in person.

How to Make a Negative Impression

- Yell, make threats, or insult the elected official
- Include racist, sexist, or other discriminatory remarks
- Tell the elected official you think he or she and everyone else is corrupt
- Hit on your elected officials
- Ramble, repeat yourself, or take longer than is necessary to get to the point
- Write, call, or e-mail multiple times per day
- Refuse to work toward a solution

Leadership and learning are indispensable to each other.
—John F. Kennedy

SCHEDULE AND HAVE A GOOD MEETING

☐ **Identify yourself and the purpose of your call or visit.** This will help the scheduler best accommodate you. Make sure to leave your contact information.

☐ **Be nice to the staff.** The staff that help legislators are hardworking, underpaid folks. They tend to be public-service minded and will bend over backward to help you, if you're polite.

☐ **Be punctual.** Meetings are often squeezed in between committees and other obligations, so if you're late you might miss your window.

☐ **Be patient.** That said, there are times when your legislator may be detained for votes or other obligations. I would generally give them fifteen to thirty minutes, then ask to reschedule.

☐ **Prepare an agenda.** While you don't need a formal agenda, it is helpful to have a focused list of things you wish to discuss in order to make the best use of your time. Order them from most to least important, in case you run out of time.

☐ **Begin with a purpose.** Open the meeting with an introduction and the purpose and goal of your visit.

☐ **Be yourself.** Give your legislator a chance to get to know you—and to like you.

☐ **Be concise.** Legislative time is highly compressed, dealing with hundreds of bills and thousands of constituents. Not everyone is equally good at getting to the point quickly, but if you don't, the legislator may never get your point at all. You can always elaborate later or if time permits.

☐ **Bring a handout.** If it's relevant, a good handout can help a legislator see your point quickly, and it gives them a tool to follow up on the issues once you leave.

☐ **Recap any action items**. At the end of the meeting, summarize what you think you're going to do for follow-up, what you think your elected official will be doing for follow-up, and the time frame for when those items will be completed.

☐ **End strong.** Close the meeting with a recap of the action you're asking for and a "Thanks for your time."

Chapter 12
Calling Your Legislators

The tyranny of a prince is not so dangerous to the public welfare as the apathy of a citizen in a democracy.
—Montesquieu

I have had many people ask me whether we look at our phone messages or e-mails when deciding how to vote on a bill. The answer is yes. We keep a log of all calls, and if a call provides feedback on a particular piece of legislation, I file its details with the bill folder so I have the benefit of that message when I'm reading the bill.

You can typically find the phone number for your legislator by going to his or her website or by visiting the website for your state legislature. If you don't have Internet access, you can call information and get the contact numbers from the phone company.

Your legislators are often not in their office due to other obligations, but they generally will get their messages. You may or may not get your legislator live, but you should be prepared either way.

Our children should learn the general framework of their government and then they should know where they come in contact with the government, where it touches their daily lives and where their influence is exerted on the government. It must not be a distant thing, someone else's business, but they must see how every cog in the wheel of a democracy is important and bears its share of responsibility for the smooth running of the entire machine.
—Eleanor Roosevelt

MAKE AN EFFECTIVE PHONE CALL

☐ **Identify yourself.** I know this seems obvious, but you'd be surprised how many people call and give some really good information but never mention who they are. If you're calling as part of an action alert from a group, you may wish to mention the group as well.

☐ **State the purpose of your call.** What are you asking for? A yes or no vote? An invitation to speak? Some information? Some help? To share an idea? You should leave this information, even in a voice mail, because it may be possible for them to look up the necessary information before they return your call.

☐ **Keep it brief.** If you leave a recorded message, keep it to sixty seconds or less with your name, phone number, and the purpose of your call. If you're calling live, aim to cover what you'd like in five minutes or less. If you need longer, ask to schedule a phone appointment.

☐ **Provide your phone number.** Again, it may seem obvious, but important calls go unreturned when your elected officials have no way to get back to you.

☐ **E-mail any lengthy stories beforehand.** If your situation is complicated, consider sending an e-mail before you call to give a more-detailed background so you can get right to the point on the phone. If there's a long history necessary for background, it's helpful if you distill it to a basic time line so your legislator can quickly get a sense of the history and start to work with you right away.

☐ **Be polite.** Manners matter. Everyone will want to work harder for someone who is courteous and respectful. It's perfectly fine to express your discontent, disapproval, or displeasure, but do so in a polite and constructive way. It will have more impact that way.

☐ **Be clear about what you're asking for.** If there's something you want your legislator to do, be clear when you ask. "Can you refer me to someone who can _____?" "I'd like to find out more information about _____." "I'd like to ask you to vote yes/no." Once in awhile we get long messages but can't figure out what the person actually wants us to do.

SAMPLE TELEPHONE SCRIPTS

Requesting support of a bill. "This is Bill Jackson. I'm a constituent of yours, and I'm calling to ask for your yes vote on HB 1000. [One sentence on why:] It's an important measure for kids in our community. Thank you for your consideration. For more information on why I support HB 1000, you can reach me at 555-555-5555."

If live, add: "Can we count on your support for HB 1000?"

Requesting opposition of a bill. "This is Maria Alvarez. I'm a constituent of yours, and I'm calling to ask that you vote no on SB 100. [One sentence on why:] I believe it limits our rights and freedoms and will have unintended consequences. For more information on why I oppose SB 100, you can reach me at 555-555-5555."

If live, add: "Can we count on your help to defeat SB 100?"

Requesting constituent help. "This is Keith Jones. I'm a constituent of yours, and I'm calling because I'm waiting to receive my teacher's license and it's been a long time. [State the problem:] I submitted all of my paperwork but can't seem to get a response. I met all the criteria, but I have a job offer that starts next month and I'll lose this job without that license. [The ask:] Can you help? My phone number is 555-555-5555, and my address is 1234 Main Street, Your City, Your State."

If live, add: "Do you have any ideas on how to help?"

Asking to consider an idea. "This is Mary Whittacre. I'm a constituent of yours, and I'm calling because I recently got my utility bill and can't really make heads or tails of it. [State the problem:] I see a lot of fees but can't really tell what they're for. [The ask:] Would you consider doing something to make utility bills more transparent and user-friendly? My phone number is 555-555-5555 and my address is 1234 Main Street, Your City, Your State."

If live, add: "What do you think? Are you open to helping clarify this?"

Extending an invitation. "This is Pete Tisdale. I'm a teacher in your district. I'm calling to invite you to attend a graduation ceremony coming up on May 14, 2011, at 10:00 AM at 2000 Main Street, City, State. We will have parking available. You can RSVP to me at 555-555-5555. Hope to see you there!"

If live, add: "Can you attend?"

Requesting sponsorship of a bill. "This is Amy Nyugen. I've been researching campaign finance laws in the fifty states and noticed some gaps in Colorado. I also noticed that you have previously carried legislation to increase campaign finance transparency. I'm calling because I have a proposal I'd like to run past you, and I want to ask if you'd be willing to sponsor legislation this session. My phone number is 555-555-5555, and my address is 1234 Main Street, Your City, Your State."

If live, add: "Would you consider carrying this bill?"

Chapter 13
E-mailing Your Legislator

That government is the strongest of which
every man feels himself a part.
—Thomas Jefferson

For many legislators, e-mail is the preferred means of contact. They can read and respond to your e-mail at any hour, late or early, so it helps with time management, whereas phone calls are typically limited to 8:00 AM–6:00 PM, and a legislator may not have any window to call during those hours because of committee hearings or floorwork. E-mail also allows the legislator to keep, print, and file your comments in bill or policy folders for follow-up.

The downside to e-mail, however, is that once in awhile your message can get caught in a spam filter, so if you haven't received a response in two weeks, you should e-mail again or call to follow up. If it's urgent, you should call to follow up within forty-eight hours. E-mail also allows you to send attachments, so if you have relevant documents to accompany your inquiry, those can be sent at the same time. The e-mail address for your legislator can typically be found on his or her website or by visiting the website for the state legislature.

Democracy is never a final achievement.
It is a call to an untiring effort.
—John F. Kennedy

WRITE AN EFFECTIVE E-MAIL

☐ **Use your subject line wisely.** The subject line itself, if used well, can help catch the recipient's attention and persuade him or her. Many legislators get such a high volume of e-mails that they use multiple e-mail filters, which usually group e-mails by subject line, to help sort them. Your subject line should be as specific as possible to get it quickly routed through the correct filter on your recipient's end. For example:

- Vote Yes on HB 100
- Invitation June 12, 3:00 PM
- Help Requested—Waiting List
- Meeting Request—Bill Idea re Job Creation

☐ **Identify yourself.** Introduce yourself and provide a sentence or two about your background and why you care about an issue. Your input can be based on life experience, work experience, education, or training.

☐ **State your purpose.** "The purpose of this e-mail is to ask you to [vote, research, help] on _____."

☐ **Keep it to one page.** An e-mail that's less than one page long is more likely to be read than one that's twenty pages. If you're sending a longer e-mail, it's very important that you add a consolidated statement of what you're asking for at the beginning and the end so it doesn't get lost.

☐ **Keep formatting simple.** It generally doesn't matter how you format your e-mail, but it's helpful if you use one 12-point or 14-point font to make reading easy. Also, writing in all caps is the e-mail version of shouting—don't do it. Paragraphs help; three pages in one block paragraph are hard to read and increase the chances that something will be missed.

☐ **State the issue.** Provide a few sentences or a paragraph to help frame the nature of the issue or the problem.

☐ **Be clear about what you're asking for.** Clearly state what it is you would like your legislator to do.

☐ **Provide your contact information.** You should include whether or not you're a constituent, your phone number, and your physical mailing address. Giving your physical address allows the recipient to confirm whose district you live in and to regionally determine the resources that may be most appropriate for you. If you have a standard e-mail signature with your name, address, and phone number, use it.

☐ **Be polite.** Manners matter. Everyone will want to work harder for someone who is courteous and respectful. It's perfectly fine to express your discontent, disapproval, or displeasure, but do so in a polite and constructive way, and avoid speculating on people's motives. Your e-mail will have more impact that way.

☐ **Include facts.** They're more helpful than conclusions. For example, we sometimes get e-mails in which a constituent will conclude that person A is a liar. But the more helpful information is to say, "This note says X, but his/her latest statement says Y—just the opposite." Also, avoid being a lay lawyer. "This person perjured himself/herself and committed fraud" is not as helpful as sharing the underlying facts that form the basis for those conclusions. You don't need to adopt legalistic language to be taken seriously, and if you're wrong about the law, it could weaken your credibility.

☐ **Give sources for your facts.** Doing so allows a legislator to verify and follow up on the material provided. If the facts are your own personal experience, that's fine—just say so. If you have data, research, or statistics, reference where the data came from.

☐ **Give a deadline or timing info.** If the nature of your inquiry requires a deadline or time frame for the help to still be beneficial, include it.

☐ **State whether your correspondence is private or public.** Most states will treat constituent communications as confidential documents, thus not subject to discovery in open records, but they may determine that it depends on the intent of the constituent. The only safe bet is to be clear. If you'd like your e-mail to be made public or to be included as part of written testimony, say so in your e-mail. If you'd like your e-mail to be private and treated confidentially, say so.

SAMPLE E-MAIL

SUBJECT: Help with Suspension, Reform Zero-Tolerance Laws

Dear Representative Smith:

My name is Jake Collins and I am writing to you confidentially as a proud but concerned parent of a high school student in your district. My son, James, was recently detained and suspended for bringing his medication to school. He has severe asthma and needs immediate access to his inhaler. I have since learned that we were supposed to notify the school of his medication needs ahead of time.

I am writing to see if you can help appeal his suspension. It makes no sense for him to be punished for a medical condition he has no control over by removing him from his class work. I am also writing because I would like you to reconsider the zero-tolerance policies adopted lately in our schools. I think they create strange and unintended consequences and go too far. We need to respond in ten days, so I'd be grateful for any help you can offer before that time.

You can reach me at jakecollins@email.com or on my cell phone at 555-555-5555. My address is 1234 Main Street, Your City, Your State.

Thank you for your time and assistance.

Sincerely,
Jake Collins

Chapter 14
Writing Your Legislators

Freedom is hammered out on the anvil of discussion, debate, and dissent.
—Hubert H. Humphrey

Letters are another appropriate medium to contact your legislators, but there are some drawbacks. Most significantly, you don't want to use snail mail for anything that's time sensitive, such as a vote, if in session. If the help you seek has a deadline, you're better off e-mailing or calling your legislators and making sure they know the deadline involved.

If time is not of the essence, the upside of an old-fashioned letter is that it has become less common to receive letters, so your letter is likely to stand out. Letters provide the option of adding a somewhat more personal touch than e-mails, but it usually takes legislators a bit longer to reply to them.

The same steps provided for effective e-mails apply to letters as well. However, in an era of heightened security, you should know that some packages or letters might be opened before they get to the legislator's desk. Because of a series of anthrax scares in recent years, you need to be careful what you put in your letters. The wrong jokes or pranks could land you in jail.

Civility is not a tactic or a sentiment. It is the determined choice of trust over cynicism, of community over chaos.
—George W. Bush

WRITE AN EFFECTIVE LETTER

Start with the steps on page 56, Write an Effective E-mail, and continue with these additons or changes.

☐ **Include your return address.** Use your return address on the envelope. Otherwise, in some states, your mail may not be delivered as a security protocol. Also, include all of your contact information in the letter itself. If the envelope gets separated from the letter, your legislator can still respond to you.

☐ **Use your legislator's title.** Until your legislator knows you well enough to say otherwise, it's safer to use his or her proper title. This can vary from state to state but is typically "Representative," "Senator," "Assemblyman/woman," or "The Honorable."

☐ **Use a regarding (RE:) line.** This is a short label identifying the subject matter of the communication, usually preceding the salutation. Some offices may have staff or volunteers who specialize in certain areas, and this can ensure your letter is routed quickly and appropriately. For example:

- RE: Waitlist for services for people with developmental disabilities
- RE: State tax policy
- RE: Public Safety

SAMPLE LETTER

Your Name
Your Address
Your City, Your State, Your Zip
Your Phone Number, Your E-mail Address

May 15, 2011

Senator Lynn Wright
Your State Capitol
123 Capitol Address
City, State, Zip

RE: General Practice Medicine

Dear Senator Wright:

I'm a constituent who lives in your district, and I'm writing to you because I'm concerned about the future of family practice general medicine in our state. I have been a family doctor in this state for thirty-two years and I remain passionate and dedicated to the patients I serve. I recently read an article in our local paper about the state experiencing a shortage of family care doctors, and I think I can shed some light on why.

My staff and I are spending an inordinate amount of time on billing matters. I didn't go to medical school to become a collections specialist, yet we find that we're constantly fighting with insurance companies to pay what's owed, even when they preapprove the procedures. Likewise, the state's Medicaid reimbursement rate is so low that we are often performing medical procedures at a loss.

The frustration of dealing with insurance billing and state reimbursement rates has made it such that it's no longer cost-effective to offer a patient-centric model of care. Please contact me at your earliest convenience so that we can discuss possible state-level reforms to attract and retain general practice family physicians. Please share this information with anyone who may find it useful, as it is my goal to raise awareness of this problem. My contact information is above.

Thank you for your time and attention.
Sincerely,

George Peterson, MD

Chapter 15
Using Petitions

*The People, though we think of a great entity
when we use the word, means nothing more than
so many millions of individual men.*
—James Bryce

Petitions can be a very effective way to get the attention of your legislators. A petition that gathers a lot of hard copy signatures is a sign of a great deal of effort and sends a strong signal that people care enough to spend time talking to others in the community about an issue. However, e-petitions can be effective too and often allow a greater

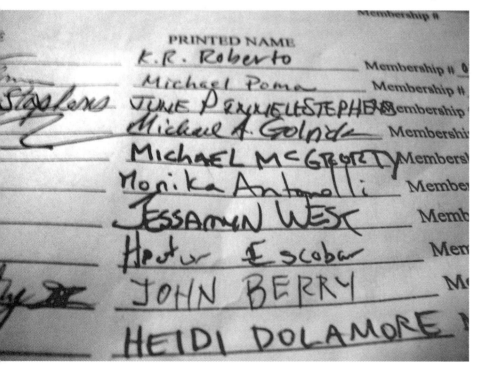

viral circulation for broader distribution of an issue.

Simply signing an existing petition that you agree with can be a time-efficient way for you to register your

support or opposition to an issue or measure. You should assume that any petition you sign will be part of a public record, so don't sign it unless you're sure you agree with it.

From a legislator's perspective, it's more time-efficient to receive one letter with a hundred signatures than it is to receive a hundred form letters. If you have time to send a personalized letter or e-mail, that will likely have greater impact than a petition. However, if you don't have time to customize your correspondence, it's probably preferable to simply add your name to an existing letter or petition.

But perhaps you'd like to start and circulate your own petition. Petitions generally take one of two forms: as a letter that simply adds a lot of signatures, or as a series of "WHEREAS" statements followed by a lot of signatures.

Petitions can be really effective. When I was working on a bill to require insurance companies to provide actuarial justification prior to rate-hike approval, it was very clear that there were many, many more insurance lobbyists in the building than consumer lobbyists. Whenever that's the case, grassroots people power is essential to overcome those odds.

ProgressNow circulated an electronic petition that included, among other things, the higher-than-average rate of insurance premium growth despite improving health statistics in Colorado that would suggest lower-than-average rates, as well as the amount of surpluses and profits currently held by the industry. We collected more than four thousand signatures from Coloradans, printed out the petition, and at hearing passed around a four-inch binder of signatures and comments from people and small businesses asking for relief from uncontrolled and unjustified healthcare insurance rate hikes. The Fair Accountable Insurance Rates Act, or the FAIR Act, passed with some bipartisan support because regular people engaged the issue and were powerful enough to prevail over a sizeable, well-funded, influential insurance lobby.

WRITE AN EFFECTIVE PETITION

☐ **State the desired action.** So it will be impossible to miss, state the desired outcome or action both at the beginning and at the end of the petition.

☐ **State the problem.** Identify the problem and include facts or research when you can. Try to offer at least three facts to support the declaration that there's a problem. Each fact should be its own sentence and include a reference citation so that the legislator can verify the source of information.

☐ **Provide reasons to support the requested action.** Offer at least three facts or researched statements to support the proposed solution.

☐ **Keep the length appropriate.** The body of a petition should be one to two pages long.

☐ **Collect signatures and addresses.** The collection of signatures should not only include names but also addresses. This helps confirm that the signatories are real people and demonstrates the geographic regions that agree with the petition.

☐ **Do NOT ask, "Do you have a minute?"** The answer is always no. Instead, lead with, "Do you support [primary principle or value behind your effort]? Would you sign a petition to [fix this problem] in our state?" Hand a clipboard to the person as you ask, and always be sure you have fact sheets or more detailed information on hand so you're ready if someone wants a full discussion. Wear a name tag and dress professionally.

☐ **Target the right places.** You'll get more signatures if you target high-population centers (grocery stores, public libraries, fairs) or areas that are likely to have a higher than average interest in the issue you're pursuing (for example, if you have a petition to support schools, target schools and school outlets). If you're starting an Internet petition, target your e-mail contact lists, Listservs or issue-oriented groups, and distribute the petition via Facebook and/or other social media sites. Remember—if you're asked to leave private property, you must do so or you're trespassing.

☐ **Present the completed petition.** While you can always just drop off a completed petition or forward it electronically, the petition will have more impact if you schedule a planned presentation in a personal meeting with a legislator or at a press conference.

I know of no safe depository of the ultimate powers
of the society but the people themselves;
and if we think them not enlightened enough
to exercise their control with a wholesome discretion,
the remedy is not to take it from them,
but inform their discretion.
—Thomas Jefferson

SAMPLE PETITION

We, the undersigned students at University Name, are writing to ask that you reinstate the state's college scholarship program that was recently cut in the state budget.

WHEREAS, the $3 million in funding negatively impacts thousands of students in the state.

WHEREAS, for many students this scholarship program is the difference between affordable and expensive college, and therefore the difference between attending and not attending.

WHEREAS, this funding is critical to ensure all young people have the opportunity to attend college, not only those who can afford it.

WHEREAS, these students have been told that if they work hard, get good grades, and apply themselves, there will be affordable college opportunities, and when the state cut this funding, they broke a promise made to our state's young people.

WHEREAS, we recognize that times are tough, but this needs to remain a top priority as it impacts job creation and job readiness in our state.

WHEREAS, we recognize there are competing interests for limited funds, but we respectfully suggest you defund Boondoggle Name instead in order to make these funds available.

WHEREAS, the reinstatement of these funds is a good investment because the state will see higher return of their investment in the form of higher earning potential and increased revenue from a future tax base.

THEREFORE, we the undersigned respectfully request that you reinstate the $3 million in proposed cuts from the state's scholarship program.

_____   _____
Name   Address

_____   _____
Name   Address

_____   _____
Name   Address

_____   _____
Name   Address

_____   _____
Name   Address

_____   _____
Name   Address

_____   _____
Name   Address

_____   _____
Name   Address

_____   _____
Name   Address

Chapter 16
Preparing Fact Sheets

*Almost always, the creative dedicated minority
has made the world better.*
—Martin Luther King Jr.

The intermediate to advanced citizen advocate may wish to consider preparing and disseminating **fact sheets**. Lobbyists and various interest groups prepare these all the time as tools to help them lobby at the capitol. As you can imagine, those "fact" sheets can sometimes be skewed, inaccurate, selective, or distorted. The single most helpful thing you can offer to help the process work better is to provide good information.

Fact sheets are typically prepared by lobbyist groups in advance of a formal vote as a tool to try to get a **vote commitment** from a legislator. The good news is that citizens can do this too, and when you take the time to do it, it often carries greater weight.

*Change your life today. Don't gamble on the future,
act now, without delay.*
—Simone de Beauvoir

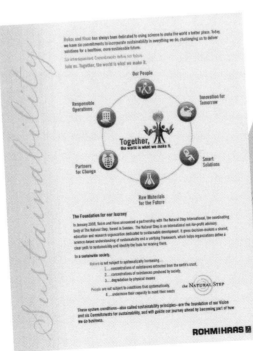

65

CREATE AN EFFECTIVE FACT SHEET

☐ **Start with a heading.** The top of your document should reference the bill number, the bill title or name, and the names of the sponsors of the measure. Legislators see hundreds or even thousands of bills and it's important that they can quickly ascertain to which measure your fact sheet pertains. This is also helpful for getting your fact sheet correctly filed with the right bill after it's been reviewed.

☐ **Use a headline ask.** For example, "Please support/oppose HB 1000." This should be very visible so if the document is merely skimmed, the reader can register whether it was in support of or in opposition to the measure.

☐ **Provide brief background.** Give any facts or background needed so that you frame the relevance of the issue.

☐ **State the problem.** Identify what's wrong with the status quo if you're seeking to support reforms, or what's wrong with the bill if you oppose it.

☐ **State the solution.** Give some policy background on what will solve or improve the problem if you support the bill, or why defeating or amending the measure is the solution if you oppose it.

☐ **Briefly describe the bill in the context of your support of or opposition to it.** If you support the measure, this description should fit with the stated problems and proposed solutions. If you're seeking to defeat or amend the measure, the description should feature the problem portions.

☐ **Acknowledge the other side.** If you can anticipate and respond to the strongest arguments on the other side, you'll have a more powerful fact sheet.

☐ **It's not all-or-nothing.** You don't have to 100 percent love or hate a measure. In fact, it can be quite helpful and persuasive to get input on why you like or dislike portions of a bill.

☐ **Establish your credibility.** You have one shot at establishing your credibility, which is extremely important to your future advocacy. Do not overstate your facts. Make sure what you include is accurate, and if you ever discover a mistake, point it out and correct it immediately so the legislator knows you can be counted on as a conscientious source of good information.

☐ **Provide your contact info and research sources.** It's helpful to add your name, contact information, and any other organizations that agree with you to the bottom of your fact sheet. You can also add source citations for any research or statistics you have included.

SAMPLE FACT SHEETS

SUPPORT SB11-72: PROTECTING COLORADO JOBS & CIVIL RIGHTS AT WORK
(M. Carroll – Levy)
FACT SHEET

Background: For 47 years it has been against the law to discriminate against workers on the basis of race, color, religion, sex and national origin…[when working for an employer who employs more than 15 people].

The Problem: The very same illegal acts of discrimination, which violate the law and a person's civil rights, are unenforceable if the person works for a company employing fewer than 15 people.

The Solution: Join the 43 other states have acted to close this loophole by providing the same rights to employees who work for companies with fewer than 15 people.

The Bill: Gives all Colorado workers the same protections found in Title VII of the Civil Rights Act of 1964 to ensure that no job loss is a result of illegal discrimination.

- A worker will still have to prove *intentional* **discrimination**, which is not easy.

- Small companies would have **3 years** to get educated and prepare for compliance.

- The bill has a **volunteer advisory committee** comprised of employers and employees to help promote awareness, education and prevention of any violation.

- **Free education and training materials** would be made available to any employer in the State of Colorado on how to comply with the law and avoid litigation in this area.

- The Colorado Civil Rights Division process includes **two phases of mediation** to help employers and employees avoid litigation.

- The bill is needed to also give enforcement to civil rights that Colorado has added as a matter of public policy: **age**, **sexual orientation** and **domestic violence status**.

The Goal: The goal is to prevent discrimination from occurring in any Colorado workplace – a practice that nearly every business in Colorado already seeks to honor.

The High Cost of Solitary Confinement

SB 176 – SOLITARY CONFINEMENT – IDENTIFIED POPULATIONS
Sponsored by Senator Morgan Carroll and Representative Claire Levy

Solitary Confinement, also known as administrative segregation, is the custody level assigned to an inmate where he or she is isolated from the general prison population and housed in a single-cell for up to 23 hours per day with severely restricted out-of-cell activities. Over the past 12 years, placement into solitary confinement has nearly tripled for inmates with developmental disabilities or mental health issues. **Currently, 37% of inmates in solitary confinement are prisoners with developmental disabilities or mental health needs.**[i] In contrast, in 1999 fifteen percent of inmates in solitary confinement were mentally ill.[ii] This drastic growth is largely attributed to significant budget cuts targeting prison services leaving solitary confinement as the default placement for many inmates with developmental disabilities or mental health care needs.

HIGH COSTS
The choice to continually place offenders with mental health issues or developmental disabilities into solitary confinement has simultaneously increased costs for incarceration, increased recidivism rates, and reduced public safety.

The two largest populations of prisoners in administrative segregation are housed in Centennial Correctional Facility and Colorado State Penitentiary,

SOLITARY CONFINEMENT FACTS
1,407 people: Current inmate total
23 hours: Daily isolation in cell
16 months: Average length of stay
$48,403: Annual cost per inmate in Centennial Correctional Facility
Colorado Department of Corrections, accessed January 18, 2011

where the state is forced to bear the cost of $48,403 and $42,642 respectively per inmate annually.[iii] Similarly situated facilities based on population size and security level, Limon and Sterling Correctional Facilities, spend only $27,709 and $26,918 respectively per inmate annually.[iv]   **The increased cost to maintain a prisoner in solitary confinement can range from $14,933 to $21,485 per inmate every year.**

Further, **nearly 41% of all prisoners released from solitary confinement are released directly into the community** either on discretionary parole (8%), mandatory parole (20%), or as a result of discharging their sentence (13%) in which they are released without any parole supervision.[v] These prisoners are not given the ability or time to readjust to human interaction with the general prison population, and thus have very limited success reintegrating into their communities at home.

Two-thirds of prisoners who were released directly from solitary confinement to the streets returned to prison within 3 years, while **inmates who transitioned from solitary confinement into the general prison population before community re-entry experienced a 6% reduction in their comparative recidivism rate** for the same time period. [vi]

In addition to the financial and human costs associated with the practice of solitary confinement, the United States of America has a long-standing moral objection to its use in the correction system. From the earliest days of American penitentiaries, dating back to

The High Cost of Solitary Confinement

Philadelphia in 1829, the use of solitary confinement has been widely denounced as an immoral tactic that undermines the innate human need for social interaction and works against the core goal of rehabilitation for correction institutions.

The decline of mental health services in the Department of Corrections, in conjunction with the conscious choice to continually place offenders with mental health issues or developmental disabilities into solitary confinement, has created a substantial financial burden for the state, exacerbated the severe human costs for prisoners with mental illness and their communities, and marred Colorado with reputation that defies our national legacy of opposition to solitary confinement.

> **In response to how history will judge Colorado's use of solitary confinement:**
>
> "Twenty, thirty, fifty years from now, they may be looking back at us and saying that wasn't a great answer, a great response, we should have known better."
>
> – *Colorado State Penitentiary Warden Susan Jones*   Denver Post, November 07, 2010

EFFICIENCY, ACCOUNTABILITY & SAFETY

As drafted, this legislation proposes to fix the high cost of solitary confinement by:

- Creating an evaluation process for prisoners with developmental disabilities or serious mental illness, while maintaining the warden's ability to restrict the confinement of any person who is a confirmed security risk;

- Ensuring all inmates placed in solitary confinement are reintegrated into the general prison population before their community release to mitigate cost and public safety issues;

- Allowing an inmate housed in solitary confinement the opportunity, based on proof of lack of disciplinary incidents, to accrue earned time to be deducted from his or her sentence and redirecting all cost savings into alternatives to solitary confinement, including mental and behavioral health programs; and,

- Strengthening existing accountability oversight to ensure mental health is considered before and during placement in solitary confinement.

COALITION MEMBERS

ACLU of Colorado
Colorado Criminal Justice Reform
  Coalition
Colorado CURE

Mental Health America of Colorado
University of Denver Civil Rights Clinic
Colorado Criminal Defense Bar

---

[i] O'Keefe, Maureen L. (2008), "Administrative Segregation for Mentally Ill Inmates," *Journal of Offender Rehabilitation,* 45:1, 149-165 at 155 and 157
[ii] O'Keefe, Maureen L. (2005), "Analysis of Colorado's Administrative Segregation," Colorado Department of Corrections at 29.
[iii] (2010), "Cost Per Offender By Facility FY 2009-2010," Colorado Department of Corrections, accessed January 18, 2011.
[iv] ibid
[v] O'Keefe, Maureen L. (2005), "Analysis of Colorado's Administrative Segregation," Colorado Department of Corrections at 23.
[vi] ibid at 25.

Chapter 17
Holding Demonstrations and Rallies

*The democracy process provides for political
and social change without violence.*
—Aung San Suu Kyi

Demonstrations and rallies can certainly have an impact on a legislator, but they're better tools for building solidarity amongst those who already agree with you, or for purposes of gaining media attention or publicity for the cause. There's nothing as effective as one-on-one targeted persuasion to each legislator whose vote you're seeking, but rallies can be good tools to raise public awareness or give a visual show of support or opposition to an issue.

Rallies are a lot of work, and a poorly attended one can send the opposite message if you're not careful.

A riot is at bottom the language of the unheard.
—Martin Luther King Jr.

HOLD AN EFFECTIVE RALLY

☐ **Choose a central location.** The capitol building is a frequent location for rallies or protests because it tends to be centrally located and the activists know there will be lawmakers inside. Pick a location that has some symbolic significance to the issue you're addressing.

☐ **Time it right.** Find a time when you won't be competing with another rally on an unrelated issue. Unless you're holding a candlelight vigil, daytime offers better visibility and you'll likely get better traffic.

☐ **Prepare visual messages.** Have signs ready to convey a visual message so if people can't hear you or are simply passing by quickly, they can get the point of your rally. A combination of professional and handmade signs can be effective. Funny or catchy signs are more likely to end up in the newspaper. As the organizer, you should have prepared the signs; having others show up with signs that are misspelled or in bad taste can actually hurt your cause.

☐ **Build a crowd.** To maximize your crowd attendance, try to plan at least two to three weeks ahead. Send notices out via e-mail and social media to your allies and supporters, and ask them to do the same. Find other groups or organizations with a shared value system and ask them to publicize the event. You may get one attendee for every hundred invites, so circulate broadly. Call on talk radio shows that would be interested in the theme of the rally to invite others to join.

☐ **Schedule a good mix of presenters.** Find a presenter lineup that includes speakers who have good name draw. Having a mix of citizen speakers and high-profile speakers can help. A rally is not a dissertation. The fastest way to de-energize your rally is to have speakers drone on and on. Generally, your speakers should be directed to keep their comments to two to three minutes. Sketch out the basic theme or content you'd like each speaker to address, and identify potential gaffes that can hurt the whole event. For example, one speaker at a Tea Party rally for less government went on to refer to state employees as "storm troopers of communism. We must defeat them. I never realized there was that much scum on the government payrolls." That comment drew boos—even from those supporters attending the rally.

☐ **Use music appropriately.** Music can help set the mood and energize a crowd. It can also minimize awkward silence while finalizing setup or in between speakers.

☐ **Use a good sound system.** Arrange access to a sound system and test it at the venue before the event to work out bugs ahead of time. Is it loud enough? Too loud? Does it distort easily and create horrid screeches of interference? Don't forget extension cords.

☐ **Get a photographer or videographer.** It's helpful if you can find someone who's willing to snap pictures or video of the event. These images can be loaded to the Internet and shared with the media to help their coverage of the event.

☐ **Devise a media plan.** Send a press release to "save the date" at least a week before the event. Send a reminder with more details about the speaker lineup and other press-worthy highlights the day before. Send a press release right after the event recapping the highlights and include photos, videos, or interesting sound files of anything that helps tell the story. Television media in particular will respond strongest to interesting, catchy, or unusual visual presentation.

☐ **Set the tone.** As organizer, it's up to you to set the atmosphere of the rally. Trust me, it'll be the one loon in the crowd who gets him- or herself in the press and becomes the icon or spokesperson for the issue, whether you want them to or not. To avoid this, be sure you set a consistent tone in your e-mails and press releases, choose your speaker lineup wisely, make and distribute signs you want used, and be sure your preferred community leaders and spokespeople are readily available to talk to the press. Generate your own flashy photo ops so the press will be less likely to search for the clown.

☐ **Begin and end with a call to action.** The point of a rally, besides drawing attention to an issue, is to get people to do something. Is there a petition you want them to sign? Calls you want them to make? E-mails to send? March to register voters? A public hearing you want them to attend? In the case of a rally, it's not just what you want your elected officials to do, but also what you'd like the attendees to accomplish. Give people something meaningful to do.

Chapter 18

Networking:
Building a Coalition and
Addressing Opposition

Teamwork divides the task and multiplies the success.
—Author unknown

Some people network naturally. I'm not one of them. It's true that one person can make a difference, but those people often do so by educating or inspiring others and growing the breadth and depth of support behind their ideas for reform. When I was first elected into office, I had a list of laws I wanted changed because I thought they were unjust. I worked diligently to research the options to change them, to write reforms to the laws, and to try to persuade my colleagues about their merits—but many of those bills died.

Legislating is a group activity, not a solo one. While my research was impeccable, my outreach wasn't, and many of my bill ideas failed as a result. There's a culture to a legislature that goes beyond party affiliation or control. The culture of the legislature prefers bills that are supported by a lot of people and organizations, are opposed by no one, are simple to understand, and that the press lavishes praise on you for running,

and for which your district thanks you. Those bills are rare, if not mythical.

To the extent you're seeking reform, you can be certain there will be opposition from interests who helped to create and protect the status quo. I made two major mistakes my first session. I didn't stop to think, *If I think this is unjust, others probably think so too,* and brainstorm a list of people or organizations that might sign on to help. I also didn't stop to think about who the organized opposition would be. It's more intuitive to network with allies and people who agree with you. It's less self-evident why one needs to also network with your likely opposition.

You can use group networking efforts to weigh in on a piece of legislation and to try to help urge its passage or defeat, or you can use group networking to try to pass your own bill.

The most straightforward goal is to grow and maximize your coalition of supporters and minimize the depth and breadth of the opposition. Both can be time consuming, but they're usually worth the effort.

Sticks in a bundle are unbreakable.
—Kenyan proverb

BUILD A COALITION
OF SUPPORTERS

☐ **Think about who you should approach.** If you're not a natural networker, ask someone who is for help brainstorming. If there's already a bill under way, then the best place to start is the sponsor—find out who's already on board. You may be able to simply offer names of other individuals or groups the sponsor hasn't included yet. (If you're running your own bill, it's a bit more work.)

☐ **Make a list**. Begin with all the people and organizations you know who would likely care about the issue you're trying to change.

☐ **Find contact info and enter it into a chart.** Create a quick reference chart or spreadsheet.

☐ **Start with the most receptive people on your list.** It's easiest to get the wheels turning if you begin with the people or groups who are most likely to take an immediate interest in your effort. Individuals are easier because they can usually just say yes or no. Organizations often need to report back to a larger board or a public policy committee to decide whether to officially support an effort—but organizational support can bring on more people and more resources to help your effort. Then ask them if they know of any other people or organizations who might be interested. The cause-based focus of most organizations means they probably know a lot of other people who would be interested. They often have members, e-mail lists, and network partners of their own. Also ask them if they have ideas or suggestions for improving the bill.

☐ **Approach organizations with care.** Ask about their approval process and what's needed for the organization to take a formal position to support a bill. You may need to write up a proposal, present at a board meeting, or ask a friendly contact within the organization to make the case for you. An organization's process can you take some time, so be sure to factor that into your plan.

☐ **Track the status of your requests.** Add a few columns to your contacts chart to keep track of the responses: Need to Contact, Pending Decision, Support, Won't Support. Many organizations have different levels of support, for example, active support, light support, support, monitor, neutral, oppose, actively oppose.

☐ **Approach the tough customers.** Once you have the most eager and active supporters lined up, you're ready for the persuasion supporters—the groups who are probably interested but might need more work, information, or persuasion to get them on board. It helps to approach these folks with your list of existing coalition members, since at this point you're asking if they're willing to join the coalition. They'll tell you if there's any additional internal procedure they need to go through to take an official position.

☐ **Spread the news.** Once you're growing a coalition, communication is key. Let others know if new people or groups have joined or if there are any meetings scheduled to work on drafting or strategy.

☐ **Ask for help.** If possible, find a lead—someone who's willing to be point person for outreach and communications with the other people and groups in the coalition. This person will often be the most dedicated to the issue and have the best follow-up skills. The role he or she takes will depend on what you and the existing coalition decide.

☐ **Consider the opposition.** The coalition of supporters should take some time to anticipate who the opposition will likely be and why. There may be small changes you can make to your effort that don't compromise the goal of the bill but that could eliminate or minimize that opposition. It's worth finding out what they don't like and what, if anything, you could do to remove or minimize their opposition. That doesn't mean you'll want to do it, but you may find that a somewhat innocuous change to the bill can sometimes do wonders to remove unnecessary obstacles.

SAMPLE SUPPORTER TRACKER

Name	Phone and E-mail	Initial Contact	Status	Position
John Smith	123-456-7890 jsmith@email.com	Yes, 3/21/11	Looking for others	Support
Katie Medina	555-700-8080	Yes	Has list of people who are interested	Support
A Group	333-333-1111 agroup@email.com	Yes, 3/25/11	Will present to board for approval	**Monitor**, will likely support pending vote
B Group	111-222-4444 bgroup@email.com	Yes, 3/12/11	Will reach out and do action alert to members, reaching out to affiliated groups, C, D.	Support
C Group	888-222-7777	No	Need initial meeting	Unknown
D Group	444-111-9999	Yes	No further action	**Won't support**, too many other issues going, not close enough to core mission

DEAL WITH THE OPPOSITION

☐ **Make a list of your likely opposition.** You may not fully learn who all would be opposed to your bill until you introduce it, but start with those you anticipate. Some of them will likely be self-evident, but you may not fully find out who the opposition is until your bill is introduced and you see who starts lobbying or working against it.

☐ **Reach out to the opposition.** In-person meetings are usually the best, but you can also reach out by phone, e-mail, and so forth. If possible, find someone in your support coalition who has a good existing relationship with the opposition. They'll be less suspicious of someone they already know and like and may try harder to find a reasonable compromise.

☐ **State your case.** Take a moment to tell them your goals and why you're pursuing legislative reform. It may seem obvious to you, but if you don't tell them, they'll make assumptions about what you're doing and why—and they may be wrong. It helps to share your big-picture goal because you may gain understanding and receptivity, which can help you reach that goal. They might even be willing to brainstorm other ways to reach your goal that would be less troublesome to them.

☐ **Respond to concerns.** Jot down any questions or concerns raised by your opposition, and respond to each, even if you have to do some research and get back to them at a later time. You may need to decide which concerns are fear based and which are fact based. The fact-based concerns are easier to address. Also, in the course of meeting with them, it's worth finding out what the nature of their opposition is—political, personal, or policy. These meetings may help you think of other ways to approach the problem, or they can let you know when you just need to agree to disagree.

SAMPLE OPPOSITION TRACKER

Opponent Name	Phone and E-mail	Initial Contact	Reason for opposition	Response
Group A	333-333-1111 agroup@email.com	Yes, 3/21/11	Thinks it isn't necessary	Provide info and data on necessity for bill
B Group	111-222-4444 bgroup@email.com	Yes, 3/12/11	Thinks it conflicts with federal law	Research federal law to see if it does, look for alternatives
State Agency	888-222-7777	No	Thinks it will increase their workload	Find more streamlined process to keep cost down
C Group	444-111-9999	Yes	Thinks it will cost them money to comply	Research to see if it has cost similar groups $ in other states

Chapter 19

Advocacy for Busy People

Nobody makes a greater mistake than he who does nothing because he could do only a little.
—Edmund Burke

You may be wondering who has time for all this. Professional lobbyists can do this work full-time and get paid for it. You can't. The reality is that most people are very busy and can't be full-time citizen advocates. Whether you work, have your hands full raising kids, or have other major commitments, there are still many things you can do to advocate that take very little time.

Your time commitment can be as little as sixty seconds—to add your name to a petition or leave a voice mail— or as much as hours, if you want to do research or testify on a bill. It can be months, if you want to prepare and run your own legislation. You can weigh in on as few issues as one per year, or as many as one per week, depending on the time you have available. The main point is that *advocacy is not all-or-nothing. Anything* you can do is always better than nothing.

But here's an interesting thought: if everyone spent as little as ten minutes a year giving input and helping to shape public policy, it would revolutionize democracy as we know it. Your elected officials would be far better representatives of you and the public, and the extremes of political rhetoric would give way to pragmatic problem solving.

Do what you can, with what you have, where you are.
—Theodore Roosevelt

BE AN ADVOCATE IN TEN MINUTES OR LESS

☐ **Sign a petition.** If you see a petition circulating that you agree with, sign it or click on the button to support. Estimated time: 15 seconds; cost: $0

☐ **Complete a survey.** If your elected official has a survey online or in hard copy, complete it so that your values and priorities can be considered. Estimated time: 5 minutes; cost: cost of a stamp, if mailed

☐ **Leave a voice mail.** Call your elected official and leave a voice mail with critical messages about your vote preferences. Estimated time: 60 seconds; cost $0

☐ **Send an e-mail.** You can send an e-mail with your ideas, suggestions, input, and vote preferences. Estimated time: 10 minutes; cost $0

☐ **Attend a town hall meeting.** Even if you do it just once a year, attend a town hall community forum with your elected official to weigh in on matters of concern to you. Estimated time: 2 hours; cost: gas or public transportation

☐ **Prepare a wish list.** It might be more time-efficient for you to sit down and brainstorm your entire wish list once a year. This can be a list of changes or reforms you'd like to see on all sorts of topics consolidated into one document that you send. Estimated time: 10 minutes; cost: $0

☐ **Write a letter to the editor.** Reach out publicly to weigh in on issues that are important to you. Even one letter to the editor per year can have an impact. Estimated time: 15 minutes; cost $0

☐ **Join a group or list.** While you may not have time to attend meetings or functions that issue groups put together, a busy person may benefit from the full-time work that certain groups put into monitoring the legislative process. This can get you on newsletter lists or action alerts for topics of interest to you. Estimated time: 10 minutes; cost: varies depending on membership dues

☐ **Sign up for legislative newsletters.** Most legislators now have electronic newsletters they send out ranging from once a week to once a month. Sign up for newsletters for all of your elected officials. Estimated time: 5 minutes; cost: $0

☐ **Follow on Facebook, Twitter, blogs, or other social media.** Admittedly, these are not for everyone, but it also doesn't take much time. If you "friend" or "like" your elected official on Facebook, you will get a stream of updates there and can sometimes give feedback as concisely as a sentence. Follow your legislators on Twitter to get a stream of brief updates. You can ignore all but those of interest to you. Estimated time: 5 minutes; cost $0

☐ **Attend candidate forums.** Many groups organize candidate forums. The League of Women Voters, Common Cause, churches, and so forth often pull together public panels and offer a chance to present debates or Q-and-As on the issues. Attending and asking your questions can have an impact. Estimated time: 2 hours (not quite 10 minutes, but you get the idea); cost $0

Chapter 20

Advocacy for Youth Under Eighteen

The young do not know enough to be prudent,
and therefore they attempt the impossible,
and achieve it, generation after generation.
—Pearl S. Buck

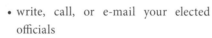

Many people assume that because one has to be eighteen years old to vote in the United States, he or she has to wait until they are eighteen to start advocating or having an impact on public policy. Not so.

In fact, your elected officials still represent you, regardless of your age, and you can make and change law even if you're not yet eighteen. So while you may not yet be old enough to vote, you can:

- write, call, or e-mail your elected officials
- testify at a legislative hearing
- help research problems and possible solutions
- intern or volunteer at the capitol or on a campaign
- start or circulate an issue petition (if not for the ballot)
- organize or attend rallies
- write or amend a law
- distribute leaflets or flyers
- hold panels or symposiums with guest speakers

- organize or attend press conferences
- write letters to the editor or guest editorial columns
- create a website for information and action
- be a spokesperson for a cause you care about
- blog, Facebook, tweet, or use other social media to mobilize and educate
- motivate your friends and family
- start an organization, nonprofit, or foundation

Young people are often even more persuasive because it's so unusual to see them involved in the legislative process and because their presence often brings out a lawmaker's best behavior.

Meet some amazing young people who have already made a difference in the world—all before the age of eighteen:

Zack Bonner created the Little Red Wagon Foundation and March Across America to raise awareness and funds for homelessness and underprivileged youth. He began his efforts in fourth grade. Learn more at http://littlered wagonfoundation.com.

Did You Know...?

Ronald Reagan was the only divorced president. He was also the only president to be head of a labor union.

Ana Dodson founded Peruvian Hearts after she visited her native Peru with her adopted family and saw extreme poverty and hardship firsthand in the orphanages. Learn more at www.peruvianhearts.org.

Ashley Shuyler was just sixteen years old when she founded AfricAid to help support education for girls in Africa. Her efforts have raised nearly $700,000. Learn more at http://africaid.com.

Bilaal Rajan was made a UNICEF Ambassador at age eight, and by thirteen he had raised awareness and funds for HIV/AIDS, natural disaster relief, orphanages, and schools. Learn more at www.bilaalrajan.com.

Mitchell Arnold started Peace is the Goal at thirteen and spread his love of soccer and message of peace in forty-one projects around the world, including Haiti and Vietnam. Learn more at www.dosomething.org/project/peace-is-the-goal.

Maya was moved to act at the age of six after she visited India and was struck by the number of children begging and living in poverty. She made crafts and toys at home, got her friends and all their pennies together, sold the items, and donated the proceeds to charity.

Obviously these are some exceptional young people, but what they have in common is that they were ordinary people who cared. They wanted to act, to do something, to make life better for other people—and they have.

*Every generation needs
a new revolution.*
—Thomas Jefferson

Meet Patty and David Skolnik

Patty and David Skolnik were an upwardly mobile professional couple traveling the country helping to establish successful preschools. They moved from Texas to Colorado in 1998 and were joined by their son, Michael, in 2000. While Patty and David were on the fast track in their

careers, Michael became an EMT and began classes at community college to get his associate's degree. His passion for helping others led him to a career as a pediatric nurse.

The idea of legislative advocacy or contacting their elected officials was far from Patty's and David's minds. They had never written, called, or contacted an elected official before. But all that changed on September 21, 2001, when, at the age of twenty-two, their only son went under the knife for brain surgery he would never recover from.

Michael had passed out once in July and once in September that year. The Skolniks were told by the neurosurgeon that Michael needed brain surgery right away, even though their family physician looked at the same results and told them, "Good news. Michael does *not* need surgery." They were told there was a cyst on Michael's brain—but a cyst was never discovered during surgery. They were *not* told that even if there was a cyst, it was not the cause of Michael's symptoms. They were *not* told that the surgery was unnecessary. They were *not* told that there was a less-invasive alternative brain surgery. They were neither advised of the risks nor that their son would also be getting a craniotomy. They were *not* advised that this surgeon lacked experience in this brain operation. They were *not* advised of all of the financial and referral relationships, which would ultimately dictate much of Michael's medical care.

The surgery took more than twice as long as it was supposed to, and the aggressive rooting around in Michael's brain caused swelling and hemorrhaging. When Michael awoke, he could no longer speak, and he was paralyzed on one side of his body and 50 percent blind in both eyes. He had a serious seizure disorder and was now psychotic, requiring twenty-four-hour care.

Following the surgery, Michael had eighty-two MRIs and was in and out of hospitals, rehab, ICU, and round-the-clock home care, with the Skolniks keeping constant vigil. The expenses for his medical care reached $4.8 million. After thirty-two excruciatingly painful months, Michael eventually succumbed to multiorgan failure and died on June 4, 2004, at 5:35 PM. David will tell you that Michael really died the day of the surgery.

The Skolniks lost their only son. When they later learned that Michael's death, and everything leading up to it was preventable, the knowledge haunted them.

Before the surgery, Patty Skolnik had checked out the profile of the neurosurgeon on the website of the Colorado Board of Medical Examiners. Nothing unusual came up, so she 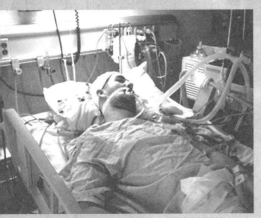 assumed they were in good hands. What she did not and could not know was that this particular neurosurgeon was being sued for the death of another patient in Atlanta, Georgia, and had operated on the wrong intervertebral disk and disabled another patient in the same city.

There is no way Patty and David would have allowed this person to open and prod their son's brain had they known this background. Realizing that patients had no meaningful access to important information about their doctors set the Skolniks on a mission that would change law forever in Colorado and in many states around the country.

Patty was galvanized into action right away; initially, it was more difficult for David to publicly share his grief. Patty created the Colorado Citizens for Accountability, which would later become a national group, Citizens for Patient Safety.

In 2007, Patty contacted me and said she wanted to run a bill that would increase transparency of critical information about doctors online so all patients could research their physicians to make informed decisions. Patty and David knew that they didn't want anyone else to ever go through what they did. Patty didn't live in my district but was told she needed a can-do legislator to help. Somehow she got my name; we met and went to work right away.

Our first challenge was that Patty had contacted me at a time in our legislative session when we were past our bill deadlines. Further, Colorado limits each legislator to five bills per session, and I was already maxed. We could get a late bill or extra bill only with the permission of leadership. For Patty, there were no obstacles—only items she needed to get done. She got a meeting with Speaker of the House Andrew Romanoff, and with what I would later call Patty Power, she got his permission both for me to carry an extra bill and to introduce it after the deadlines.

Our next step was to figure out specifically what we needed and wanted in our bill. Patty's focus was twofold: (1) relevant background was not made publicly available on the state's website; and (2) a doctor could move from state to state and his or her prior disciplinary history would not necessarily be captured and made available. So we divided up the work. I had our legislative council write a research memo on what

information each state's board of medical examiners made available online, and I asked Patty to create a wish list of all information patients should have the right to know when choosing their doctor.

Patty found a good resource in Public Citizen, a national nonprofit advocacy organization that had recently completed a report comparing the content on the states' medical board websites. She identified Massachusetts as a state that seemed to be ahead of the curve on these transparency issues. The wish list started to take shape:

- A patient should be able to know what education, training, certifications, or specialties a doctor has.
- A patient should have easy access to the disciplinary history or malpractice history of a physician in any state.
- A patient should be able to find out if the provider has ever been turned down for malpractice insurance, lost drug-prescribing or hospital privileges, and the nature and extent of the financial ownership relationships a provider has with other medically related companies and investments.

We gave the full wish list to the drafter and then began to work on the hard part—getting it passed. Patty met with every legislator and said, "I'm a mom. I would like a meeting with you and to take a few minutes to show you a video." The video was an excerpt about Michael's story from *The Today Show*. One meeting at a time, she moved people and began to grow our support. Many legislators were surprised to find out that this medical information wasn't already available online.

Patty met with the Colorado Medical Society, who, to our great delight, was supportive of the effort. But it was important to them to include a disclaimer to give some context on the malpractice information, basically stating that some specialties are inherently higher risk than others. We discussed the disclaimer and decided it was factually true and didn't hurt the bill—and having the support of the medical society made our job easier.

Patty met with everyone she could, and with every meeting our support grew. Hospitals began to see that the information we wanted available could be useful in making hiring decisions. But here was the test—COPIC. COPIC is Colorado's physician-owned malpractice carrier that underwrites most of the malpractice insurance in Colorado. They spend a great deal of their time and money defending physicians in malpractice actions. Yet, COPIC was also able to see that preventing malpractice in the first place with better information and education for consumers was a win-win for everyone—they too came on board. I was simply amazed.

There was another challenge: we didn't want this to be a partisan bill. Both Democrats and Republicans go to the hospital. People of any political party deserve good information with which to make good decisions. So Patty made sure she had both a Democratic helper and a Republican helper so that she could have these conversations on both sides of the aisle. It shouldn't matter, but sometimes it does. The messenger can have everything to do with how the policy or bill idea is received.

With no legislative experience whatsoever, Patty was able to get support for her idea at every turn. Then we hit our next bump when the drafter told us that in Colorado we don't name bills after people. Patty, David, and I wanted this to be the Michael Skolnik Medical Transparency Act. It was important to us that it bear his name in his memory and in his honor. The bill, after all, was about real people; it was about Michael. It was about the millions of people who enter a hospital every year and trust the advice of their physicians. I told the drafter we were naming it the Michael Skolnik Medical Transparency Act—period. And that was that.

I had a lot of work to do to live up to what the Skolniks deserved. They'd been let down by a lot of people in the system, and I felt a bit intimated by the responsibility of taking this on and doing it well. What if it failed? Fortunately, for Patty, failure was not an option. Meanwhile, I did a significant amount of research on medical error in our country. I found out that there are an estimated 98,000 preventable deaths due to medical error every year and that it was the eighth leading cause of death in the United States. I found out that a very small percentage of physicians are responsible for the majority of the malpractice incidents. I found other research suggesting that a doctor on average commits thirteen acts of medical negligence before losing his or her license to practice medicine. Wouldn't you want to know if your doctor was one of them?

Before our first legislative hearing in the House (I was in the House at the time), Patty met with every member on the House Health and Human Services Committee. She asked for their support. I asked for their support. Patty brought a legion of unlikely and unusual allies to the table—all in support of the bill. We showed the video news clip. Our allies testified in support, offering many policy reasons why this level of transparency for informed decision making was a good idea. Patty and David testified. Everyone forgot to breathe. Patty explained what happened to their son and what information was and wasn't available to the public that could have meant a different outcome for Michael. It could have happened to anyone, but it didn't need to happen at all. Legislators began to see *their* children, *their* parents, and *their* spouse at risk for something similar.

David testified and took a moment to begin. He pulled out his written comments, took a deep breath, and paused. Then he put his prepared comments aside and told the committee that he needed to speak from the heart. He did—and reached every soul in the room that day. They began to see that the information we wanted available could be a matter of life and death for any of us. The bill passed unanimously on a vote of 11–0.

Our next challenge was a stop at the House Appropriations Committee. While the bill didn't cost much, there would be some need to reprogram the state's computers at the Department of Regulatory Agencies. We have a balanced-budget amendment in Colorado's constitution, so we can't create any new law or policy without having a way to pay for it. (We also have the TABOR amendment, which has limited the state's ability to raise revenue). We needed to find a way to pay for the technology changes and a little extra initial staff time to help physicians through the new filing system. By adding thirteen to nineteen dollars to the renewal fee of the health professional's license, we found our way to pay for it and the organizations representing physicians agreed to it. The Michael Skolnik Medical Transparency Act (HB07-1331) passed House Appropriations Committee 13–0. The bill then passed the House on a final recorded vote of 65–0.

We asked Senator Lois Tochtrop to be the Senate sponsor for the bill because she's an experienced nurse and seasoned legislator. She agreed. In the Senate, the bill was assigned to the Business, Labor, and Technology Committee, and it passed after another round of strong testimony, on a vote of 7–0. Then it passed the Senate Appropriations Committee on a vote of 9–0. We were nearing the final stretch of the session and needed to get it passed. The bill passed the Senate on a final recorded vote of 34–1. Only one no vote in the whole process—not bad.

The Michael Skolnik Medical Transparency Act was signed by then governor Bill Ritter on May 24, 2007, with a signing ceremony.

The Colorado Board of Medical Examiners then took to heart implementation of the act and included us in all key phases of implementing the bill. In 2009, we carried a

cleanup bill to help with some logistical issues on implementation and to give clearer definitions to some of the requirements. That bill (HB 09-1188) also passed, and the website went live with new and meaningful information, available as a complete physician profile as each physician renewed his or her license (www.dora.state.co.us/pls/cproweb/hpps_search_gui.search_form). In 2010, we extended the same type of provider transparency to other key health professionals (dentists, nurses, psychologists, chiropractors, acupuncturists, physician assistants, midwives, and physical therapists) in SB 10-124.

Patty and David Skolnik passed three bills in three years, even though they never imagined they'd be involved in the legislative process. They didn't stop there. They've continued to work on other key healthcare reforms and participate in educational efforts with providers and the public on patient safety. Colorado's bill expanded the transparency available beyond that of most other states, and ours has now become a model for other states. Once the bill was enacted, the Skolniks continued to engage in public service announcements to help the public know that they now had a right to this information and where to find this information on health providers.

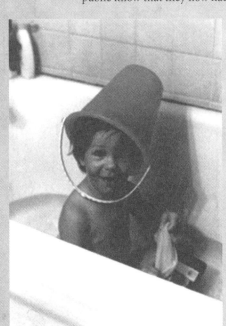

They did it for Michael. They did it for you. You can do it too.

Patty and David have this advice for you. If you're interested in making or changing law, Patty says, "Anyone can do it. Don't be afraid of the process. Find a champion, and they will help you." David's power is sharing the raw, unpolished truth and letting others see it for what it is. He says, "Speak from the heart and reach people on a human level."

Part Three

Intermediate
Advocacy

Chapter 21

Researching Problems
and Solutions

It always seems impossible until it is done.
—Nelson Mandela

Which Level of Government Is Right for Reform?

As a practical matter, most average citizens who get involved in the democratic process will be responding to a bill that has already been introduced, and many times the most rewarding work can be to participate in finding the right solutions to real problems. Most elected officials have some ideas about how to solve some problems when they get elected, but even if they care deeply about an issue, they may not have a clear idea about *how* to solve a particular problem.

Our **federalist** and layered system of government is an important part of the foundation of this country. Our founders believed levels of government (city, county, state, federal) are as key to checks and balances as is the **separation of powers** between branches of government (legislative, executive, judicial). Yet, it can also be a source of frustration and confusion for citizen advocates. Our multiple levels of government can leave people feeling like there's too much bureaucracy or that they're getting the runaround.

If you have identified a problem where you believe government has a role, one of the most important first steps is to decide at what level of government the problem needs to be solved.

Federal issue. In some cases, the federal government may have exclusive jurisdiction over a policy, which means that if you want reforms, you'll need to pursue it at that level. This can include matters such as international foreign policy, US currency, or military policy, which are *only* addressable at the federal level, or it could include issues such as education or transportation, over which multiple layers of government have jurisdiction (education, for example, is addressable at the federal, state, and local school board levels).

State issue. Under the Tenth Amendment to the US Constitution, matters not expressly given to the federal government are reserved to the states. Therefore, a profound majority of policy issues are actually decided by state law. In some instances, the states may have exclusive authority over a topic (for example, water or custody matters), and in other cases the states may have concurrent jurisdiction to legislate in an area where the federal government does as well, so long as it doesn't directly conflict with federal law. This can also be known as **preemption**: when federal and state law conflict, federal law prevails. It is rooted in the supremacy clause of the US Constitution.

Municipal issues. Each incorporated city has a creating document and a series of city-based laws, often called ordinances. The problem you want to address could be resolved at the city level if it's a matter of city ordinances, which often address neighborhood issues and amenities, zoning and development requirements, and local licensing or permits. However, some licenses or permits may be at the state level, and some may require both state and municipal licensing. If a city is a home-rule city, it means that its laws can be different than state laws unless it's a matter of statewide concern. If a city is not a home-rule city, then its ordinances generally must be in areas not covered by the state or that don't conflict with state law.

Elected specialty boards. Most regions have elected school boards, library district boards, water boards, and transportation boards. These are local and specialized based on subject matter. The problem you'd like solved may be best addressed through one of these direct, local governing entities.

New trends in government. Recently, depending on the part of the country in which you live, there has been a real surge in homeowners associations (or HOAs), special districts, and metropolitan districts. Some of these entities are private, public, or a hybrid. Yet they typically have the ability to assess fees, dues, or taxes and can put a lien on or foreclose on property if they go unpaid. They also typically have the ability to create binding laws about behavior or use of personal property. These entities are so new in most regions that state laws have often not caught up on basic tenets of democracy: election access, budget and decision disclosure, speech rights for impacted persons, due process before decisions, or ability to challenge those decisions.

The problem you wish to address may need to be solved at one or multiple levels, and determining on which to focus is not always easy. For example, let's say you want to focus on high-school dropout rates. There can be federal implications through the US Department of Education, federal grants, or federal laws such as No Child Left Behind. The states can be involved in determining direct funding, graduation criteria, or policies about creating alternative choices for kids who may not thrive in traditional academic settings. And the school boards are likely involved as the most direct governing entity over a school district. It may be that a solution would best include reforms at multiple levels of government.

Determine the Appropriate Level of Government for Your Problem

- **Start with your elected officials at the most local level of government.** Not only are most issues that arise solved or solvable at a local level, but you're also more likely to get a real response (not a form letter, or a response at all!) from a real person. They can also help direct you to the correct level if it's not the local level.

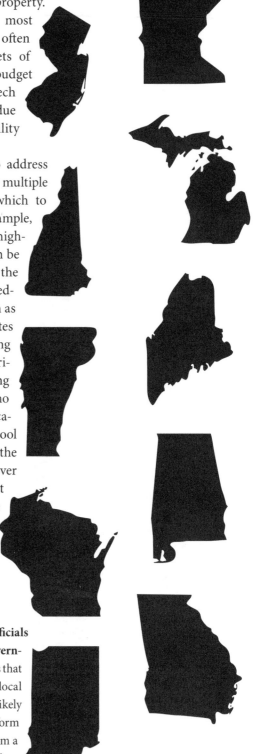

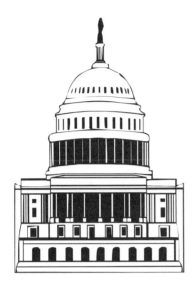

Did You Know…?

New Mexico has the highest percentage of Latino legislators in the country: 40 percent.

- **Know the source of the problem—it will give you your answer.** For example you may know that the problem you wish to address is a federal or state law you don't like or a city ordinance that drives you bonkers. In that case, you want to go to the entity that made the law or policy to seek to repeal or reform it.
- **Use your library.** Libraries are fantastic (and free) resources. Not only are they likely to have materials that can help you find the answer to your question, but the librarians can personally help you.

Which Branch of Government Is Right for Reform?

If you determine that the state or federal government is the right level to focus on for reforms, next you need to consider which branch of government is the right one to approach.

Legislative. The legislative branch writes the laws. If the question is one of making or changing law, then you need to be reaching out to your elected legislators for your reform efforts.

Executive. The executive branch implements the laws. They're typically implemented through various agencies and departments under the executive branch who are not elected but appointed. If the law is okay but the issue is how a law is or is not being implemented, then you likely need to focus your advocacy on the agencies or departments of the executive branch who are charged with implementing the laws. The accountability for the functioning of agencies and departments rests with the governor or president, but they aren't typically the most effective place to go for reforms. Instead, talk to the director or public liaison for the department. The devil can be in the details of laws, and agencies or departments typically enact further rules to put specific implementation details on state laws.

Judicial. The judicial branch interprets the laws. If there's a specific situation in which you feel your rights have been violated under existing law, then a court will interpret the laws as they apply to the specific facts in your case. The courts can be a source of bigger reforms if you believe the harm in your case violates the Constitution or state law. However, you'll notice this is the only area of advocacy that's not free, so it generally isn't the best place to start if there are other remedies or options available.

When in doubt, start with your local elected officials. They should be able to help you or put you in touch with someone who can.

What Is the Right Reform to Pursue?

The next two pages outline a process to help you find the best solutions to pursue in your reform efforts. Those solutions may eventually inform changes in law and policy that *you* get through the legislature.

Know how to ask. There is nothing more difficult
for some people, nor for others, easier.
—Baltasar Gracian

FIND A SOLUTION

☐ **Identify the problem.** The first step is to identify the problem you wish to solve or at least improve.

☐ **Identify possible causes.** The next step is to begin brainstorming the causes of the problem.

☐ **Find research or data on causes.** Follow up by searching for evidence, data, research, or anecdotes that seem to best illustrate or explain the causes. Be sure to also look for materials suggesting ideas that are different than yours or those that may even conflict with your initial inclinations.

☐ **Select among multiple reasons.** Okay, so there are lots of reasons or causes behind the problem you want to resolve. You'll likely need to focus on one or a few. Which reason you choose to emphasize will have a significant impact on the solution you pursue. So how do you choose?

- **Root cause.** You may wish to go for either the most central or root cause on the rationale that if you solve that, you may have the biggest impact.
- **Low-hanging fruit.** You may wish to look for the easiest change to grab—the smallest change that's most likely to pass that can have the biggest impact.
- **Greatest justice principle.** You may consider picking the solution with the greatest implications for your sense of justice or principle. In other words, one area may stick out as being about fundamental fairness or your sense of right and wrong.
- **Best-supported cause.** Among multiple possible causes, you may find that research and evidence is strongest behind one approach in particular. If you select a cause that's well researched and reasoned, it may be easier to persuade others on the strength of the data.

Once you've investigated the possible and likely causes or reasons behind the problem you want to improve, it'll help inform how you approach the solution. For example, if you want to address a high school dropout rate, your solution will be different depending on whether you conclude the primary cause is boredom, teen pregnancy, lack of available tutoring, lack of interest in subject matter, problems at home, substance abuse, mental health problems, lack of parental support, or financial problems requiring a student to work full time.

What you emphasize in that former step might direct whether you think the solution is making school more interesting and relevant for young people, addressing health and sex education, adding resources for tutoring, adding school nurses and counselors, or addressing the bigger economic picture for parents.

☐ **Brainstorm possible solutions.** It's helpful to jot down as many ideas as you can about how you think one might address the stated problem. Start with as many ideas as possible, because as you get further you may realize you need to abandon some ideas as potentially creating unintended consequences, costing too much money, being politically unrealistic, or having been tried and failed elsewhere. This will also give you more flexibility in how you ultimately draft or amend possible legislation so you don't have everything riding on one idea alone.

☐ **Research solutions.** Depending on the causes you select as your primary focus, you'll then be able to research possible solutions. The following is a list of some sources for ideas.

- **Government publications.** At this point, you can research what has been tried elsewhere with what results. As you begin to ascertain what has worked and what hasn't, you can brainstorm how it might be done better. You can get information from some organizations like National Conference of State Legislatures, American Legislative Exchange Council, Council of State Governments West, and dozens of others. As with everything, some organizations are more neutral than others, so you should just be prepared to use your own filter on whether you actually like any of these ideas.
- **Academic articles.** Depending on the subject area you're investigating, you may find that there's a significant body of research on what works. Trade publications, university publications, and scientific journals can include some excellent research and data, which may help you decide the best approach. You should look at who's authoring the article and who's funding the research in order to best filter any potential bias.
- **Nonprofit articles.** Some of the best research on what works can come from various nonprofits and foundations. For example, Pew has done an extraordinary review of criminal justice reforms to help sort out fads and politics from data about what actually reduces recidivism, increases public safety, and delivers better bang for the criminal justice buck.
- **Professional and trade articles.** Many occupations have some type of trade membership organization. They'll typically be well versed in what policies they think best help or hurt their trade in the fifty states. A reader just needs to consider that what's best for one trade is not necessarily always the best public policy for society at large, but is worth reviewing.
- **Asking others.** Call legislators or people in other states you read about with experience on a related issue in their state, and ask their opinion on what worked, what didn't, and what they would do differently. It may help you avoid replicating avoidable mistakes that have occurred elsewhere.

- **Your own creativity or common sense.** Don't dismiss your thoughts just because no one else has tried them before. One may be the best idea out there! You may see what others are missing because they're too close to it or have been around it too long.

    For example, after a tow-truck driver was recently dragged to death in Colorado Springs while he was in the middle of hooking up a vehicle to tow, a concerned citizen contacted us. He wasn't a tow-truck driver or a lobbyist, and he didn't even know the people involved, but he was bothered by the incident and truly thought this type of death was preventable. His suggestion: put a visible sticker or magnet on the driver's side of a vehicle when a tow is initiated so no driver can say they didn't know. Seems like common sense, right? But no one else had thought of it, and he made his idea a reality and changed law in the process.

☐ **Devise a strategy for passage.** Once you've focused on your preferred solution, it's time to consider some strategy for passage. What reform you ultimately pursue doesn't occur in a vacuum of research but in a larger context of reality. So what other considerations may impact what reform you pursue?

- **Who can help you?** One person can introduce ideas and prevail, but it's far more likely you'll see your reform enacted into law if you have help. The help you could muster may vary depending on which solution you pursue. Brainstorm a list of people or organizations you know will help you and continue the list with people who might help, if asked.
- **Can you build a coalition?** If so, it'll be much easier to get your reform passed. See chapter 18, Networking, for how to build your coalition.
- **Who might oppose your efforts?** You'll want to figure this out and minimize their opposition. The more people or organizations working against your reform effort, the more difficult it may be to secure the votes for passage. See chapter 18, Networking, for how to deal with the opposition.
- **Who is your preferred legislative sponsor?** You'll need a legislative sponsor to get your bill introduced. Who you choose can affect whether or not your bill gets passed. See chapter 22, Introducing Your Own Bill, for tips for selecting a sponsor.

How much support you can muster may impact which solution you pursue. A solution with lots of support and little opposition may be more appealing and help you select between options. Likewise, a solution with a lot of opposition and not much support may get ruled out.

Ultimately, you'll decide the right reform based on your values, trial and error, feedback from other people, your research, and practical considerations based on votes you need to pass the reform.

Chapter 22

Introducing Your Own Bill

If you want it done right, do it yourself.
—Your parents

There are hundreds of bills introduced every year, most of which might be fully lobbied but will never receive any public input. There are many opportunities to find issues that merit your support or issues that should galvanize your opposition efforts. However, when I take a status sheet (a chart of all introduced bills) to my town hall meetings, the most common thing I hear is "Don't you guys have anything better to do?" That's because the overwhelming majority of bills introduced are mundane, technical, or seemingly irrelevant to people's lives.

That's where you come in. *You don't have be elected to public office to be able to make or change law.* Introducing your own bill is admittedly a bit more advanced; a tiny fraction of people will ever even try, and it takes a bit more time and effort to personally create and shepherd a bill through the entire process than it does to weigh in with your support or opposition on existing bills.

You may be so familiar with an issue that you've long known what needs to be changed with the law and have assumed that surely somebody else will introduce it. If that's the case, you should seriously consider doing it yourself.

How wonderful it is that nobody need wait a single moment before starting to improve the world.
—Anne Frank

INTRODUCE YOUR OWN BILL

☐ **Do your research.** Research the problem, the possible solutions, and the results of the solutions anywhere they've been tried. This will give you fertile ground for ideas and start you thinking about other people with whom you should talk (see chapter 21, Researching Problems and Solutions).

☐ **Find a legislative sponsor.** In sponsoring a measure, the legislator is agreeing to be the bill's author and primary advocate within the legislature. You only need one legislative sponsor, and once you have this ally in your camp, he or she can help you find someone else to carry it in the other chamber and help you with strategy for passage both inside and outside the capitol. It's okay if you don't know or feel comfortable with all of the legislative rules or protocols; your sponsor can be a great mentor and help walk you through the entire process. Once you've done it, you'll be hooked.

☐ **Write an initial draft of the bill.** Your legislative sponsor will have access to professional drafters, so you don't need to be a lawyer or drafter to begin this process. They can give the drafter permission to work with you.

☐ **Proofread and reread your draft.** Make sure your bill does what you think it does, and give it a markup with any questions you have for the drafter to avoid any embarrassing mistakes prior to introduction.

☐ **Build a coalition of allies.** See chapter 18, Networking. As you build your coalition, they may have other ideas that prompt drafting changes in the bill. Supporters typically want to see a copy of a bill draft before definitively signing on.

☐ **Devise a bill-passage strategy.** Map out the path for the bill and how you're going to build the support and votes necessary for each step of the process. Sequence matters. Spending a lot of time working for the governor's support won't help if you can't get a bill hearing or passage (in states where it isn't guaranteed) or out of the first committee. Your strategy should not only include each required step in the process, but also what media, outreach, or publicity you plan to use to raise awareness of the issue and create a climate where public opinion supports your efforts.

☐ **Identify and meet with the opposition.** See chapter 18, Networking. Identify and meet with any people or groups that you anticipate might oppose the measure to see if you can find common ground or address their concerns. If not, a meeting may still change the character of their opposition because they'll likely at least appreciate that you tried.

☐ **Count your votes.** Lobbyists do it, legislators do it, and you can do it too. A vote count is simply the process whereby you ask whether a legislator is planning to vote yes or no on a bill. See chapter 25, Vote Counting.

☐ **Secure a committee hearing.** You may need to exercise your citizen lobbyist skills to persuade the chairperson to hold a hearing. Find out the criteria the chair uses to decide, research the types of issues that have warranted hearings before, and find the similarities between those and your bill.

☐ **Line up supporters to testify.** A legislative hearing is nowhere as formal as a court proceeding. However, besides your own testimony, you may want to work with your allied coalition to see who among them would testify. Picking the right witnesses is helpful. I've watched really good issues get derailed because of a witness who is overly combative, too dogmatic, or unfocused.

☐ **Prepare fact sheets.** Prepare and distribute your fact sheets to the legislators who have a vote, the press, and your allies. See chapter 16, Preparing Fact Sheets.

☐ **Execute your plan.** At each phase you want to have a strategy for successful passage. Consider any new barriers or challenges at each step to see if they suggest revisions to your initial plan.

☐ **Get the governor on board.** Each governor has a slightly different style or criteria he or she uses to determine whether to sign or veto legislation. Some give deference to the legislative branch and only veto if they feel there's an extremely compelling reason to do so. Others will simply veto a measure if they don't like it or if they have been heavily lobbied to do so. The governor will likely have legislative or policy staff. Meet with them, pitch your bill, and see if the governor has any concerns or red flags *before* the bill is in the second chamber, if possible. You may be able to amend your bill to get a skeptical governor on board, but you can't change the bill once it hits his or her desk for action.

☐ **Debrief the mission.** If your bill passes, celebrate! Include everyone who helped with your effort and make sure to thank everyone who made it happen (legislators who voted their support, staff, allied groups, the governor who signed it, and so forth). Not all bills pass the first year. Some of the most important legislation in this nation's history took multiple years to pass. Don't give up! Debrief with your allies: what went right, what went wrong, what would you do differently next time.

SELECT A LEGISLATIVE SPONSOR

☐ **Start with legislators you know.** See chapter 11, Meeting Your Legislators, if you haven't yet met any of your elected officials. They might agree to do it, or they'll at least be likely to help brainstorm with you about who would be best.

☐ **Think about committee assignments.** Consider selecting a legislative sponsor based on the committees he or she serves on. It can be helpful to have a legislative sponsor who has a vote on the subject matter committee that's likely to be assigned the bill.

☐ **Consider approaching leadership and chairs.** The fate of your bill can be greatly helped by having the chair of the committee, or another member of leadership, carry your measure. It certainly can't hurt!

☐ **Review track records.** Consider selecting a sponsor with a good track record for passing bills. This can be a sign that he or she has good navigation skills through the process or is well liked and respected by colleagues.

☐ **Find someone with subject matter expertise.** Choosing a legislative sponsor who knows the subject matter particularly well or who is passionate and dedicated to the issue or cause you're pursuing can be quite helpful. If the sponsor really believes in the reform effort, he or she will work harder for its passage.

Meet Mark and Cappi

Mark has always had strong opinions about right and wrong and has never been shy about expressing them, but he was not always involved in the legislature (Mark has now completed more legislative sessions than any serving legislator). By the age of twenty-three, he was already a successful businessman, running an appliance, service, repair, and construction operation in Vail, Colorado. He and his wife had a ten-month-old son and another child on the way. Life was looking pretty good.

In 1984, Mark was working when a twenty-seven-ton mobile home fell on him. The concrete blocks holding it up collapsed, nearly severing him in half. He remembers pushing a coworker out of the way and being pinned. The Jaws of Life were used to lift the mobile home, but it was his brother who crawled under and pulled him out because the emergency personnel deemed it too risky. The blood loss was so severe that the first hospital in Vail ran out, and Mark needed to be airlifted by helicopter to a hospital in Glenwood Springs. His reaction: "Damn, I always wanted to ride in a helicopter and I can't even see out the window."

He awoke from a coma six weeks later. His doctors and his family didn't expect him to live. His pelvis was broken in thirty-eight places, and he sustained profound and permanent organ damage. He was immobilized and on a liquid diet. Mark has had forty-two surgeries to rebuild his bones and organs, many of which were experimental in nature because most people don't live through injuries that severe. His doctor, an army medic by training, once opined that the only time he had seen injuries this severe was when people were blasted in combat—and they didn't survive.

Mark was an inpatient for a year, five months of which was spent immobilized in a weightlessness chamber so his pinned-together body could try to heal without the impact of gravity. He was discharged to a rehab hospital and was kicked out after five weeks because, well…they were probably driving each other crazy. Mark has always been *very* independent. It didn't help that they told him he would spend the rest of his life in a wheelchair and would need someone to take care of him 24-7.

Mark was dealing with legal battles at the same time as he was facing medical and health battles. Despite being a business owner obviously hurt on the job, Mark's claims were denied by the insurance company on a series of technicalities. So even though they took his insurance premiums all those years and received his regular employee reports, they tried to allege he wasn't covered. His financial world was turned upside down. The insurance company told him they would never pay his claim and actually called his doctors, who were in the process of trying to save his life, to notify them that they had no intention of ever paying his claim; if they wanted to keep treating him, it would be "at their own risk."

One thing became clear to Mark right away. People were behaving this way because *the law* allowed them to behave this way. In 1986, we didn't really have in-home healthcare services for Medicaid. The choices—Mark's choices—were either nursing home care or self-care at home. He wasn't ready to be pushed into a nursing home, but his care needs were a bit much for a nonprofessional caregiver. A bill came up that would provide a third option, which could keep many disabled people out of a nursing home and increase their options for relatively independent living at home. He was all over it.

Mark began to meet other disability advocates through ADAPT, a grassroots community of disability activists, and the Atlantis Community, an independent living center for people with disabilities. Some of the greatest threats to personal, civil, and human rights of people with disabilities have come in the form of over-institutionalization and lack of public access to basic amenities—and Mark's been ready to fight those battles at every stage. When he began his legislative advocacy, the state capitol wasn't even wheelchair accessible. Access of any kind is really about the right to live and participate in the community, and even though the Americans with Disabilities Act has been on the books awhile now, there remains poor understanding and compliance, and the law itself has been unduly weakened by recent court decisions.

Mark also became a sorely needed voice for injured workers. Very few people understand the workers' compensation system or its problems until or unless they or a loved one gets hurt on the job. As he met more injured workers, some trends became clear. An injured worker could expect denials, delays, interference with medical care by the insurance company, and difficulty getting access to medical providers who weren't controlled by the insurance company. Workers were routinely having problems getting the benefits the law said they were supposed to receive. Workers were regularly harassed with unwarranted surveillance to try to pressure them into settling for less than they were owed. They were regularly being forced to go to court to get the benefits the law already said they were supposed to receive.

It was 1991—a bad year for injured workers in Colorado. It represented the culmination of an effort by the insurance and business lobby to gut rights for injured workers in the name of cost savings. They eliminated the right to vocational rehabilitation and made it much more difficult for catastrophically injured people, who could never work again, to receive "permanent total" benefits. Yet, despite the momentum going the other direction, Mark helped get two important amendments on the legislation that was otherwise clearly a step backward for injured workers.

One reason insurance noncompliance was so rampant at the time was that the penalty for failing to follow the law was only $100 maximum per incident per day. It was cheaper in many cases for carriers *not* to comply with the law, earn interest on unpaid claims, and simply pay the $100 if ordered. Mark got the penalty revised to $500 per incident per day. The second amendment he got on the bill allows an injured worker to take a worker's comp order from the administrative law to district

court and convert those orders into an enforceable judgment. His own insurance company kept losing in court, but refused to pay anyway.

Mark has now testified for or against countless bills, introduced and passed his own legislation, and written a book, and he continues to serve on countless boards, commissions, and citizen organizations. Mark has made himself at home anywhere that public policy is debated or made. He's known to all who serve at the capitol as a force to be reckoned with. Over the span of Mark's citizen lobbying career, he has arguably had more impact on legislation and public policy than any elected official. Legislators come and go; he has decided he's there to stay.

Cappi is Mark's best friend and service dog, and they are both familiar faces at the legislature. As Mark says, "Cappi is famous and I'm infamous." He's not afraid to be a troublemaker. Legislators know that if Mark sees an injustice, he'll be there every year until it's fixed. Somehow, he's managed to maintain an unstoppable sense of humor; his persistence and stubbornness may be the only reason he's still alive.

Mark knows who he is and what he wants. He knows that he's blessed with an incredible wife and family. After fighting so hard for his life, his rights, his medical care, and his freedoms, one might suspect Mark would be tired. But now he's fighting for your rights.

Mark has been involved in legislation every year since 1986. At this point, even he may have lost track of how many bills he has run or amended. He's now mentoring others who are new to the process. His advice for you: "Rule number one: smile. If you can't put a smile on your face, don't walk in the door. Rule number two: *always* have good manners. Rule number three: always respect the office, even if you can't stand the legislator personally. Rule number four: *always* be nice to the staff. Rule number five: *never* lie."

Chapter 23

Building Support for Your Bill and Addressing the Opposition

*If I have seen further than others,
it is by standing upon the shoulders of giants.*
—Isaac Newton

Now that you know you're introducing a bill, presumably you'd like it to pass. If your idea is uncontroversial and you get a bit of luck, it can be possible to pass a bill without allied support, but your chances of success are much greater if you have it. If you're thinking, *Well, I'm not an insider so I don't know who all might be supportive*, don't worry. Chapter 18, Networking, has most of the information you need to start building support for your bill and addressing the opposition; however, I must emphasize two key points. First, when you're running your own bill, it's *much* more important to build support and minimize opposition than if you're simply weighing in on an existing bill. Second, this process must begin much, much earlier—that is, prior to the introduction of the bill.

There are a few steps in addition to those listed in chapter 18 for building support that you should include when running your own bill (see page 98).

For a number of reasons, it's usually beneficial to reach out to the opposition prior to introducing your bill. First, they may not actually be opposed if you take the time to explain what you're doing. Second, the degree of opposition will usually be stronger if they're caught by surprise. Third, you may find that they have ideas or suggestions that could improve the bill or at least remove their opposition. For example, they might be on board if you use this definition instead of that one, or if you give them a bit more time to come into compliance.

If *you* are the opposition, it's generally regarded as a courtesy to the sponsor to let him or her know that you're opposed and the reasons for your opposition.

As with building support, there are some additional steps you should take in addressing the opposition when running your own bill (see page 98).

*If your heart is large enough to envelop your adversaries,
you can see right through them and avoid their attacks.
And once you envelop them, you will be able to guide them
along the path indicated to you by heaven and earth.*
—Morihei Ureshiba

CONTINUE TO BUILD SUPPORT FOR YOUR BILL

☐ **Ask your coalition if they have other policy ideas.** One of the benefits of bringing other people in is that they'll likely have some experience or expertise and may have ideas that can improve your bill.

☐ **Research organizations and tailor your approach.** If you're asking an organization to support a bill, it's helpful if you've looked up their mission statement so you can tailor your request and explanation as to why it fits the group's mission or purpose. It may not always be obvious, so it's always a good idea to spell it out. For example, reaching out to education-related groups may seem a bit like a stretch for a criminal justice reform bill, but if K–12 education is taking cuts because of the growth of the prison budget, they might care about corrections reform.

☐ **Identify your common ground and lead with it.** There will always be something you can agree on with another person or organization, so start with that. Reform, at times, can make for strange bedfellows who seem to be pretty far apart on most issues but then come together on some issues.

☐ **Listen.** If your own allies have ideas, suggestions, or concerns, be sure to listen. There may be changes you need to make to your bill in order to keep the coalition together and actually working for your bill.

☐ **Be aware of support "in the building" versus "out of the building."** As you can imagine, there can be a wide gulf between public opinion and the opinions of the people who are frequent participants at the capitol. In the best scenario, it's nice to have support from both. But many times they're at variance. If the people support what you're doing but the traditional actors at the capitol don't, you'll need greater reliance on media and grassroots organizations to help get the votes you need in the legislature.

☐ **Be honest about strengths and weaknesses.** You'll build more credibility among your allies if you're up front in identifying the likely strengths and weaknesses in your bill. Likewise, if your supporters are caught by surprise with unanticipated problems, they may feel blindsided.

☐ **Divide the work.** One of the greatest benefits of building a support coalition is that the amount of work can be shared. When you hold a coalition meeting, try to have an agenda to keep folks focused, and track any to-do items, who's doing them, and when. This will help prevent too much burden being placed on any one supporter and will help allies feel that you're making good use of their time. Recap those to-do assignments at the close of the meeting.

CONTINUE ENGAGING YOUR OPPOSITION

☐ **Brainstorm potential reasons for opposition and an appropriate response to each one**. As you assess these issues or reasons for opposition, you'll generally find that they fall into one of the following categories:

- A faulty assumption that you can (sometimes) clarify with facts and research.
- A valid point that you can work on substantively in negotiations to find other ways to do what you want in ways that don't cause the identified problem.
- A valid point on which you may have to agree to disagree. For instance, the disagreement may center around competing values, where you can understand the reason for the opposition, but the justice principle you're pursuing is a higher priority to you than the basis of their opposition.

☐ **Offer a solution or alternative, if you can.** There will be less resistance to passing your measure and reduced incentive to undermine or repeal your effort if you can keep your opposition to a minimum. Some of your strongest support witnesses can be former opponents who, through negotiations, are now on board with your effort.

☐ **Mine your allies for information.** Have they dealt with these organizations before? Do they know what their style is? Do they have ideas for how to best address the opposition's concerns? Past experience is a great predictor of future behavior.

Sometimes, however, the nature of the opposition is a more generic fear or resistance to change, profiling based on the sponsors' political party, or a symbolic stand. Those amorphous reasons can be far more difficult to address. That said, you'll always learn something useful by reaching out and talking with your opposition.

Chapter 24

Media and
Public Support

*All of us who professionally use the mass media
are the shapers of society. We can vulgarize that society.
We can brutalize it. Or we can help lift it onto a higher level.*
—William Bernbach

The **mainstream media** has often been referred to as the **Fourth Estate**, and for good reason. While we generally know about the legislative, executive, and judicial branches of government, the media is a necessary conduit between the people and their government. If functioning properly, the press should act as a **check and balance** to the other branches of government. Of course, the media isn't a branch of government; in its current form, it's a series of individual or corporately owned operations or chains.

The independence and vitality of an **independent press** function is critical if the public is going to have access to information about their own government. While there are some important higher-level discussions about how we maximize and preserve a free press, for purposes of this book I will focus on how and when to use different media to get your message out.

The first thing you should understand is that there is no singular media. You will want to study all of the different components of your media market because they are different and should be approached as such. The next big point is that the more resistance you encounter at the capitol, the more you will need a really good media plan to offset that resistance. If you find that an overwhelming majority of the traditional professional lobbyists oppose your idea, the most likely outcome is that most legislators will oppose it too...unless they get a clear and overwhelming sense that the court of public opinion (average citizens) is strongly leaning the other way. That's where you and opportunities for good media strategy come in.

I am by no means a press expert (and you don't have to be, either), but I've found the press to be indispensable to the process, particularly when there's a mismatch between what capitol lobbyists want and what the public would want.

WORK WITH THE MEDIA

☐ **Identify your local media outlets.** This can be quite a project for a first step, but it's well worth doing. Break down your list by type of media: newspapers, radio stations, radio shows, television stations (network, cable), key local blogs, and so forth.

☐ **Find the right contacts at each outlet.** For example, you'll have one set of contacts if you're writing Op-Ed pieces or letters to the editor and a different one if you're trying to pitch a news reporter or blogger.

☐ **Create a database for all your media outlets and contacts.** Particularly with press releases, you want to be able to get word out quickly. Keeping a database of all your contacts and addresses allows you to do that, though you'll need to update it periodically because of turnover in the profession.

☐ **Get to know reporters and bloggers.** Reporters have very different styles and interests, but most of them are interested and take pride in covering significant and meaningful stories. Even if their work is ultimately truncated, or if they're assigned to filler or puff pieces, the inspiration for becoming a reporter is generally a passion for empowering the public and uncovering important stories that affect people's lives. Many influential bloggers share the same passion.

☐ **Use a press release.** Press releases can be used to announce a press conference, an event, or the release of a key finding or report, or they can be used to issue a statement, to feature key developments in your bill, or to put a human interest feature on an important policy issue, among other things. Press releases essentially give notice to reporters and their editors but by themselves are insufficient.

- **Content.** Be relevant, timely, catchy, and brief. The tone of your release will be different depending on whether you're in delicate negotiations with your opposition or throwing bombs once they've locked down. The release should include a headline, a possible subheading, and a basic description of who, what, when, where, and why. If you include facts or statistics, provide the sources so reporters can easily track them down for themselves. Consider including one or two quotes, and add any photo, video clip, or sound file if it helps tell the story. Every press release should be able to convey why the subject matters very concisely. Try to keep it to a page or less, and format it so your main point is never buried—you want busy people skimming the release to immediately see its importance. See the sample on page 105.
- **A press release versus the scoop.** A press release is useful when you're aiming to give everyone notice of a key event or turn of events of public interest. Sometimes the fact that other outlets are carrying the story creates the expectation that a media group might be missing something if they fail to report it too. However, it can have the opposite effect—because they know the rest of the media has the release, it wouldn't be unique, and therefore they might choose not to report it. When you have something big to uncover in the form of a discovery or an investigation, it's often better to scoop it instead. By that I mean working with one good reporter at one outlet, giving them the exclusive opportunity to work it up and feature it. Most news organizations covet original and newsworthy materials. Until you have relationships built with individual reporters, you may need to rely on press releases. A scoop is a good way to build a relationship with a reporter, *but* you should never offer a scoop and then proceed to share the story with others—that's a no-no.

☐ ***Never* lie to a reporter or any other media contact.** That probably seems pretty obvious, but there's no surer way to blow up your reputation and hurt your cause than to lie to a reporter. If you ever find a mistake in information you've provided, it's your responsibility to contact the reporter and correct it as soon as possible. If you don't know an answer, say so. If you think you're about to be ambushed, then you either need a good response plan or to abstain from the story altogether—but never, never, never lie to a reporter.

☐ **Ask about deadlines.** If you're contacted by a reporter, one of your first questions after "What's your story about?" should be "When is your deadline?" TV reporters will usually need interviews and footage at least two hours before airing, but they'll tell you because you can lose coverage just based on timing alone. Newspaper reporters will often need their information finalized by around 3:00 PM the day before they go to press. Edited radio stories usually need to be finalized by the day before they air. Talk radio interviews can happen on the same day as airing, but radio personalities usually try to sketch out their programs at least twenty-four hours in advance. The point is that the deadline will vary by media outlet and you should always ask.

☐ **Help with sources, interviews, and quotes.** You may have ideas on people to interview for a story, other people who may have inside tips, or sources who would be able to offer good quotes. Feel free to offer those. A reporter can sort through who would best complete the story within the given deadline. If you help them look good, compelling, and accurate, you'll likely have a good rapport for future issues.

☐ **Pitch your idea.** As you get to know reporters, you may want to give them tips or leads, or to pitch an idea to see if they think there would be interest in an article on it.

☐ **Assume you're on the record.** When talking to a reporter, blogger, or interviewer, you should always assume you're on the record. That simply means that anything you're saying is fair game for use in the story. If you're in a position where you want to give a reporter information but cannot or do not want your comments to appear in print or on camera, you need to expressly say, "This part is off the record." A reporter will respect that but prefers to be able to use, quote, and source information on the record whenever possible.

☐ **Be compelling.** You'll often hear "If it leads, it bleeds." To some extent this is true, but the less cynical version of the idea is that a story has to be compelling. A pothole in your street is not a story. A pothole in your neighborhood because a local decision maker is getting kickbacks to fill potholes in rich neighborhoods first is a story. Controversy, corruption, matters of life-and-death, public safety, natural disasters, economic survival, heroes and villains—those are stories.

☐ **Look for a way to appeal to a broad audience.** Most media outlets have to appeal to a broad audience, so being able to explain how your issue could affect every man and woman at home can be the key to explaining your issue's greater relevance. Your efforts may be centered around autism, for which it may seem like there's only a small audience, but the story may show that at autism's current incident rate, everyone will know someone who's impacted by the disorder, or that autism will have broader implications on the future workforce. Look for a universal human theme, even for a seemingly narrower topic. You don't want to simply preach to the choir.

☐ **Respect the reporter, blogger, or interviewer.** Reporters are used to people trying to manipulate them. They're used to spin and being pitched. Just know that they can see through that a mile away, and while such techniques might get you a quote in the short term, you'll lose their long-term respect, and they'll search elsewhere for a good source for information. These are generally pretty intelligent people who actually care about getting their stories right.

☐ **Provide quality in a crunch.** The modern work environment makes it very difficult for reporters to spend much time on any given topic. To the extent errors are made, they can usually be traced to a rushed atmosphere where reporters are covering multiple issues on a very short deadline. You can help by being brief, concise, and accurate.

☐ **Request an editorial board meeting.** An editorial board exists largely in the realm of the print news media, and they typically write the opinion editorial pieces for newspapers and some magazines. If you know you're going to be facing a David-and-Goliath-type issue at the capitol for legislative reform, an editorial board meeting can be helpful. It's up to the board to decide whether to schedule a meeting or how much time to give you, but these are important opinion leaders in your community. This is a time for strong facts. Be able to describe the problem, your proposed solution, and the obstacles you're likely to face. Getting a good editorial can really help your effort, and even if they don't end up supporting your effort, they're likely to at least understand it better. When it comes to vote counting a key legislative vote (see chapter 25), you'll appreciate a strong editorial in a local paper.

☐ **Foster relationships.** While some news stories are one-time hits, if you plan on being engaged with reform for any length of time, you should appreciate that working with the news media is like anything else—it's about relationships, and it's about your credibility.

☐ **Don't be afraid of controversy (at least in the media).** In the media world, controversy is your friend—it increases media interest and coverage and therefore attention to your story or reform effort. Welcome controversy as far as media is concerned. (This can run at odds with your legislative strategy, however. Many legislators are by disposition uncomfortable with controversy and would prefer to see only measures where "everyone" agrees. Consensus can be a rare and wonderful thing, but many important reforms couldn't or can't happen by consensus, for example, voting rights for women or minorities.)

☐ **Find an experienced media mentor.** This is a dynamic and tricky world, and it can really help to have someone with media experience at the helm to help you.

TELEVISION

Many TV news stories originate from press wires, such as the Associated Press, but they try to include local tips to make stories relevant to a particular regional audience. Television timing is almost always same day, so if you want TV coverage, you need to be flexible and quick to accommodate their timing. Remember that for TV they need to visually show the story as well as tell it often in sixty seconds or less. Many people are getting their news from TV these days, so even if the time you're allotted is inadequate, you can't afford to skip it.

☐ **Props, photos, video, or other visual information can help you make your point quickly.**

☐ **If you're going to appear on camera, avoid busy patterns or flashy jewelry.**

NEWS RADIO

There are a number of radio formats, but one potential format for your message is news radio reporting. News radio formats will either pick up stories from a newswire or do independent investigative radio journalism. It's different than talk radio in that news radio still tries to give equal time to different views, relies upon verifiable sources for news information, and generally refrains from blending editorial comment with the news. Most news radio reports are recorded, edited, and played during a news cycle. They may ask you to interview in the studio or over the phone. If you're doing a phone interview, they usually prefer you use a landline to avoid interference or dropped calls.

☐ **Answer questions and offer any facts you can in a conversational tone.**

☐ **With limited time, ask yourself what is the single most important thing you want the public to get out of the interview and include an action item.** "If people are interested in this issue, call your legislators and let them know… or attend the hearing this Thursday."

TALK RADIO

Talk shows are rarely neutral or balanced anymore, and even though they often market themselves as news, they differ in a few key respects. The content is largely driven by whomever the radio personality is, and they tend to be longer on opinion than they are on fact.

☐ **Therefore, you should know the show before you go on.** You'll be able to tell whether or not these are generally friendly audiences or not.

☐ **Don't limit yourself to friendly audiences only, but understand that some hosts are so hostile that you'll be wasting your time**. A shouting match on air doesn't really get your point across.

☐ **Know the personality's protocol.** Each host has a different culture for how they handle callers who disagree with them. Some will respect the caller, give you space to speak, and then debate you. But others will simply talk or even yell over you, or simply cut the microphone when you're saying something they don't want to hear. But if the host agrees with you and is planning for your interview, you can often get five-, ten-, or even occasionally twenty-minute segments to unfold a great deal of facts, discussion, and action items.

NEWSPAPERS

Our newspapers have become much more multimedia to compete in the modern news market. A good newspaper story can live on long after its original print in an online version that search engines may pick up in perpetuity. The same is true for a bad news story.

☐ **Think in terms of headlines.** While the journalist may or may not be able to select his or her own headline, it helps you create the angle of the story and stay focused.

☐ **Ask the reporter for a deadline.** Many local papers have now moved to a weekly rather than daily format, and a later deadline may give you more time to look up and include other key facts or information.

☐ **Suggest other contacts, especially the opposition.** Be ready to suggest who the reporter should talk to in order to get the other side of the story.

MAGAZINES

Most magazines print monthly and have a very specific theme. If a magazine reporter is interested in covering your topic, you may get the benefit of a more in-depth feature, but because they print less often, your issue has less opportunity to be featured. Magazine coverage is better when there's no urgent deadline behind the story and when the topic is as likely to be relevant in thirty days as it is today. So, legislation coverage doesn't lend itself well to magazine inclusion since it can change quite dynamically in twenty-four hours. That said, if you have a person, a story, or a problem that should be featured, it's worth aiming for magazine coverage as well.

THE BLOGOSPHERE

You have the most control over your content and your message in the online world of blogs (short for "Weblog"). The quality of blogs varies greatly, but you ignore blogging at your peril. It's helpful if you can get guest-blogger privileges on existing, well-established blogs. This allows you to author original posts (as opposed to just commenting on someone else's post) and you should take advantage of the opportunity to say directly what you want people to know. Reporters now follow most key political or legislative blogs, and some have suggested that blogs are now taking the place of press releases as far as providing tips to reporters on possible stories. Your blog could be one of them!

☐ **Comment on blogs.** At minimum, you should create a commenter login on all relevant blogs so you can directly respond or post where relevant.

☐ **Don't use multiple screen names.** Whether you're commenting on other people's blogs or publishing your own posts, use only one screen name. If you're dedicated to a real, specific public policy reform, you're more credible if you use your real name. If you want the freedom to speak truth to power without concern for reprisal (but also without accountability), then you may wish to post under a pseudonym.

☐ **Be careful with cross-posting.** While spurring a theme of discussions on multiple blogs with your comments is okay, simply doing a cut-and-paste across the blogs can wear out your welcome.

☐ **Be respectful.** While you'll find other people who habitually post toxic or vicious remarks, you shouldn't be one of them. You'll hurt your ongoing online credibility, even if it's attached to a pseudonym.

Media Plans

As you're preparing to create your own legislation or impact an existing bill, it's a good idea to have a media, press, or public relations plan. There's no shortage of professional firms who can help with this, but if you're like most of us, there won't be a budget for that and you should be prepared to run your own plan.

A media plan should include four basic components: (1) a timeline; (2) the action; (3) the topic, theme, or angle with each phase; and (4) which media outlets will be used. I also suggest a Notes column, where you can record other relevant info.

Whoever controls the media, controls the mind.
—Jim Morrison

SAMPLE MEDIA PLAN

Timing	Action	Topic	Outlet	Notes
November 15	Exposé #1	Human-interest story illustrating problem	**Local TV**	Breaks to larger story
November 21	Exposé #2	Another human-interest story, pattern emerging	**Local TV**, followed by press release about emerging pattern	Larger story
December 1	Overview	The problem with the system; data, facts, stats, the cause(s)	**Press release:** All outlets	
December 8	Editorial run	Why is no one doing anything about this?	**Print outlets, talk radio, blogs**	Inaction unacceptable
January 3	Announcement	Recap problem; will take action on problem	**Press release:** All outlets	Coalition
Session Begins	Announcement	Bill introduced, new angle	**Press release:** All outlets	Coalition
January 20	Preview	Bill gets a hearing, preview of controversy, testimony	**Press release:** All outlets	Coalition
January 20	2nd Editorial run	Support for proposed solution	**Print outlets, talk radio, blogs**	Inaction unacceptable
January 22	Recap and next steps	Hearing outcome, highlights from testimony	**Press release:** All outlets	Coalition
January 30	Recap	Bill passes chamber, what it means for public at large; backstory	**Scoop:** the backstory, favorite reporter #1	
March 1	Bill-signing ceremony	What the new law means for you	**Press release:** All outlets	Coalition
Effective date of bill	Press conference	Public service announcement: understanding new law; your new rights, remedies, or responsibilities	**Press release:** All outlets	Coalition

SAMPLE PRESS RELEASE

COLORADO STATE SENATE
DEMOCRATIC MAJORITY

FOR IMMEDIATE RELEASE
Thursday, May 5, 2011

CONTACT:
Eddie Stern, Communications Director, (303) 866-4882, edward.stern@state.co.us
Jack Wylie, Deputy Communications Director, (303) 866-3005, jack.wylie@state.co.us

LOCAL FOODS, LOCAL JOBS ACT PASSED SENATE
Senator Schwartz's bill will support Colorado farmers and stimulate job creation

DENVER—The Senate passed a bill by **Senator Gail Schwartz (D–Snowmass)** to promote local foods and create local jobs. Senate Bill 258, the "Local Foods, Local Jobs Act" will increase the availability of healthy, locally produced food by fostering direct connections between agricultural producers and consumers. The bill will support local farmers by allowing them to increase the selection of foods sold in farmers markets. The bill will also ensure Coloradans have access to a year round supply of healthy, local food. Senate Bill 258 now goes to the House for consideration.

Senator Schwartz offered the following comment on the passage of Senate Bill 258:

"This bill is good for all of Colorado. This bill supports farmers, local markets, local communities, and local jobs. By making adjustments to state regulations, we can support our economy, continue to protect our food supply, and provide our communities and visitors with more healthy food options."

Under the provisions of Senate Bill 258, baked goods, jams and jellies, preserved whole foods, eggs, dehydrated produce and spices may be sold by growers directly to consumers at farmers markets, on farms and through CSAs (Community Supported Agricultural organizations). Making locally produced foods more easily available to all consumers will support our economy, stimulate entrepreneurial activities, create new jobs and increase agritourism in our state. Senate Bill 258 also encourages the creation of farm-to-school food programs.

Mark Guttridge, owner of Ollin Farms in Longmont, CO wrote about the Local Foods, Local Jobs Act:

"[Senate Bill 258] has major implications for farmers, farmers markets, and consumers interested in year round supply of local, nutritious food. The bill would allow farmers to bake, dehydrate, or prepare products in their home kitchens and be able to sell those products directly to consumers either at farmstands, farmers markets, or through community supported agriculture programs."

A tool for finding local farmers markets is located at coloradosenate.org.

Chapter 25
Vote Counting

*Counting is the religion of this generation;
it is its hope and its salvation.*
—Gertrude Stein

Vote counting is simply the process by which a legislator, a lobbyist, or *you* track how each legislator says they're going to vote. It sounds straightforward, but it's more of an art than a science. The purpose of counting votes is to know if a bill you care about is going to pass or fail—and it'll help you make a variety of other strategic decisions. While you can be very involved and still have an impact without this process, the secret of vote counting is one of the key advantages that professional lobbyists can have over regular citizens. If you master this, you've just leveled the playing field.

When you count votes, you're just tracking responses of legislators who have votes at each key stage so you know whether or not they're likely to support or oppose a measure.

COUNT VOTES

☐ **Make a list or spreadsheet of those you need to contact.** You may not have to start from scratch. Ask anyone you know who's pretty active and see if he or she already has such a list. If not, go to the website for the state legislature and search for "contacts" or "directory." If the site allows mass export, then your work is done. If not, you'll need to copy and paste (a) name of the legislator, (b) district number, (c) political party, (d) e-mail address, (e) telephone number, (f) mailing address, and (g) committees the legislator serves on into a spreadsheet or a database. Then update it every two years as results come in from new elections. It's best to design this in a way that allows you to sort and search your list. For example, you might want to sort by name or political party, or search to find all legislators on the House Education Committee.

☐ **Ask conversationally.** Call your legislators and give a ten-second description of the bill. If you support the bill, follow with, "Do you know if you are supporting bill X? Do you have any questions about bill X?" or "Can we count on your support for bill X?" If you oppose the bill, follow the description with, "Let me tell you my main concerns with bill X...Do you share any of those concerns?" or "I have a fact sheet summarizing the key points of the bill. Do you have any questions?" and "Can I count on your no vote to help defeat this measure?" You can always elaborate later, but if you start too long, they may have to leave before you can finish.

☐ **Start with leadership.** If you get the leadership of the chamber in your court early, it can help determine which way many of the other legislators will vote. If leadership supports an effort, it's likely to pass, and if leadership opposes an effort, it's more likely to fail. While you'll benefit most immediately from the majority leadership, you'll find other benefits to working with the minority party leadership as well.

☐ **Count the chairperson.** The next critical vote is the chairperson of the committee to which your bill has or will likely be assigned. The chair's support or opposition of a measure will likely determine whether or not the bill will get out of committee. If the chairperson doesn't support a bill that you do, it's important to ask, "What, if any, changes to the bill would need to be made to the bill to get your support?"

SAMPLE VOTE COUNT

Senators	Yes	Lean Yes	Undecided	Lean No	No	Comment
Adams	X					
Galoyan				X		
Hernandez		X				
Jackson	X					
Lovell			X			Needs to read it
Martin					X	Hates the bill
Nunez			X			
Sanderson				X		Wants amendment
Tipton			X			
Vischer	X					
Walker			X			
TOTAL	3	1	4	2	1	
	4		4	3		

☐ **Count the committee members.** You'll need a majority of votes to get a measure out of committee. For example, on an eleven-member committee you'll need six votes to pass your bill. Bills can fail on a simple matter of attendance, so the closer your vote count is, the better your strategy needs to be. *Ask for everyone's vote*, regardless of party, even if it already looks like you have enough votes.

After an initial count, you can see that you have more yes votes than no votes, which looks like good news (if you want it to pass), but you could still lose the bill. In this example, you need a minimum of six committed yes votes to pass your measure. You don't have six votes yet. You have four undecided legislators and the bill could still fail.

☐ **Shore up your weak support.** If you're trying to pass a measure, you want to strengthen your lean-yes votes to move them into the yes column. So in the example above, you would talk to Senator Hernandez and find out if she needs any more information to be a solid yes or if she has any questions you can help answer.

☐ **Focus on the undecideds.** You can have the biggest impact on the margin. In the sample count, you're two votes short of passage and if you persuade them to vote yes, the bill

passes. As a citizen activist, you'd try to get meetings with, send e-mails to, or make phone calls to senators Lovell, Nunez, Tipton, and Walker. They're your swing voters. Find out if they need more information, if they have questions, or if they have suggestions for language they want to see changed in the bill to get their support. This is where doing background research on and actually *knowing* each legislator helps. Ideally, you would like to know what principles drive each decision maker, who they find persuasive, and how your bill does or doesn't fit into their value system. While you're unlikely to change a legislator's core value system, you can help them see how your efforts may fit within their value system.

☐ **Recount.** After you take an initial count to see where each legislator's initial inclinations take him or her, you'll be doing follow-up with your swing votes. Then you need to count your votes again. You may or may not get a different result. Start by following up with anyone who simply needed more time to review the bill. It's helpful to have fact sheets with you for each conversation. Your second count can confirm that you have your votes, or it can confirm that you'll need to make changes to your bill in order to pick up enough votes. This is how compromises happen in the process.

☐ **Start early.** The earlier you start counting your votes, the better. It gives legislators more time to digest information and it gives you more time to adjust your strategy, if you need to, in order to achieve your goal. Also, ideally you should wait to hear the bill until you're pretty certain you have your votes. This, of course, is not always possible, and you should bring your best effort to hearing.

☐ **Understand that votes can change.** Sometimes legislators change their vote. If you're counting votes on a bill, you are counting it *as written*. That doesn't necessarily indicate how a legislator will vote on a particular amendment or if a legislator changes his or her mind if an amendment gets on the bill. Sometimes legislators forget what they told someone about their intended vote. Sometimes a legislator will change or make up his or her mind when hearing the actual testimony. There's a strong culture in most legislatures to keep a vote commitment, but it's more important to get the public policy right, and if a legislator hears new and important information, their ultimate obligation is to their district and their conscience. It can be very frustrating when a flip happens because it can mean a bill that should have died passes or that a bill expected to pass dies.

☐ **Count the floor.** You'll also need to be ready to act quickly to count the floor if your bill gets out of committee. That simply means counting the remainder of the legislators in the chamber who'll be hearing the bill. Your vote count chart would look the same except it would include every member of the chamber. This is where having coalition allies can be quite helpful. You could divide up the vote count among allies and report back. For any no vote, it's helpful to ascertain their reason (you may or may not be able to address it).

☐ **Identify opinion leaders.** All votes are equal when it comes to the math, but not all votes are equal in terms of your passage strategy. It's important to identify who the issue or opinion leaders are on given topics. Some legislators will defer to the expertise of others because they believe they have a greater knowledge or mastery of the issues in some areas. Identify who those folks are and try to get them on your side of the issue.

Vote counting is as much about persuasion and style as it is about substance. Many of us have a natural tendency to debate people who disagree with us. But in seven years of serving, I can say that debating or arguing with a legislator is not the best way to persuade him or her. The most effective people I have witnessed listen and observe. They listen to the values basis of the legislator and the key assumptions beneath a legislator's position. The effective advocate can then describe their effort through the legislator's own values frame and offer information that can help shift key assumptions. A soft sell seems to work better than a hard sell. Pushing too hard can actually cement a position in the other direction. A good skill set of vote counting can help you pass or defeat measures that are important to you and help you make the right strategy decisions about your effort.

Democracy is only an experiment in government, and it has the obvious disadvantage of merely counting votes instead of weighing them.
—Dean Inge

Chapter 26
Amending a Bill

*All men can see these tactics whereby I conquer,
but what none can see is the strategy
out of which victory is evolved.*
—Sun Tzu

Amendments are simply proposed changes to the bill language after it's introduced. Most bills undergo some amendments or changes in the process. However, amendments can be one of the most frustrating aspects to being a citizen lobbyist. They're not typically made public ahead of time. Therefore, your ability to get an advance copy is likely to hinge on asking the bill sponsor if they'll share any amendments they know of with you.

Reasons to Amend a Bill

- **To correct errors in the original draft.** This happens when proponents agree on what the bill is meant to do, but there were errors in the bill that weren't caught prior to introduction.
- **To define terms.** Amendments may add definitions to terms used in the bill that aren't defined elsewhere, or they may change existing definitions.
- **To gain support or remove opposition.** These types of amendments usually stem from discussions and negotiations, and they range from technical to substantive.
- **To insert a poison pill.** These amendments are generally suggested in an effort to kill the bill. Proponents of this type of amendment know that if it gets on the bill, there will no longer be enough votes to pass the bill, or it will create a defect that

renders the bill unenforceable, unconstitutional, or simply distasteful.

- **To avoid conflicts with other laws.** Amendments can be offered to avoid conflicts with other provisions of state law, other pending legislation, or federal law. In other words, they can be offered to help the bill work better with other existing laws.
- **To create exceptions to the law.** Most laws start off as general principles that apply to everyone, but as they linger over time, invariably someone will come up with some occasion to start exempting people.
- **To remove or prevent unintended consequences.** Unintended consequences are by their nature unplanned. Sometimes these can become clearer after the bill has been introduced and there's more public discussion on the measure.
- **To improve implementation.** Sometimes those individuals, groups, or departments who are expected to enforce the law will request more specifics as to enforcement. Other times they'll ask for more flexibility for enforcement.
- **To make a symbolic statement.** These amendments are offered more to make a particular point than to actually adopt as part of the law. It can afford someone the opportunity to debate or get his or her talking points or rhetoric on the record.

- **To reduce costs.** Amendments may be needed to reduce or eliminate costs of a bill.
- **To create a campaign piece.** Some amendments are offered simply to get legislators on the record for a campaign mailer—a legislator wants to be able to tell his or her district that he or she tried to do X. Other legislators offer amendments knowing they can get a partisan recorded vote that'll sound bad to the general electorate, who won't have the benefit of having all of the information.
- **To resuscitate a dead bill.** Some amendments are really whole bills in their own right. If a bill is killed in committee or can't get scheduled for a hearing, a legislator can try to amend it onto someone else's bill that's further on in the process. Sometimes this is done with the consent of the other bill sponsor.
- **To amendment filibuster.** The amendment filibuster is not really a filibuster, but it's a time-stalling tactic implemented either to wear out the proponents of the bill, get media attention, or run out the clock so a final vote cannot be taken. These can present as a marathon of amendments if you're in a state that doesn't have a prior vetting process for amendments.

A Few Technical Points on Amendments

- **Your bill drafter is also your amendment drafter.** If you're advocating on an issue and want an amendment, you'll need to ask to have it prepared. That typically means having a legislator make the request on your behalf. Anyone can draft an amendment, but to be properly introduced, it's usually required that the finished amendment product be written and prepared by the legislative drafters.
- **Stipulations on single subject or germaneness.** Depending on the state, there may be a requirement that an amendment be germane or on the same topic.
- **Know the rules—or ask.** The process for amending can vary widely. In some states, anyone can offer an amendment on anything. In others, there might be a separate committee that determines or preapproves which amendments can be offered. There can be timing, notice, and page-length limitations.
- **Order matters.** In some chambers there are "settled questions" (issues that have already been presented and voted upon), which effectively preclude the same amendment from being offered more than once or from repeatedly amending the same portion of the bill. (So, the first legislator to raise the issue and get a final vote may be able to stop subsequent amendments to the same area addressing the same issue.) Therefore, if your chambers have settled questions, you want your amendment to come up for a vote first. If there aren't settled questions in the chamber, the rule may be that the last amendment adopted is the final language, in which case you want your amendment offered and adopted last.
- **Substitute amendments.** Typically an amendment is offered and the vote is taken before any other amendments on the same bill are offered. But sometimes a second amendment is offered before the original vote is taken—this is known as a substitute amendment. If a vote is taken on the substitute amendment and it passes, then it essentially kills the first underlying amendment. If the vote on the substitute amendment fails, then the group returns to the original underlying amendment for a vote.
- **Severed amendments.** Once in awhile an amendment will have several parts to it, and a legislator may like some portions of the amendment but not others. The request can be made to sever the amendment and vote on

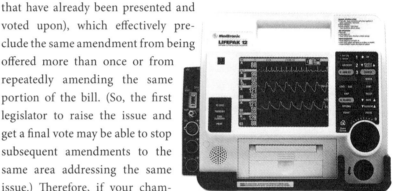

Did You Know...?

The Bill of Rights originally consisted of twelve proposed amendments, but two were ultimately rejected. The first ensured one representative for every 30,000 people in an effort to keep district sizes manageable. The second failed amendment was a measure to limit increases in congressional salaries. Even though it originally failed, it was later adopted as the Twenty-seventh Amendment to the US Constitution in 1992, prohibiting pay increases from taking effect until the beginning of the following term.

each portion separately. It's usually up to the chair to rule whether or not an amendment may be severed.

- **An amendment to strike the enactment clause.** This type of amendment kills the bill. A bill cannot have the effect of law without an enactment clause. This is an aggressive maneuver usually meant to play tricks on people who aren't paying enough attention to the proceedings.
- **A strike-below or striking everything below the enacting clause (SEBEC) amendment.** This type of amendment doesn't kill the bill. The amendment keeps the bill number but rewrites everything else. It's really a completely new bill that uses the existing bill number and, if adopted, moves forward in the process without having to start over again with a new hearing and new committee votes.
- **Count votes for amendments.** The same reasons for and process of counting votes on bills also apply to any amendments to the bill (see chapter 25, Vote Counting).
- **Amendments matter.** They can make a bad bill good or a good bill bad. A single word can reverse the entire meaning of the bill.

Honestly, amendment strategies can be highly complex and confusing, making this one of the most difficult arenas for citizen activists to navigate. Citizen participation is by no means all-or-nothing, and if you want to leave the amendment details to someone else at first, who could blame you?

But the more you observe the process, the more approachable it'll seem, and before you know it, you'll have your own amendment ideas. After all, an amendment is simply seeking a change to a bill. There'll also be drafters, legislators, mentors, or staff available to help walk you through the process. If you can master this, you can do anything.

However beautiful the strategy,
you should occasionally look at the results.
—Winston Churchill

Chapter 27

Paying for Your Bill— Fiscal Note Analysis

There is no dignity quite so impressive, and no one independence quite so important, as living within your means.
—Calvin Coolidge

Most states have a process where a financial estimate is prepared to anticipate any costs associated with passing or implementing a piece of legislation. This is often called a **fiscal note.** A draft of the bill is usually shared with the impacted state agencies in order to solicit their estimates of potential costs. This is a seemingly innocuous and nonpolitical part of the process, but it's loaded with both challenges and opportunities. Fiscal notes are often available online for you to read alongside the text of any given bill.

The Hidden Power of a Fiscal Note

Some of the reasons fiscal notes are important may be fairly obvious, but others less so.

- **Expensive=bad; cost savings=good.** Even if you have a great idea, the more your proposed legislation is estimated to cost, the less likely it will garner the votes it needs to pass, for a number of reasons. One important one: many states have been facing significant budget shortfalls, and some have balanced budget requirements.
- **An additional committee assignment may be required.** If your bill requires an appropriation to implement it, then you'll have an added

stop at the appropriations committee, where you'll need to garner a majority of votes—again—to pass your bill. Now you need to count votes not only on how you're going to fund your bill, but also on the bill's merits. A legislator in appropriations committee might support how you're paying for your bill, but not the bill itself, which means he or she would be a no vote. In other words, counting votes in appropriations means asking legislators (1) if they're okay with the bill, and (2) if they're okay with the funding mechanism. Strictly speaking, the narrower focus of an appropriations committee is really not supposed to be about the merits, but it'll influence how people vote nonetheless.

- **The cheat sheet version.** The fiscal note analysts usually include a plain-English summary of what a bill does. Many legislators and members of the public will read the fiscal note summary instead of the actual bill, amplifying the unofficial importance of the note.

Some Unspoken Truths about Fiscal Notes

- If a department or agency doesn't like your bill, it always seems to cost more, but if they like your bill, it seems to cost less.

SAMPLE FISCAL NOTES

SB11-025

Colorado Legislative Council Staff Fiscal Note

FINAL
FISCAL NOTE

Drafting Number: LLS 11-0226	**Date:** June 14, 2011
Prime Sponsor(s): Sen. Carroll	**Bill Status:** Signed into Law
Rep. Ferrandino	**Fiscal Analyst:** Bill Zepernick (303-866-4777)

TITLE: CONCERNING ACCOUNTABILITY FOR STATE PROCUREMENT, AND, IN CONNECTION THEREWITH, ENACTING THE "COLORADO TAXPAYER EMPOWERMENT ACT OF 2011".

Fiscal Impact Summary	FY 2011-2012	FY 2012-2013
State Revenue		
State Expenditures	See State Expenditures section.	
FTE Position Change		
Effective Date: The bill was signed into law by the Governor on April 8, 2011, and takes effect on July 1, 2011.		
Appropriation Summary for FY 2011-2012: None required.		
Local Government Impact: None.		

Summary of Legislation

This bill requires that personal services contracts of more than $100,000 entered into under the state procurement code specify that the contract and its performance measures and standards are open to public inspection, unless prohibited by federal law. Access to these types of documents are governed by the Colorado Open Records Act (CORA). The bill also clarifies that procurement information and contracts are public records. Current law requires that performance measures and standards are developed by the contracting governmental body specifically for each personal services contract and negotiated with the vendor prior to execution of the contract. The bill also makes the agreements with certified employee organizations (e.g., Colorado WINS) open to public inspection.

State Expenditures

The bill could increase the workload of state agencies for responding to open records requests. However, this analysis assumes that the volume of requests will be relatively small and that no additional appropriations are required at this time.

Departments Contacted

All Departments

SB11-200

Colorado Legislative Council Staff Fiscal Note

FINAL
FISCAL NOTE

Drafting Number: LLS 11-0249	**Date:**	June 20, 2011
Prime Sponsor(s): Sen. Boyd	**Bill Status:**	Signed into Law
Rep. Stephens	**Fiscal Analyst:**	Kerry White (303-866-3469)

TITLE: CONCERNING A COLORADO HEALTH BENEFIT EXCHANGE, AND, IN CONNECTION THEREWITH, CREATING A PROCESS FOR THE IMPLEMENTATION OF A HEALTH BENEFIT EXCHANGE IN COLORADO.

Fiscal Impact Summary	FY 2011-2012	FY 2012-2013
State Revenue		
State Expenditures General Fund	$29,638	$29,638
FTE Position Change	0.4 FTE	0.4 FTE
Effective Date: The bill was signed into law by the Governor and took effect on June 1, 2011.		
Appropriation Summary for FY 2011-2012: See State Appropriations section.		
Local Government Impact: None.		

Summary of Legislation

This bill creates the Colorado Health Benefit Exchange Act in connection with federal health care laws enacted in 2010. It establishes a non-profit organization that is an instrumentality of the state to oversee the establishment and operation of a competitive insurance marketplace (exchange) in Colorado. The exchange will be governed by a board of directors consisting of 12 members, including 9 voting members of certain qualifications appointed by the Governor and legislative leadership, and 3 non-voting members representing the Department of Health Care Policy and Financing, the Commissioner of Insurance, and the director of the Office of Economic Development and International Trade. Board qualifications, powers, and duties are specified, to include:

- appointing an executive director and creating an initial operational and financial plan;
- applying for gifts, grants, and donations to fund the planning, establishment, and operation of the exchange;
- creating technical and advisory groups as needed;
- preparing and presenting a written report, on or before January 15 of each year, concerning the status of the exchange;
- reviewing the internet portal and templates for citizens to access information on health plans offered through the exchange;

- identifying the structure of the exchange, including whether to separate the individual and small employer markets and the appropriate size of the small employer market; and
- considering the unique needs of rural Coloradans.

All board members serve without compensation, although per diem and expenses may be reimbursed from gifts, grants, and donations. All other expenses of the exchange are to be paid with gifts, grants, and donations received by the board. Financial information is to be reported to the Legislative Audit Committee, which may audit moneys received by the board.

A 10-member Legislative Health Benefit Exchange Implementation Review Committee (review committee) is created to guide implementation of the exchange, make recommendations, and carry legislation. Members are appointed by legislative leadership and serve without compensation, although per diem and travel expenses may be provided. The committee is to meet on or before August 1, 2011, and may meet up to five times per year thereafter to review the exchange's financial and operational plans and grants applications. Legislative Council Staff is directed to assist the committee.

The bill clarifies that no General Fund moneys are to be used to implement the bill except as required to reimburse legislators serving on review committee and to pay for legislative service agency staff costs. The legislative service agencies are also required to conduct a post-enactment review within 5 years of the bill becoming law. As amended, the bill also clarifies that the General Assembly has sufficient resources to implement the bill within existing appropriations.

State Expenditures

This bill will increase state expenditures by up to $29,638 in FY 2011-12 and FY 2012-13 to support the review committee created under the bill, as described in Table 1 and the discussion that follows.

Table 1. Expenditures Under SB11-200		
Cost Components	**FY 2011-2012**	**FY 2012-2013**
Personal Services	$20,288	$20,288
FTE Senior Research Assistant (0.3 FTE) and Staff Attorney (0.1 FTE)	0.4	0.4
Legislative Per Diem and Travel (10 members x $187 x up to 5 meetings)	9,350	9,350
TOTAL	**$29,638**	**$29,638**

Legislative branch. Expenditures will increase by $29,638 General Fund and 0.4 FTE per year, beginning in FY 2011-12. The review committee includes 10 legislators, for whom per diem and travel reimbursements may be paid. Assuming the committee meets up to 5 times per year at a cost of $187 per member, costs are estimated to be up to $9,350 per year. Legislative Council staff is tasked with providing research, and the fiscal note assumes that resources will be required to staff the committee and prepare legislation. Personal services costs total $20,288 and 0.4 FTE per year.

The Office of the State Auditor may experience an increase in workload if the Legislative Audit Committee chooses to audit moneys received by the board of directors of the exchange. Costs for post-enactment review are expected to be minimal.

State agencies. Representatives from the Governor's Office, and the Departments of Health Care Policy and Financing and Regulatory Agencies are to serve on the committee. Participation is expected to have a minimal impact on agency workload, but does not require a new appropriation.

Board of directors of the exchange. The bill specifies that board expenses are to be paid with gifts, grants, and donations. To the extent that the board requires any services provided by state agencies and reimburses board members for per diem and travel expenses, these costs will be paid with gifts, grants, and donations.

Expenditures Not Included

Pursuant to a Joint Budget Committee policy, certain costs associated with this bill are addressed through the annual budget process and centrally appropriated in the Long Bill or supplemental appropriations bills, rather than in this bill. The centrally appropriated costs subject to this policy are summarized in Table 2.

Table 2. Expenditures Not Included Under SB11-200*		
Cost Components	**FY 2011-12**	**FY 2012-13**
Employee Insurance (Health, Life, Dental, and Short-term Disability)	$2,840	$2,840
Supplemental Employee Retirement Payments	918	1,082
TOTAL	**$3,758**	**$3,922**

More information is available at: http://colorado.gov/fiscalnotes

State Appropriations

Due to the Legislative Council's approval of this committee, no separate appropriations are required for FY 2011-12. The Legislature is budgeted each year with resources to support a limited number of interim committees of the General Assembly (5). While this committee is anticipated to be ongoing, its costs will be paid from the portion of the budget reserved for interim committees.

Departments Contacted

Governor's Office
Health Care Policy & Financing
Regulatory Agencies

Governor's Office of Information Technology
Legislative Branch
State Auditor

- Every possible cost of your bill will be itemized. The departments will often err on the high side, but cost savings are generally not quantified. So, policy ideas that may require some initial short-term funding to ultimately yield high long-term savings will not necessarily get the commonsense analysis they deserve.
- Secondary benefits aren't usually included in the analysis. So, for example, if your bill keeps 5 percent more students in school until high school graduation, the fiscal note will show the added cost of educating those students, but it won't show the reduction in criminal activity or the resulting cost savings associated with prisons, nor will it show the increased earning potential of those students postgraduation and the net financial revenue increase to the state.

ENGAGE EFFECTIVELY IN THE FISCAL NOTE PROCESS

☐ **Ask to see the draft of your fiscal note** *before* **it's finalized.** This means having your legislative sponsor ask to see the note ahead of time. You may find errors or omissions, or you might have better or additional data you can provide the analyst.

☐ **Ask to see the raw responses from the departments.** The fiscal note analyst will contact the relevant departments to get their estimates of the financial impact of the bill. The departments will spell out their assumptions as well as their estimates. Their assumptions may not be well supported, and you may be able either to provide information to that effect or to amend the bill to be clearer about how something will work.

☐ **Look for inefficiencies.** Within a fiscal note or the department analysis, you may find that some of the things that drive costs up result from inefficiencies. For instance, do they really need a new IT system or a new computer programmer, or can they use the current ones? How many employees are they estimating, and is there a more-streamlined process that can put fewer demands on employee time?

☐ **Ask the analyst to spell out the cost drivers.** As a good steward of public funds, you should be looking for ways to remove or reduce cost drivers, particularly if they aren't even central to the importance of your bill. This discussion may lead to amendments to the bill.

☐ **Share your own data.** If you have research, data, or statistics about the experience of other states or about real past behavior, it can help offset inflated estimates. The earlier you can get that to your analyst, the more useful it is to them.

☐ **Do it within your existing resources.** There's one amendment (that departments hate to see) that can zero out the financial cost or appropriation on your bill: an amendment that the bill shall be implemented within existing resources. This requires good judgment on your part. If your bill creates a new position where someone is clearly going to need to be hired, then it isn't realistic to expect the department to do that within existing resources. But if they're trying to add cost for something more amorphous like answering a few more phone calls, this is an important amendment strategy to keep in mind.

☐ **Change the effective date.** Fiscal note analysts don't track the financial implications of a bill in perpetuity, but will generally only itemize the first few years. One short-term approach is to put the effective date of a bill out beyond the analysis window of the analyst. This is generally frowned upon, however, because if there's a real cost, then you're essentially putting out unfunded mandates into the future.

☐ **Fiscal notes can be a good way to kill a bill.** If your advocacy involves trying to get the defeat of a piece of legislation, a fiscal note revealing its costs can be good news. Even if people like the idea of a bill, if it drives up a cost, there's an increased chance you can find the votes to defeat it.

☐ **Long-term memory and comparisons across bills can be helpful.** Sometimes departments that are generally feeling underfunded may try to make up that shortfall on the back of your bill. Remember, the fiscal note for your bill is only supposed to be for any cost of implementing new laws, not backfilling for funding shortages in existing laws. Having some history to show where departments' trends were inflated versus the actual cost can help keep down the anticipated cost for your bill. Also, you may find that they're double billing for the same feature. For example, you may find that a department included a cost for a new computer system on another bill and they're trying to attach the same cost to your bill, even if they can use the same system.

Like amending a bill, fiscal note analysis is a fairly sophisticated level of involvement, but you don't have to know this level of detail to have an impact on public policy. But because fiscal notes can determine whether a bill passes or dies, it's important that you have this information. Experienced advocates or legislators can help walk you through a fiscal note strategy on your legislation.

Money is better than poverty, if only for financial reasons.
—Woody Allen

Chapter 28
Lobbying the State Budget

We can tell our values by looking at our checkbook stubs.
—Gloria Steinem

The state budget is the most important (and my least favorite) part of the legislative arena. In it, there's fierce competition among laudable interests for scarce resources. The budget can be opaque, it can read like an eight-hundred-page Excel spreadsheet, and it's laced with a strange vocabulary of acronyms, econ-speak, and wonky concepts. Because of its complexity, the budget is an arena that's particularly at risk for takeover by professional lobbyists, leaving ordinary citizens in the cold. The good news is that in the modern age, every budget should be online in its entirety, accessible to anyone. And—more good news—the budget is like any other bill, and changes to it are an amendment like any other, with one exception—in order to add funds in one area, you must also identify where you're making the equivalent cut in another area.

Why You Should Advocate on Budget Issues

Almost anything you care about will eventually lead you to the state budget. Do you think your taxes are too high or not spent in the right ways? Do you think classroom sizes are too large and teachers are underpaid? Do you think college tuition rates are too high? Do you want to see more economic development or tourism in the state? Do you want to see improved services for people with developmental disabilities, or better early childhood education? Do you think child-protective services are too quick to snatch kids from their homes or too slow to act with known cases of abuse? Do you think prison sentences are too short or too long? Do you hate sitting in traffic or realigning your tires after hitting too many potholes? Do you hate standing in line at the driver's license locations? Do you care about having clean air to breathe, clean water to drink, and uncontaminated food to eat? Do you want to know that your doctor is licensed and qualified to operate on you? The list is nearly endless, and everything is influenced by the budget.

All state budgets seem unwieldy and large because we're so accustomed to a household budget. It's important to remember that a budget serves millions of people. The per-person cost is one good way to get a sense of how much bang for your buck you're getting from your taxes in relation to the amount of public services provided. *Everyone* uses public services, but very few people are conscious

Did You Know...?

Before winning the election in 1860, Abraham Lincoln lost eight previous elections for various offices.

of what they're accessing or what value they'd put on that service. There's no such thing as someone who uses no public or publicly subsidized services.

A Thought Experiment

Keep a detailed journal of everything you do for one day and consider to what extent you use a public service or publicly subsidized product. Do you:

- use roads or a public bus or train system?
- drink water or flush toilets?
- eat at restaurants? (Regulated by public health departments)
- send your kids to public school or college?
- use parks or recreation areas?
- live in a house or use buildings? (They must pass safety inspections.)
- have family or friends with mental health problems or disabilities? (Many receive help to live independently.)
- rely on police and fire departments to keep your homes and neighborhoods safe?
- have elderly parents who receive in-home service or live in nursing homes?
- go to work and get paid at least minimum wage, or receive Social Security benefits?
- go to the doctor? (Or any other medical professional who needs a license?)

This is just a short list of services, so you'll likely miss some even if you aim to be quite complete in your list.

The budget matters because it reflects our values. What are your priorities, and what do you think should be the top priorities for your state budget? Where would you make cuts and why?

How to Read a Budget

The most important thing for you to know about a budget is that, like a bill, you can read and decipher it, even if you aren't an accountant or economist.

Summary chart. There's usually a summary chart that captures the whole state budget at a glance. This overview is a good place to begin. (See example on opposite page.)

Organization by department. The budget staff usually organizes a budget by department, with subcategories called line items under each department. (See bottom example on opposite page.)

Comparison. There'll typically be a comparison between this year's appropriation and last year's appropriation, so you can see if total funding has gone up or down.

An increase may really be a decrease. Watch for budget categories that are caseload or person driven. For example, a Medicaid budget can show a net increase in appropriations, but the recipients will be receiving a cut. Why is that? It's possible for the number of applicants to Medicaid (caseload) to go up, even if the individual benefit amounts are cut per person. The net growth in caseload can mask the per-person cuts. Another example might be K–12 education. The total funding line may appear to increase, but if the number of enrolled students has increased, it could still indicate a per-pupil cut to K–12 education.

Funding sources. There'll also usually be columns for different funding sources, depending on how your state is financially structured. For example, funding sources might include General Fund, Cash Funds, Federal Funds, Transferred Funds, and so forth.

Budget narrative. This is the most useful component for reading and understanding a budget; the budge narrative is the plain-English description of key actions or items in the budget. This will be where you can best ascertain the values, priorities, and reasons behind the ultimate budget document. (See example in sidebar on page 126.)

SUMMARY OF PROPOSED LONG BILL APPROPRIATIONS FOR FY 2011-12

Department	TOTAL	General Fund	Cash Funds	Reappropriated Funds	Federal Funds
Agriculture	$38,833,345	$5,237,048	$28,550,895	$1,042,342	$4,003,060
Corrections	727,033,121	641,840,769	40,223,222	44,250,443	718,687
Education	4,561,372,393	3,294,711,018	617,275,069	23,433,557	625,952,749
Governor	168,262,296	11,275,530	7,722,770	125,392,860	23,871,136
Health Care Policy and Financing	5,052,388,319	1,781,255,499	761,306,727	7,535,185	2,502,290,908
Higher Education	2,880,156,988	624,242,230	1,697,237,745	539,636,738	19,040,275
Human Services	2,090,960,535	618,764,498	331,392,727	450,967,546	689,835,764
Judicial	479,976,040	346,258,755	113,762,155	14,744,832	5,210,298
Labor and Employment	159,534,454	0	61,271,465	756,026	97,506,963
Law	53,477,430	9,573,187	10,460,741	31,920,410	1,523,092
Legislature	2,905,149	2,655,149	0	250,000	0
Local Affairs	345,478,643	10,449,980	230,570,470	7,181,744	97,276,449
Military and Veterans Affairs	221,373,748	5,478,155	1,210,964	803,509	213,881,120
Natural Resources	224,108,586	23,806,367	171,931,889	8,493,047	19,877,283
Personnel and Administration	157,336,679	5,239,847	8,836,054	143,260,778	0
Public Health and Environment	477,519,100	27,640,974	152,176,076	29,773,850	267,928,200
Public Safety	265,590,140	82,795,856	128,883,205	24,248,440	29,662,639
Regulatory Agencies	76,585,985	1,623,241	69,481,273	4,286,845	1,194,626
Revenue	292,735,425	70,546,702	220,125,899	1,339,123	723,701
State	18,770,239	0	18,770,239	0	0
Transportation	1,108,403,517	0	699,360,251	4,898,243	404,145,023
Treasury	386,470,593	27,932,150	358,538,443	0	0
LONG BILL OPERATING TOTAL	**$19,789,272,725**	**$7,591,326,955**	**$5,729,088,279**	**$1,464,215,518**	**$5,004,641,973**

PART I
DEPARTMENT OF AGRICULTURE

(1) COMMISSIONER'S OFFICE AND ADMINISTRATIVE SERVICES

	TOTAL	General Fund		Reappropriated Funds	Federal Funds
Personal Services	1,309,998 (14.7 FTE)	294,625		18,031ᵃ	997,342ᵇ
Health, Life, and Dental	1,631,507	285,788		1,284,766ᶜ	60,953
Short-term Disability	25,447	5,387		18,358ᶜ	1,702
S.B. 04-257 Amortization Equalization Disbursement	403,551	86,230		290,403ᶜ	26,918
S.B. 06-235 Supplemental Amortization Equalization Disbursement	324,736	69,745		233,360ᶜ	21,631
Workers' Compensation	176,054	28,153		147,901ᶜ	
Operating Expenses	117,122	112,622		4,500ᶜ	
Legal Services for 4,653 hours	352,279	105,770		246,509ᶜ	
Purchase of Services from Computer Center	520,491	382,813		137,678ᶜ	
Multiuse Network Payments	182,691	71,404		111,287ᶜ	
Management and Administration of OIT	134,856	104,395		30,461ᶜ	
Payment to Risk Management and Property Funds	108,062	29,403		78,659ᶜ	
Vehicle Lease Payments	208,951	73,377		133,521ᶜ	2,053
Information Technology Asset Maintenance	153,031	34,705		118,326ᶜ	
Leased Space	110,751	43,026		67,725ᶜ	
Capitol Complex Leased Space	171,145	139,608		31,537ᶜ	
Communication Services Payments	14,542	9,283		5,259ᶜ	
Utilities	146,318	66,939		79,379ᶜ	

Department of Corrections—The bill includes a net decrease of $14.0 million. This primarily reflects the following reductions: (1) $17.2 million for the external capacity program based on the projected inmate population; (2) $5.6 million to reflect a 1.5 percent reduction for Personal Services line items; (3) $4.5 million associated with FY 2010–11 supplemental adjustments; (4) $3.0 million for academic and vocational programs offered to inmates; and (5) $2.0 million for prison operations and prison therapeutic communities. These reductions are primarily offset by the following increases: (1) $9.8 million to restore one-time personal services reductions for FY 2010–11, including a 1.0 percent General Fund reduction for certain Personal Services line items, and a reduced State contribution to the Public Employees' Retirement Association (PERA) pursuant to S.B. 10-146; (2) $5.9 million for adjustments to centrally appropriated line items; and (3) and $2.6 million related to the impact of prior year decision items and legislation.

Briefing documents or memos. The best analytical information often comes from budget staff in the form of these documents, which provide a more in-depth analysis of cost drivers and cost savings in certain areas within the budget. Most of this information is online and available for you to read yourself.

> *Government is a trust, and the officers of the government are trustees; and both the trust and the trustees are created for the benefit of the people.*
> —Henry Clay

LOBBY YOUR STATE BUDGET

☐ **Make friends with someone on the budget committee.** Seriously. Those legislators know the process, rules, and math better than anyone else. If you need guidance on how to accomplish what you want or where to find a funding source, they're your best ally.

☐ **Pick a department.** The entire budget is a bit overwhelming. Find an area that's of particular interest to you and try to make an impact there.

☐ **Apply the strategies for influencing legislation that you already know.** All of the prior discussions on building coalitions, minimizing opposition, and so forth still apply. The tips on e-mail and phone calls are just as applicable in the budget arena. See chapters 3–18.

☐ **Identify your funding source.** It may seem frustrating as an ordinary citizen to have to identify how you're going to pay for something, but if you want to increase funding for Meals on Wheels, you need to know where you're getting the money from or else be up front about the fact that you don't know. Adding funding in any one portion of the budget necessitates cutting from somewhere else in the budget—particularly if you're in a balanced budget state.

☐ **Be specific.** If you're going to ask for increased funding, you should be prepared to state exactly how the funds would be used. Saying a budget is too big or too small is too vague. What would you cut? Where would you invest?

☐ **Show that your request is a good investment.** It's helpful if you can find research demonstrating why what you're seeking is a good investment.

☐ **Demonstrate the cost of *not* appropriating funds.** Sometimes there's a short-term or long-term cost to not appropriating certain funds. For example, deferring maintenance on a public building can mean a higher repair bill for taxpayers in the future, or a depreciated asset for the state.

If you engage in a budget debate or try to advocate to shift priorities within a budget, you'll no doubt be among a very small group of citizens who do. But your presence and involvement as a nonlobbyist will catch the attention of decision makers, and real people can and do change and impact budget decisions.

Chapter 29
Resolutions

Democracy cannot succeed unless those who express their choice are prepared to choose wisely. The real safeguard of democracy, therefore, is education.
—Franklin D. Roosevelt

Resolutions are different than bills in a few key ways. Resolutions don't change the law. Some issues or causes are as much about awareness or education as they are about the law. So if you want to raise awareness but don't have a law you want changed, consider a resolution.

Resolutions can be on virtually any topic. As with a bill, you need a legislative sponsor to introduce your resolution. Here are some examples of actual resolutions we've heard:

- Holocaust Memorial—Remembering the causes and consequence of genocide
- Different Cancers—Know the signs, get-tested-early messages, find a cure
- Other Disease Awareness—Know the signs, get-tested-early messages, find a cure

- Equal Pay—Updating the statistics on the pay gap between men and women
- Mediation—Alternative dispute resolution options
- Fallen Soldiers—Tribute to veterans who gave their lives
- Martin Luther King Jr.—Paying tribute to extraordinary historical people
- Mental Health Issues—Prevent, detect, and treat
- Honoring Single Parents

Most resolutions are easier to pass than bills. They don't typically get routed to committees, so they don't face the usual hurdle of committee passage to make it onto the floor. Also, legislators tend to be a bit more lenient with resolutions because they aren't actually creating law.

If liberty and equality, as is thought by some, are chiefly to be found in democracy, they will be best attained when all persons alike share in government to the utmost.
—Aristotle

WRITE AN EFFECTIVE RESOLUTION

☐ **Pick a topic you feel strongly about.** A resolution about minor or trivial issues will not get the same respect or attention as a more substantial topic.

☐ **Include good research.** The substance of a resolution is typically a series of "WHEREAS" statements using facts and sources that are important for the public to know.

☐ **Include an action statement.** What do you want the listener to do? After someone hears your resolution, what reaction do you wish to evoke? For example, do you want the audience to donate blood to the local blood bank, or call their member of US Congress to ask that they support or oppose a federal measure?

☐ **Avoid ideological extremes.** A resolution is typically something everyone can get behind. If you stick to the facts, you're better off, and a unanimous vote sends a stronger message.

☐ **Coordinate timing with the majority leader if you have guests.** Sometimes resolutions are run at a time when special guests are expected. If your resolution is time-sensitive (either because it's Child Abuse Awareness Month or because there are groups making a special trip to the capitol) make sure you have also planned the timing with the majority leader. There are many competing time demands on the calendar, and it can be awkward for you to bring people down for a resolution that doesn't happen that day.

☐ **Specify who the resolution will be sent to.** At the end of a resolution, include the statement "Copies shall be provided to _____." This is your opportunity to provide copies to decision makers and other organizations who might be in a position to benefit from the information or act on it.

☐ **Share the resolution with the media.** Have one or two people impacted by the resolution's topic who are willing to talk with the media about its importance. So, if the topic is education, you want as many people to know about it as possible.

Part Four

Beyond Legislation

Chapter 30
Other Ways to Be Involved

Democracy is the worst form of government, except all those other forms that have been tried from time to time.
—Winston Churchill

Participating in the legislative process can be very rewarding, and your participation increases transparency of your government and helps ensure that your elected officials are working for you. Below are other things you can do outside of the legislative process to make an impact. Maybe some of these are right for you. (If your schedule doesn't allow much time, check out chapter 19, Advocacy for Busy People, for other, quick ways to be involved.)

- **Join a board or commission.** Most states, counties, and cities have a host of boards and commissions that serve a very important function, and key positions often go unfilled. These offer a very broad range of possible topics, so the chances are pretty good that you'll find some area of interest to you (for example, citizen budget group, civil rights commission, police oversight boards, water boards, economic development, the environment, tourism, and so forth). These boards and commissions often have citizen appointment positions with important oversight functions. Most jurisdictions have a list of vacancies on their website. There's also a wide range of time commitments (some meet monthly, some quarterly), so you can pick what best fits your schedule. The first step is simply to apply.

- **Become a regular attendee of town hall meetings.** Hopefully, most of your elected officials hold regular town hall meetings (if they don't, you should ask why not). These meetings will typically include people from various political perspectives, some of your neighbors, friends, and coworkers. Town halls may be an open format, such as a coffee talk, to just chat about the latest updates and seek your input on priorities; or they may be a panel of speakers on a specific topic allowing for questions from the audience. Most people at town halls are interesting, engaged, and polite. You'll often hear the latest announcements and discussion of bills that will never appear in any newspaper.

- **Volunteer at the capitol.** If you're in a position where you have time to offer, you can volunteer at your capitol. It's a great way to see the process up close and see for yourself what you think is or isn't effective.

- **Talk to canvassers.** At the local level, you're likely to have your representatives walking door-to-door, either asking for your vote or asking for your priorities. While the interruption may at times be unwelcome, the input that's gathered has a real impact. I walk my district every year with some volunteers to see what issue priorities people want me to work on for the next year. Your input helps ensure that your elected officials are actually working on what you want them to.

- **Use technology.** It's now so easy and so cheap to have a website, write a blog, and use social media that an online presence can be a great way to have an impact. Create your own blog and disseminate information you care about on your own website. Follow your elected officials, and share links for information you want them to have on their pages. A word of caution: the apparent anonymity or impersonality of this medium means that it isn't for everyone, and your e-credibility can be hurt by being toxic, bombastic, or loose with your facts. Use your real name whenever possible.

- **Vote.** If you're old enough to vote, please vote. For most of human history and still today in many countries people cannot vote, their votes risk violent reprisals, or the elections are rigged. While our elections may not be perfect, you have a right in this country that most people will never have. Great men and women died for this right as the most basic, precious, and central to a democracy. No one will ever agree with you 100 percent of the time, but find the candidate that most closely mirrors not only your policy values but also your process values. If you really,

really don't like any of the candidates, then get involved in recruiting *different* people to run for office—someone you could be excited about. Heck, maybe that's even you (see chapter 31, Run for Office).

- **Join issue groups or nonprofits you believe in.** There are a lot of organizations that are formed around specific issues and values. If you find one that reflects your interests, join the organization, get on their newsletter and action-alert list, get involved. While not every idea needs a group, if you don't find an organization that's already dedicated to an issue you believe in, maybe you should form one.

- **The audit function.** Most states have an audit function of some type. If you have questions about possible waste, duplication, gaps, or noncompliance with current law by any agency or department of state government and you suspect it may be a systemic problem, request an audit. Audits are generally conducted by nonpartisan professionals who do an in-depth analysis of what is or isn't working, and they generally conclude with findings and recommendations for how government can work better. Audits can be the source of significant cost savings or efficiencies and can be fertile ground for possible ideas for legislative improvements. The process is a bit different in each state, so start by reaching out to your elected officials. Ask them to explain how the audit function works in your state and the process by which an audit is requested or approved.

Did You Know...?

Nebraska is the only state in the Union with a unicameral legislature, meaning the legislature consists of just one house. It's also the only state to have a nonpartisan legislature, meaning the political party of the candidate isn't listed on the ballot.

Problems cannot be solved
by the same level of thinking that created them.
—Albert Einstein

Meet Rhonda Fields

Rhonda Fields was a single mother of two kids who besides working full-time was taking care of her elderly mother and making sure her children graduated high school and college. She was used to fitting forty hours of life activities into a twenty-four-hour day. Rhonda described herself as living a little at the margins of society, but somehow pulling it together—working, and being active in her church. Her son and daughter were bright, successful, and family- and goal-oriented people who would make any parent proud. She had never before written to her elected officials.

Her life changed forever on July 4, 2004, when her son, Javad Fields, and his fiancée, Vivian Wolfe, witnessed a murder. In the past, Javad organized annual July Fourth barbecue parties at a park. He would emcee the events with live hip-hop and urban entertainment. As they were closing down the event that year, his friend Greg Vann went over and asked a guy, "Why did you bring a gun to my party?" Sir Mario Owens shot Greg point-blank in the chest, and after he fell shot him twice more.

Javad and Greg's brother pursued Greg's murderer on foot. Javad was shot in the arm and the leg as unmistakable warning shots. Yet Javad survived, and he worked with the police department as a key witness in the murder investigation. Javad identified Robert Ray as the driver of the getaway car, which carried Sir Mario Owens in the front passenger seat. He attended numerous court proceedings, and as Owens's murder trial—and Javad's witness testimony—drew closer, he began receiving threats.

Despite the fact that he was a shooting victim of the man on trial, the obvious risks of testifying in a high-profile murder trial, and the verbal threats made prior to the trial, Javad was never offered any witness protection. He wasn't advised of any rights he might have or any witness-protection measures that could be offered as he was about to take the stand against a murderer.

Meanwhile, Javad successfully graduated from Colorado State University in May 2005 and was discussing graduate school plans on the East Coast with his fiancée, Vivian. But Javad Fields would never testify at the murder trial, because he and Vivian were murdered in a drive-by shooting on June 20, 2005.

Rhonda heard her son had been shot and rushed to the hospital, where she couldn't get a basic answer as to whether he was alive or dead for at least forty-five minutes. Then she heard he was dead—had died at the scene. Rhonda wanted answers, but few were forthcoming.

Rhonda wanted to know why witness protection wasn't offered to her son. Why would the police and prosecutors ask someone to testify against a dangerous murderer without advising him and his family of all of their rights for protective services? She eventually found out that police departments were not routinely trained in witness-protection efforts, that Colorado lacked a statewide witness-protection program, and that the state lacked a risk-assessment tool to determine when and how to best protect important high-profile witnesses to crimes. How is law enforcement supposed to expect witnesses to come forward and testify against dangerous criminals if basic protections aren't offered? Rhonda was told Javad didn't get witness protection because he didn't ask for it.

Rhonda was having a hard time getting answers from the hospital, the police, and the district attorney, so she took matters into her own hands by holding a press conference a few days after the murder to talk to the public about what happened and what had failed to happen, leading to the death of her son. The more Rhonda talked about her son and his fiancée, the more public interest grew, and her personal questions were now becoming public questions.

Finding answers became her full-time mission. She hired private investigators and dedicated every waking moment she could into finding out as much as she could. Rhonda and her daughter, Maisha, did some of their own investigating and came up with leads and clues that would later prove useful to the police department and prosecutors. Her legal saga was complicated and difficult and ultimately led to the trial and conviction of those responsible. But why did it happen? Was Javad's death preventable? The sad answer was yes.

By 2006, Rhonda contacted her state representative, Michael Garcia, and told him what happened. Garcia was disturbed by what he heard, and he agreed to look further into Colorado's witness-protection laws and those of other states. He then reached out to Representative Terrance Carroll, because Carroll chaired the judiciary committee and had a background in law enforcement. Carroll would later become Speaker of the Colorado House of Representatives. Together, they worked on some proposed legislative ideas with Rhonda to increase training, funding, screening, and notice of witness-protection rights in Colorado.

Not even a year after her son's death, Rhonda had already passed her first bill in the legislature: HB 06-1379, which required statewide training and materials to implement witness-protection programs. I was honored to be on the House Judiciary Committee at the time we heard Rhonda's bill, and I'll never forget her testimony and that of Christine Wolfe, Vivian's mom. Still asking questions about what else could be done to make witnesses safer, Rhonda came back the next year with another bill.

House Bill 07-1147 provided *in camera* review (in judge's chambers) of witness-protection materials for possible redaction of (blacking out) sensitive witness information before it was handed over to a dangerous defendant. A defendant would still get materials necessary for the defense, but for highly dangerous crimes, sensitive information such as a witness's home address could be redacted. Rhonda passed that bill too.

She continued to work full-time but was now joining victims' advocacy groups around the state and country. She learned more about her rights, what rights her son had, and where the fragmented criminal justice system fails so many victims. Rhonda Fields, Christine Wolfe, and Colorado State University created the Fields Wolfe Memorial Fund (www.fieldswolfememorialfund.org). The scholarship foundation has now sent seven kids to college, three of whom have already graduated. The organization profiles courageous citizens in the community and ensures they're recognized for their courage.

Rhonda has worked around the clock for reforms, and advocacy has become a way of life for her—so much so that she is now serving in the Colorado General Assembly. Representative Karen Middleton was vacating her seat to move to California, so she asked Rhonda to consider running for her seat. Rhonda prayed and thought about the decision and two weeks later announced she would run for office.

Rhonda saw the opportunity to continue fighting for all types of justice reforms in the legislature. She ran for office in 2008 and won her election handily. The local community embraced her because they knew she would be a champion for them too.

She has this advice for you: "You have power. We all have personal power we can exercise. Power is *not* in our elected officials, but in all of us. We have the power to influence and persuade those around us and in office. Power is not at the state capitol. It's in the community. Tap into your personal power and don't tolerate any inadequacies or inequities. Don't take no for an answer and don't hesitate to tell your story."

Chapter 31

Run for Office— Yep, You!

If your actions inspire others to dream more, learn more,
do more and become more, you are a leader.
—John Quincy Adams

You'll never agree 100 percent of the time with your elected officials, but if you find yourself lamenting a lack of choices for candidates you can really believe in, then you have two choices: find someone you think would be great and get him or her to run for office, or run for office yourself. If you're like most people, maybe you assume that running for political office is something other people do. Or maybe you think you have to be a corrupt scumbag to want to run for office. Not true. Running for and serving in a public office is something you can actually do to directly serve your community and ensure people have good choices.

If you want the majority of elected officials to be public-service minded, then you want the candidates who run for office, from any political party, to be people with integrity who care about the community in which they live. The initial selection of who gets on the ballot may feel like an insider's game, but you have a powerful role to play in recruiting and encouraging the right people to run.

Some of the best and brightest have never considered running for office but should. *You* should consider it. How do you know if it's right for you? You should run for office:

- **if you care** about people, issues, and your community.
- **if you can listen** as much or more than you speak.
- **if you're curious;** if you're willing and interested to ask a lot of questions and do a good amount of research to find solutions to problems.
- **if you're a critical thinker;** if you can think for yourself and resist pressure to do what others want if it's wrong in principle or wrong for your community. It's necessary to stand up to lobbyists or even your own political party at times.
- **if you have ideas** and are willing to explore others for improvements in public policy. If you don't have ideas, lobbyists will fill the void and give you bills to run.
- **if you're a problem solver**—and you're open to finding solutions, regardless of who gets or takes credit.
- **if you aren't turned off by customer service.** Elected office is essentially a customer service position with a lot of responsibility, and if you like helping or serving other people, you'll love this job.
- **if you have a strong work ethic.** The job will require a great deal of time and effort to do it well. This means a lot of time reading (the bills, mail, e-mail), responding, and problem solving.

• **if you can put your ego aside.** This occupation can attract some serious egos. Just remember it isn't really about you; it's about your district, its needs, and its priorities. A common mistake candidates make is talking on and on about themselves. Voters want *some* background on you, but mostly they want to know what you can do for them.

Perhaps one of the best things I can do is clear up what you don't have to be. You don't have to be an attorney, a political insider, or have any particular resume to run for office. You don't have to be rich, well connected, or well known. It's up to you and your district to decide what qualifications are important. I think a varied mix improves the overall system. I've had the privilege of working with teachers, business owners, construction workers, stay-at-home moms, retirees, public sector employees, nurses, doctors, lawyers, police officers, ministers, chefs, realtors, social workers, students, and nonprofit workers. Many people eliminate themselves from even asking the question because they assume they have to be something they aren't.

You don't have to be a saint. It's okay to be a real person with actual flaws and imperfections, but learn from them, be honest, and be willing to admit your mistakes. The people who fall the hardest are people who invest a great deal in trying to cultivate a perfect image and wind up actually living a double life and getting caught. You *do* need to be authentic, and it helps if you're secure with yourself. You'll have a lot of new "friends" willing to offer gifts, perks, flattery, or even seduction, and you need to be confident enough that you don't get hooked into that.

Those who shouldn't run for office are people who are looking for power, perks, or a resume builder. People who are self-centered, vindictive, or purely partisan should leave the job for someone else. A good leader can recognize ideas from any corner and articulate a vision or goal of how we can get there. A good leader will unify, rather than divide, to find a common goal or purpose.

It's okay to be different. The profile of who is running for office is changing. At one point the field was predominantly wealthier (white) heterosexual men, married with kids. More women are running, more ethnic minorities, more openly gay, lesbian, and transgender people, and more divorced or single people. More young people and more people with disabilities are running—and winning. People are increasingly willing to look past a caricature of a politician in favor of a real person if that person is willing to work hard and be responsive to the needs of the district.

There are a lot of resources out there to help you figure out *how* to run for office. I just want to encourage you to think about running for office and let you know that you don't have start off knowing how it all works—you can find that out later. People are very willing to mentor, and some of our very best elected officials are people who had previously never even considered running for office. We need talent and conscientiousness at all levels of public office if our democracy is to work the way our Founders envisioned. Even if you don't run for office, please take an active role in searching for and encouraging people you like and respect to run.

Did You Know...?

Thomas Jefferson was the first president to shake hands with guests. Previously, citizens bowed to presidents.

Do not follow where the path may lead. Go instead where
there is no path and leave a trail.
—Harold R. McAlindon

RUN FOR OFFICE

☐ **Find a mentor.** First and foremost, talk to someone who has run for office and won, and someone else who has run for office and lost. In fact, find as many mentors as possible. You'll get different advice from different people, and it's not all equally good advice. This does wonders to get you relevant advice, but it also helps you clear the biggest hurdle just by demystifying the process and the job.

☐ **Be honest about your motives.** Spend some quality time thinking about why you want to run and what you'd like to do in office. Soul searching can not only lead you to a clear vision, but it can also help you connect with voters as well. Your motive for running will generally be one of the following:

- **To run, win, and lead.** Most people who run for office are running to win. This takes the greatest amount of time commitment, effort, and work. But if you're running to win, you want to have an excellent campaign plan and stick to it. There are people, organizations, and resources dedicated to candidate recruitment and assistance, so it doesn't matter if you don't currently know how to run a campaign—as long as you're willing to learn and ask for help.
- **To drive a discussion.** Another valid reason to run is to give voters an option and drive a debate—even if it's a very politically one-sided district. Having multiple perspectives tends to help give some depth to the discussion and round out the policy choices.
- **To be a placeholder.** A placeholder candidate is one who doesn't really intend to win and may not do all of the work typically required of a viable campaign. It can be disturbing to see some races for office blanked out in their entirety. But if you're running to be a placeholder, you should know it could hurt your future electoral opportunities if you're blown out of the water. You should also be prepared for what happens if you win. It's rare, but it's happened—where no one was more surprised on Election Day than the candidate who thought he or she was simply a placeholder wound up winning.

☐ **Consult your family and friends.** It's a good idea to float the idea and have a discussion to get the reaction of those closest to you. Would they be supportive or resistant to the idea? You'll need the time, emotional support, and financial help of those closest to you. If your significant other is flat-out opposed to the idea, neither your electoral bid nor your relationship will end well.

☐ **Talk with local party leaders.** Under the current system, the overwhelming majority of candidates are placed on the ballot through the political party system. It's possible to run unaffiliated, but it's much, much harder. If you're affiliated with a party, talk to the local party leadership to get their insight and suggestions and to make sure you're on their radar. They'll often know what "the bench" looks like—you can find out the depth of existing interest and the number of other possible candidates already looking at a seat. Party leaders are generally not a fan of primaries because they prefer to focus party time and money resources on one candidate. You're more likely to get their support if you run for a position in which they think you're needed, not always where you might prefer to run.

☐ **Determine the right district.** Spend some time deciding which is the right office and the right district for you. It's easier to start with smaller districts because you have a better opportunity to personally meet more voters. Run where you live; some states have a residency requirement, but even if they don't, your local roots will be important to your district. District boundaries change every ten years with the census, so you should look at neighboring districts as well, because even if you stay put, your boundaries might not. It's easier to start where there's a natural vacuum—where there isn't already a candidate or an incumbent. There are plenty of people who can help you analyze which is the best office or the right district.

☐ **Choose the right time.** Timing matters and can have a lot to do with whether you win or lose. Preparing a good campaign takes some time, and while it's possible to jump in later in a campaign season and win, it's far harder and riskier that way. Pick a time that makes sense for you and your family. Is it better to run in a wave year (a year in which electorate political party trends heavily favor one political party) or not? If you have term limits, who will be term limited which years, or do you want to run against an incumbent?

☐ **Consider whose support you can expect.** Think of which friends, family, neighbors, colleagues, and activists you know who might be willing to support you if you run for office and ask their opinion. If you're the only one who thinks you should run for office, that doesn't bode well. These are people who, as a practical matter, you would need to ask for volunteer help and donations to get you started.

Chapter 32

How Does Your State Measure Up?

*High achievement always takes place
in the framework of high expectation.*
—Charles F. Kettering

Each state has somewhat different laws and rules pertaining to their legislative process. The goal should be to maximize transparency and citizen participation. Below is a list of positive government reforms that can be a sign of how user-friendly your state government is. You may wish to start your reform activities by identifying in which areas your state is weak and push for some of these improvements.

Guaranteed public hearings. Does your state ensure that every bill that's introduced has a full, fair public hearing? If so, can everyone who wants to testify do so, or does it require prior approval? The most citizen-accessible process guarantees a public hearing and the right for any member of the public to testify without prior notice or approval. In many states, a hearing is granted only if the chair of the committee or leadership decides to schedule it. This is sometimes referred to as a pocket veto, which essentially kills the bill without a hearing or a vote.

Audio/video proceedings. Does your state audio or video record its committee and floor vote activity? If not, it should. This allows citizens to monitor proceedings even if they cannot attend in person, and it facilitates obtaining archives of prior proceedings if needed for research. It can also help you decide if your elected official is living up to your expectations.

Online campaign finance disclosures. Does your state have comprehensive campaign finance disclosure laws that put the campaign finance information online so that any member of the public can easily search to find out who has contributed to each elected official? If not, accountability to the public is inadequate. If you want to look up political campaign contributions to see who's donating to your legislators, or if you want to determine the adequacy of your state's campaign finance disclosure laws, go to www.fec.gov/pubrec/cfsdd .shtml and click on your state.

Online legislation. Does your state legislature put all legislation online so that the public can download and read it for themselves? This is critical so that you can read and judge for yourself whether or not you like a measure.

Online voting records. Does your state legislature's website post the recorded votes of all legislators and all bills? This is critical for holding your elected officials accountable.

Online lobbying activity. Does your state require that all professional lobbyists register, identify all of their paying clients, and disclose the amount of the contract and what legislation they're supporting or opposing? This is important to change the backroom culture of deals that gives more clout to the lobby corps than to citizens. It's also important so citizens can see what special interests are lining up for and against each measure.

Prohibition of lobbying gifts. Does your state prohibit or limit gifts from lobbyists to lawmakers? This is important to avoid corruption, to restore public confidence about the legislative process, and to ensure the process will be equally open to the average citizen who cannot or should not be expected to offer gifts to be heard and have influence. Typically no legislator thinks *he* is impacted by gifts, but social science research suggests that *all* people are impacted by gifts with a natural human inclination for gratitude and an impulse to reciprocate. This is a problem when public policy is involved.

Sunshine, open meetings, and open records. These are your state's laws pertaining to public notice of public meetings and the right for the public to request and receive public records. What are your state's laws on open meetings and open records? Does it err on the side of transparency or secrecy? Do the exemptions swallow the rule?

Government contracting. Does your state's procurement system contemplate seeking and obtaining multiple bidders, objective criteria for evaluation, and transparency of the contracts? Does your state rate and track performance of vendors so that poor-performing vendors are not awarded future contracts? Does your state prohibit gifting, wining, and dining of those with the power to award contracts by those who are seeking state contracts?

State budget and finances online. Does your state put its budget, finances, and expenditures online so that citizens can follow their money?

Single subject rules. Does your state require that there be only one subject or topic in each bill? This ensures that everyone can understand what's in the bill and prevents vote trading on unrelated matters in one bill. Single subject rules help ensure that each individual topic gets its own separate vote on its merits.

No man is good enough to govern another man
without that other's consent.
—Abraham Lincoln

Chapter 33
Putting It In Perspective

Vision is the art of seeing what is invisible to others.
—Jonathan Swift

In the end, there's only one thing that matters—that you get involved. Pick and choose what works for you on topics you care about. You don't need to know or do everything in this book. You can write, run, and pass your own laws, or you can simply make one sixty-second phone call per year to share your wishes with your elected leaders. The danger is for citizens to cede their power to the professional lobbyists through disengagement or inaction. When citizens don't engage, there's 100 percent certainty that the wealthier lobbying interests are shaping public policy. That may not *always* be a bad thing, but it's rarely reflective of what the people actually want and many times can actually be harmful to you and your interests. While my hope is to share tips on how to be most effective, you should know that there's no wrong way to be involved. Don't let the pomp and circumstance or formal traditions get in the way. All of the process is incidental and can be learned quickly. When in doubt, don't be afraid to ask.

For all the civics, government, or political science classes out there, we rarely get practical information on what it takes for citizens to have an impact on their government. I believe elected officials generally do a poor job of inviting the public in and making this process approachable and comfortable for people. The capitol is *your* building filled with *your* elected officials who work for *you*. "The government" is you—all of us—and in a healthy democracy it's a shared responsibility to make it what *we* want it to be. No one else will do this for us. The danger of a public that's increasingly cynical about its government is that it replaces action with apathy, ideas with anger. If the public checks out of their own government in a democracy, what's left behind will surely be a self-fulfilling prophecy revealing our lowest common denominator.

This isn't about party. It isn't even about a specific issue. It's about whether or not we, the people, claim our inheritance of freedom, liberty, and democracy and make our government work *for* us. Complaining is easy. Fixing it is the work of real patriots. The keys to the capitol are yours—make yourself at home.

I have been impressed with the urgency of doing.
Knowing is not enough; we must apply.
Being willing is not enough; we must do.
—Leonardo da Vinci

Glossary

adhere. A procedural motion of amending a bill in which the original house votes to stick with the language as it passed the original chamber, unamended. This forces the second chamber to acquiesce to exactly the language of the first chamber. Or, if the second chamber also votes to adhere to its own language, the bill dies because it failed to pass both chambers with the exact same language.

administrative law. The body of law that governs administrative agencies and regulations. It typically consists of a rule-making process, which is a more-detailed description of how statutes are to be implemented or enforced by the agencies. This is sometimes referred to as public law.

act. A bill that has passed the necessary legislative steps to become a law.

amendment. A change to a bill. It must receive a majority of votes in order to be adopted as part of the bill.

appropriation. The legislative authorization to expend some public money for a particular purpose. An appropriation clause is the provision added to a piece of legislation to enable the expenditure of the identified funds.

bill. A proposed law that is introduced in the legislature.

bill number. A unique number assigned to a piece of legislation upon introduction. This is the number that will be used subsequently for scheduling or other public action on the bill.

campaign contribution. A monetary or in-kind donation made by an individual or a group to a political candidate for purposes of election or reelection.

caucus. A closed meeting of a group of elected members within the same political party (for example, the Democratic Caucus, or the Republican Caucus). A caucus can also be issue based (for example, the Transportation Caucus or the Mental Health Caucus).

chair or chairperson. The legislative member who leads or governs the committee rules and procedure. He or she presides over the meeting and makes decisions on how a committee will be run. The leadership of the majority party usually appoints this person.

chambers. The different houses in a bicameral legislature. Typically the House is one chamber and the Senate is the other.

checks and balances. The idea enshrined in the US Constitution that includes both the concept of separation of powers and the ability to limit powers by other entities or people. Its purpose is to prevent consolidation of power and limit the potential for abuse of power.

citation. A unique series of numbers and letters to identify each provision of law. A statutory citation provides a unique combination of numbers and letters to indicate in which title, article, or section one will find a specific law. A case citation provides a unique combination of name and numbers to identify a particular court opinion.

citizen lobbyist. An unpaid member of the public who does not represent a particular group and who engages and advocates in the legislative process with the goal of impacting the outcome.

civil law. The body of law that addresses private rights, responsibilities, and remedies. It governs disputes between private parties.

committee hearing. A public meeting where decisions can be made on legislation or recommendations to the larger membership. This is the phase where public testimony can be accommodated on the merits or demerits of bills.

concur. A procedural motion of agreeing or acquiescing to the changes in language made to the bill in the other chamber.

conference committee. The process by which a bill that has passed between the two chambers with different language is reconciled. Usually conducted by a small working group of appointees from both chambers and both parties who seek to find one common wording for passage in each chamber.

constituent. In the narrow sense, a person who lives within the district of a legislator. In a broader sense, a member of the public. A constituency can be a group of people with shared interests in policy even if they don't share the same geographic region.

contract lobbyist. A professional (paid) lobbyist who works for a variety of different clients, representing multiple groups and interests and facing a high potential for possible conflicts of interest between the groups he or she represents. This person is a free agent of sorts, not tied to one interest.

cosponsor. A legislator who has decided to indicate his or her support of a bill by jointly sponsoring the measure alongside the prime sponsor, even if he or she is not the author of the measure.

criminal law. The body of law that prohibits certain acts deemed to cause public harm and to be a threat to public safety, and that provides punishment as consequences for violation.

democracy. A form of government in which rule is by the people. Typical features include free and fair elections; a multiparty system; freedom of speech, religion, and the media; the right to criticize one's government and elected officials without reprisal; "one person, one vote"; and the absence of corruption.

department. The unit of organization of the executive branch. Departments are tasked with implementing specific areas of law and responsibility (for example, the Department of Labor and Employment).

dictatorship. A form of government in which powers are consolidated behind one person or one regime. Typical features include an authoritarian regime; few or no checks and balances; a lack of free or fair elections with meaningful choices; little or no ability to criticize the government; and the use of military powers to suppress political dissenters.

district. A political unit of geography from which an electorate selects the representatives of their choice. Districts are generally drawn to ensure that there is "one person, one vote" and that an elected official can concentrate on serving the regional needs and preferences of the people they represent. Districts are generally redrawn every ten years, upon receipt of updated US Census population figures.

division. A subunit of an agency or department tasked with the implementation of a specific function of the executive branch. Or, a division vote is one where the voting members are asked to either sit or stand to have their votes counted. Votes are not recorded for each individual member, but a numerical count is taken, unlike a voice vote.

effective date. The date on which the provisions of the law take effect and can be enforced. Most laws are not retroactive.

enforcement mechanism. The means by which a law is to be enforced. Most laws will be enforced by one or more of the following: agencies or departments; police and prosecutors; or private right of action in courts. Most laws are not self-enforcing, and a law without an enforcement mechanism may have no actual effect.

executive branch. One of the three traditionally recognized branches, responsible for implementing laws. Typically consists of a lead executive, such as the president of the United States or governor, and includes their staff, departments, or agencies.

fact sheet. An advocate's simple summation of key facts or reasons to support or oppose a particular piece of legislation. These are often used to help focus conversations with elected officials and to try to persuade a legislator's vote.

federalism. The distribution of power between a central authority and local political authorities.

First Amendment. So named for its primary location in the Bill of Rights, which are the first ten amendments to the US Constitution. It provides, "Congress shall make no law respecting an establishment of religion, or prohibiting the free exercise thereof; or abridging the freedom of speech, or of the press; or the right of the people peaceably to assemble, and to petition the Government for a redress of grievances."

first reading. The part of the legislative process in which a bill is introduced. A measure changes from a private idea to a public bill and is assigned a bill number and a legislative committee.

fiscal note. The analysis provided for a piece of legislation about the possible costs associated to state government, if any. This analysis determines what appropriation may be needed if the bill is adopted, and it can also identify possible cost savings to the state.

floor debates. The part of the process in which a bill has made it out of committee and has an opportunity to be debated by every legislator within the chamber.

floorwork. The portion of a legislative calendar during which action is taken by the entire chamber. It can include second reading of bills, third reading of bills, resolutions, or acting to accept or reject amendments made in the other chamber. It basically includes everything that's not committee work.

Fourth Estate. The concept that the media is an essential component of a functioning democracy because of its role for checks and balances and the role it plays in educating the public about the activities of their government.

framers. The drafters and signers of the US Constitution. There were fifty-five people who were delegates, thirty-nine of whom actually attended and signed the US Constitution.

government lobbyist or liaison. A person who works for an executive department and is paid to advocate for the department before the legislative branch. Government lobbyists are not authorized in all states.

House of Representatives. One of two chambers in bicameral legislatures. Historically derived from the British parliament's House of Commons, or lower chamber, as distinguished from the House of Lords, or upper chamber. The branch of government designed to be closest to the people.

idealist. A person who lives under the influence of ideals.

independent press. The portion of the media that's generally beholden to neither government nor oligopolistic chain ownership.

judicial branch. One of the three traditionally recognized branches. Responsible for interpreting the laws as they apply to specific people and facts, is intended to be independent of the trends and tides of public opinion, and aspires to be impartial. Judicial interpretations of states' laws are the final laws unless changed by the legislature.

legislation. One or more bills introduced by lawmakers. Can be used to describe bills either before passage or after adoption.

legislative branch. One of the three traditionally recognized branches. Representatives elected by the people responsible for writing laws on their behalf, levying and collecting taxes, and making financial appropriations. This branch generally makes the policy decisions.

legislative calendar. A public document indicating what bills will be heard in committee or on the floor. Serves as public notice for where a bill is in the legislative process.

legislative declaration. A section of a bill that describes the intent or purpose of the bill. It is not substantive law but can be used by the courts or the public if ambiguity about the intent of the legislation ever arises.

legislator. Someone elected to make the laws for the people within a particular political subdivision.

lobby corps. Collectively, the group of professional lobbyists who advocate at the capitol.

lobbyist. Person who advocates in the legislative process. Professional lobbyists are paid, volunteer lobbyists are not. Volunteer lobbyists are different than citizen lobbyists or advocates because a citizen lobbyist represents their own interests and values not necessarily those of a special interest group.

loophole. An ambiguity or omission in a law's provision that allows someone to evade the law's reach. Occurs when applicability of the law is inconsistent or not universal and if uncorrected can mean that the original intent of legislation is thwarted.

mainstream media. Where most people get their information and news and includes the more traditional media of newspapers, television, radio, and magazines. These are generally prepared for a broad, general audience.

majority leader. The majority party legislator elected by caucus to represent the majority. Serves as a spokesperson for the members of the majority party and typically gets to appoint their majority members to committees and has the prerogative to determine timing and sequence in running the floor calendar.

majority party. The political party whose members compose more than half of the legislature. It's easier for the majority party to get its bills through and it typically gets to determine who chairs committees or presides over the chamber. The majority political party has significantly more power in the legislative process than the minority party.

minority leader. The legislator elected by the caucus in the minority to represent them. Serves as a spokesperson for the members of the minority party and typically gets to appoint their minority members to committees.

minority party. The political party whose members compose less than half of the legislature. It's more difficult for the minority party to get its bills through and it typically does not get to chair committees or preside over the chamber. The minority political party has significantly less power in the legislative process than the majority party.

party affiliation. The party you select when registering to vote. More broadly, it can be the party you most closely identify with, regardless of how you're registered to vote.

political ideology. System of beliefs about what goals should be pursued in a society and the process by which they should be achieved. In some contexts, political ideologies become synonymous with inflexibility in putting abstract ideas over the practical needs and considerations of real people.

political party. An organization that seeks to influence politics and public policy by nominating candidates of its choice and creating a platform of issues and values.

politics. The process by which different groups in a society make decisions that impact everyone.

populist. A believer in the rights of the common people.

preemption. A doctrine based on the supremacy clause of the US Constitution that holds that when federal and state law conflict, federal law overrides or replaces state law.

president of the Senate. The leader of the Senate, elected by the majority caucus. Presides over the Senate when meeting as the Senate and has a great deal of influence over bills at all stages; makes numerous appointments and determines the committees to which bills will be assigned.

prime sponsor. The legislator who files and authors the bill in the originating chamber and shepherds the measure through the process.

private rights of action. An enforcement mechanism that allows ordinary citizens to act to enforce their rights, usually in court. It provides for citizens to be less dependent on the will of other government actors to enforce their rights, but also usually means they bear the time, cost, and responsibility of enforcing their rights.

professional captive lobbyist. A paid lobbyist who advocates for one organization.

quid pro quo. Something for something. While historically this meant an exchange of items of basically equal value, in a political context it has come to mean favor trading: if you do this for me, I'll do that for you.

recede. A procedural motion of amending a bill in which the chamber can abandon the amendments made in chamber and ultimately acquiesce to the amendments and language adopted in the other chamber.

reject. A procedural motion of rejecting the amendments made in the second chamber; typically followed by a request for a conference committee to try to work out the differences in language.

remedy. A redress one receives if a right has been violated. The purpose is to try to make a person whole who has had one or more of their rights violated.

representative democracy. A form of government founded on the premise of elected individuals representing the people in their government.

republic. A form of government in which the people or their elected representatives retain the sovereign power of the state.

resolution. A formal statement of opinion or information by a legislature that is then adopted. It is not a law.

right. A legal guarantee of something; usually ensures a freedom or protection to someone against the actions of someone else.

right to petition. The right for citizens to approach their elected officials with grievances or suggestions, found in the First Amendment to the US Constitution. It incorporates the right for citizens to approach their elected officials with grievances or suggestions.

second reading. The legislative phase in which a bill has passed out of committee and is considered for debate by the full chamber.

Senate. One of two chambers in bicameral legislatures (and the only chamber in Nebraska). Historically derived from the British parliament's House of Lords, or upper chamber, as distinguished from the House of Commons.

separation of powers. The idea enshrined in democracies that there are different functions of government and that their respective powers should be separated so they can offer a check and balance to other parts of government.

session, legislative. The period of time in which a legislature is convened for the purpose of making laws. Most legislatures don't meet year-round, and the length and timing of each legislature depends on the state. A legislator can work on constituent matters all year but only has the power to create and pass legislation when they're convened in session.

single subject. The idea that there should not be more than one subject or idea in each piece of legislation. This is a requirement by law or rule in some states. It can be a mechanism for preventing unrelated amendments or ideas from getting onto a bill. This can prevent riders or pork-barrel projects from getting appended to an unrelated measure.

social media outlets. Communication outlets that are Web or technology based, allow for interaction and networking, and encourage the exchange of user-generated content. This includes blogs, Facebook, Twitter, MySpace, YouTube, wikis, podcasts, and dozens of other online networking and communication applications.

Speaker of the House. The leader of the House of Representatives, elected by the majority caucus. Presides over the House when meeting as a house and has a great deal of influence over bills at all stages. Makes numerous appointments and determines committees to which bills will be assigned.

special interests. Interests that impact a narrower subset of the general public. Can connote a special expertise or interest, but is often used to describe something that may not be in line with the general or public interest.

sponsor. A legislator who authors a piece of legislation and serves as the lead person or shepherd of the bill in each chamber throughout the legislative process.

statute. A law. Also a collective term for the books of laws adopted by the legislature (as opposed to interpretations by the court).

term limit. The maximum number of years or terms an elected official can serve in a particular office. Term limits were a popular trend in response to a perception of unfair incumbency advantages and an effort to eliminate career politicians. Common criticisms of unintended consequences include loss of expertise and a shift of knowledge and power away from elected people and toward unelected people such as lobbyists and staff.

testimony. Public comments offered at a legislative hearing that become part of the record and reason to support or oppose a particular bill. Legislative testimony can also include fact-finding or investigative efforts.

third reading. The final phase of legislation in a chamber during which a final vote is taken and recorded by each voting legislator. In the vote history of a bill, it's usually this vote that is recorded and made public.

under the dome. A phrase that differentiates between the inner workings of regular participants at the capitol and the rest of the world. It highlights the difference that can be present between insiders and outsiders and connotes a unique culture that develops amongst the people who spend the majority of their time at the capitol. Can be used to emphasize a difference of opinion or priorities that can exist between legislators and lobbyists and the public at large.

volunteer lobbyist. An unpaid advocate of a specific group or organization.

veto. The executive power to reject legislation passed by the legislative body; prevents a bill from becoming a law. Overriding a veto typically requires a two-thirds majority vote of the legislature.

voice vote. Process for calling a vote whereby individual votes are not recorded but rather the group is asked to vote verbally en masse. For example, "All in favor say aye; all opposed say no."

vote commitment. A promise or indication by a legislator that he or she will vote yes or no on a particular bill or amendment. A vote commitment is more than an initial inclination on a vote and typically triggers an expectation that others are entitled to rely on that promised vote.

vote counting. The process whereby a person asks voting legislators how they intend to vote and tracks the total number of votes in support or opposition to determine whether a bill or amendment is likely to pass or fail.

Appendix A
Online Legislative Contact Information

State	Webpage Name	Web Address
Alabama	Alabama House of Representatives	www.legislature.state.al.us/house/representatives/houseroster_alpha.html
	Alabama State Senate	www.legislature.state.al.us/senate/senators/senateroster_alpha.html
Alaska	House of Representatives	http://w3.legis.state.ak.us/house/house.php
	State Senate	http://w3.legis.state.ak.us/senate/senate.php
Arizona	Arizona State Legislature	www.azleg.state.az.us/MemberRoster.asp
Arkansas	Arkansas House of Representatives	www.arkansashouse.org
	Arkansas Senate	www.arkansas.gov/senate/senators.html
California	California State Assembly	www.assembly.ca.gov/acs/acsframeset7text.htm
	California State Senate	http://senate.ca.gov/senators
Colorado	House Members	www.leg.state.co.us/Clics/CLICS2009A/csl.nsf/DirectoryHou?openframeset
	Senate Members	www.leg.state.co.us/Clics/CLICS2009A/csl.nsf/DirectorySen?openframeset
Connecticut	House of Representatives Members	ww.cga.ct.gov/asp/menu/hlist.asp
	Senate Members	www.cga.ct.gov/asp/menu/slist.asp
Delaware	Delaware General Assembly—Representatives	http://legis.delaware.gov/legislature.nsf/Reps?openview&Count=75&nav=house&count=75
	Delaware General Assembly—Senators	http://legis.delaware.gov/legislature.nsf/sen?openview&nav=senate
District of Columbia	Council of the District of Columbia Directory	www.dccouncil.washington.dc.us/councildirectory
Florida	Florida House of Representatives	www.myfloridahouse.com/Sections/Representatives/representatives.aspx
	Florida Senate	www.flsenate.gov/Senators

State	Webpage Name	Web Address
Georgia	Georgia House of Representatives	www1.legis.ga.gov/legis/2009_10/house/alpha.html
Georgia	Georgia State Senate	www1.legis.ga.gov/legis/2009_10/senate/senatelist.php
Guam	Guam Legislature Senators	www.guamlegislature.com/senators.htm
Hawaii	Hawaii State Legislature Directory of Representatives	www.capitol.hawaii.gov/members/legislators.aspx?chamber=H
Hawaii	Hawaii State Legislature Senate Members	www.capitol.hawaii.gov/members/senate/legislators .aspx?chamber=S
Idaho	Idaho Legislature House Membership	www.legislature.idaho.gov/house/membership.cfm
Idaho	Idaho Legislature Senate Membership	www.legislature.idaho.gov/senate/membership.cfm
Illinois	Illinois State Representatives	www.ilga.gov/house
Illinois	Illinois State Senators	www.ilga.gov/senate
Indiana	Indiana General Assembly Legislators	www.in.gov/legislative/legislators/listing.html
Iowa	Iowa Legislature General Assembly	www3.legis.state.ia.us/ga/legislators.do
Kansas	Kansas Legislature House Roster	www.kslegislature.org/li/chamber/house/roster
Kansas	Kansas Legislature Senate Roster	www.kslegislature.org/li/chamber/senate/roster
Kentucky	Kentucky Legislature House Members	www.lrc.ky.gov/house/hsemembers.htm
Kentucky	Kentucky Legislature Senate Members	www.lrc.ky.gov/senate/senmembers.htm
Louisiana	Louisiana House of Representatives	http://house.louisiana.gov/H_Reps/H_Reps_FullInfo.asp
Louisiana	Louisiana State Senate	http://senate.legis.state.la.us/Senators/offices.asp
Maine	Members of the Maine House of Representatives	www.maine.gov/legis/house/hbiolist.htm
Maine	Maine State Senators	www.maine.gov/legis/senate/Senator-Alpha-List.html
Maryland	Maryland House of Delegates	www.msa.md.gov/msa/mdmanual/06hse/html/hseal.html
Maryland	Maryland Senate	www.msa.md.gov/msa/mdmanual/05sen/html/senal.html
Massachusetts	Members of the House of Representatives	www.malegislature.gov/People/House
Massachusetts	Members of the Senate	www.malegislature.gov/People/Senate
Michigan	Michigan House of Representatives	www.house.mi.gov/replist.asp
Michigan	Michigan Senate	www.senate.michigan.gov/members/alphamemberlist.htm

State	Webpage Name	Web Address
Minnesota	Minnesota House of Representatives	www.house.leg.state.mn.us/members/housemembers.asp
	Minnesota Senate	www.senate.leg.state.mn.us/members/member_list.php?sort=a&ls=86##header
Mississippi	House of Representatives	http://billstatus.ls.state.ms.us/members/hr_membs.xml; http://billstatus.ls.state.ms.us/members/h_roster.pdf (printable)
	Mississippi State Senate	http://billstatus.ls.state.ms.us/members/ss_membs.xml; http://billstatus.ls.state.ms.us/members/s_roster.pdf (printable)
Missouri	Missouri House of Representatives	www.house.mo.gov/member.aspx
	Missouri Senate	www.senate.mo.gov/11info/senalpha.htm
Montana	Montana House Roster	http://leg.mt.gov/css/Sessions/61st/roster.asp?HouseID=1&SessionID=94
	Montana Senate Roster	http://leg.mt.gov/css/Sessions/61st/roster.asp?HouseID=2&SessionID=94
Nebraska	Senator's Web Pages (unicameral legislature)	www.nebraskalegislature.gov/senators/senator_list.php
Nevada	Assembly Member Contact Information	www.leg.state.nv.us/75th2009/legislators/Assembly/alist.cfm
	Senate Leadership and Members	www.leg.state.nv.us/75th2009/Legislators/Senators
New Hampshire	House Members	www.gencourt.state.nh.us/house/members/housemembers.html
	Senate Roster	www.gencourt.state.nh.us/Senate/members/senate_roster.aspx
New Jersey	New Jersey Legislative Roster	www.njleg.state.nj.us/members/roster.asp
New Mexico	New Mexico House of Representatives	www.nmlegis.gov/lcs/lcsdocs/HouseMailingList.PDF
	New Mexico State Senate	www.nmlegis.gov/lcs/lcsdocs/SenateMailingList.PDF
New York	New York State Assembly	http://assembly.state.ny.us/mem
	New York State Senate	www.nysenate.gov/senators
North Carolina	North Carolina House of Representatives Members	www.ncga.state.nc.us/gascripts/members/memberList.pl?sChamber=House
	North Carolina Senators	www.ncga.state.nc.us/gascripts/members/memberList.pl?sChamber=Senate
North Dakota	North Dakota Senators	www.legis.nd.gov/assembly/61-2009/senate/members/last-name.html
	North Dakota Representatives	www.legis.nd.gov/assembly/61-2009/house/members/last-name.html

State	Webpage Name	Web Address
Northern Mariana Islands	Members of the House of Representatives	www.cnmileg.gov.mp/members.asp?secID=1&legsID=17
	Members of the Senate	www.cnmileg.gov.mp/members.asp?secID=2&legsID=17
Ohio	House of Representatives Members Directory	www.house.state.oh.us/index.php?option=com_displaymembers&Itemid=55
	Ohio Senate Members	www.ohiosenate.gov/directory.html
Oklahoma	House of Representatives	www.okhouse.gov/Members/Default.aspx
	Senate Members	www.oksenate.gov/Senators/Default.aspx?selectedtab=0
Oregon	Oregon House of Representatives	www.leg.state.or.us/house
	Oregon State Senate	http://www.leg.state.or.us/senate
Pennsylvania	Members of the House of Representatives	www.legis.state.pa.us/cfdocs/legis/home/member_information/representatives_alpha.cfm
	Members of the Senate	www.legis.state.pa.us/cfdocs/legis/home/member_information/senators_alpha.cfm
Puerto Rico	Puerto Rico Senators	www.senadopr.us/senadores/Pages/Senadores%20Acumulacion.aspx
	House of Representatives	www.camaraderepresentantes.org/legsv.asp
Rhode Island	Rhode Island House of Representatives	www.rilin.state.ri.us/House
	Rhode Island Senate	www.rilin.state.ri.us/Senate
South Carolina	Members of the House	www.scstatehouse.gov/html-pages/housemembers.html
	Members of the Senate	www.scstatehouse.gov/html-pages/senatemembers.html
South Dakota	Who Are My Legislators?	http://legis.state.sd.us/sessions/2007/mem.htm
Tennessee	The House of Representatives	www.capitol.tn.gov/house/members
	The Senate	www.capitol.tn.gov/senate/members
Texas	Texas House of Representatives	www.house.state.tx.us/members
	Texas Senators	www.senate.state.tx.us/75r/senate/Members.htm
Utah	Utah House of Representatives	www.le.state.ut.us/house/members/membertable1add.asp
	Utah State Senate	www.utahsenate.org/aspx/roster.aspx
Vermont	Vermont Legislative Council	www.leg.state.vt.us/legdir/legdirmain.cfm
Virgin Islands	Legislature of the Virgin Islands	www.legvi.org/index.php?option=com_content&view=article&id=170&Itemid=47
Virginia	Virginia House of Delegates	http://dela.state.va.us/dela/MemBios.nsf/MWebsiteTL?OpenView
	Senate of Virginia	http://sov.state.va.us/SenatorDB.nsf/$$Viewtemplate+for+WMembershipHome?OpenForm

State	Webpage Name	Web Address
Washington	House of Representatives Roster of Members	http://apps.leg.wa.gov/rosters/Members.aspx?Chamber=H
	Senate Roster of Members	http://apps.leg.wa.gov/rosters/Members.aspx?Chamber=S
West Virginia	House of Delegates Members	www.legis.state.wv.us/House/members/delmemview1.cfm
	Senate Members	www.legis.state.wv.us/Senate1/members/senmemview.cfm
Wisconsin	Wisconsin State Representatives	http://legis.wisconsin.gov/w3asp/contact/legislatorslist.aspx?house=assembly
	Wisconsin State Senators	http://legis.wisconsin.gov/w3asp/contact/legislatorslist.aspx?house=senate
Wyoming	House Members	http://legisweb.state.wy.us/LegislatorSummary/LegislatorList.aspx?strHouse=H&strStatus=N
	Senate Members	http://legisweb.state.wy.us/LegislatorSummary/LegislatorList.aspx?strHouse=S&strStatus=N

Appendix B

Length and Timing of Legislative Sessions

Source: National Conference of State Legislatures

Constitutional, Statutory, or Chamber Provisions on the
Convening and Adjourning of Regular Legislative Sessions
As of December 22, 2010

State	Convening Date	Limit on Session Length
Alabama	*Statute:* Commencing in the year 1999, the annual sessions of the Alabama Legislature shall commence on the first Tuesday in March of the first year of the term of office of the legislators, on the first Tuesday of February of the second and third years of the term and on the second Tuesday in January of the fourth year of the term.	*Statute:* The annual sessions shall not continue longer than 30 legislative days and 105 calendar days.
Alaska	*Statute:* The legislature shall convene at the capital each year on the second Monday in January at 10:00 AM; however, following a gubernatorial election year, the legislature shall convene on the third Tuesday in January at 10:00 AM.	*Constitution:* The legislature shall adjourn from regular session no later than one hundred twenty consecutive calendar days from the date it convenes except that a regular session may be extended once for up to ten consecutive calendar days. 120 calendar days. *Statute:* Sec. 24.05.150. Adjournment. (b) The legislature shall adjourn from a regular session within 90 consecutive calendar days, including the day the legislature first convenes in that regular session.
Arizona	*Constitution:* The sessions of the legislature shall be held annually at the capitol of the state, and shall commence on the second Monday of January of each year.	*Chamber rule:* Regular sessions shall be adjourned sine die no later than Saturday of the week in which the one hundredth day from the beginning of each regular session falls. The President or Speaker may by declaration authorize the extension of the session for a period not to exceed seven additional days. Thereafter the session can be extended only by a majority vote of the Senate or House.

State	Convening Date	Limit on Session Length
Arkansas	*Constitution amendment in 2008:* Odd year—The General Assembly shall meet in regular session on the second Monday in January of each odd-numbered year. The General Assembly may alter the time at which the regular session begins. Even year—Beginning in 2010, the General Assembly shall meet in fiscal session on the second Monday in February of each even-numbered year to consider only appropriation bills. A bill other than an appropriation bill may be considered if 2/3 of the members of each house of the General Assembly approve consideration of the bill. *Statute:* The General Assembly shall meet in regular biennial session at 12:00 noon on the second Monday in January in each odd-numbered year. However, in any odd-numbered year following the election of a nonincumbent governor, the General Assembly upon convening at 12:00 noon on the second Monday in January may remain in session only for such time, not to exceed two (2) days, as is necessary to open and publish the votes for various constitutional offices, to swear in the state constitutional officers and members of the General Assembly, to organize and select officers, and to otherwise prepare for the regular session. It may then stand in recess for a period of not to exceed thirty (30) days.	*Constitution amendment in 2008:* Odd year—The regular biennial sessions shall not exceed sixty days in duration, unless by a vote of two-thirds of the members elected to each house of said General Assembly. The session shall not exceed 75 calendar days, unless extended by a vote of ¾ of the members elected to each house of the General Assembly. Even year—A fiscal session shall not exceed 30 calendar days, except that by a vote of ¾ of the members elected to each house of the General Assembly a fiscal session may be extended one time by no more than 15 calendar days.
California	*Constitution:* (a) The Legislature shall convene in regular session at noon on the first Monday in December of each even-numbered year and each house shall immediately organize.	*Constitution:* Each session of the Legislature shall adjourn sine die by operation of the Constitution at midnight on November 30 of the following even-numbered year. *Chamber rule:* Odd year—The Legislature shall be in recess from September 12 until the first Monday in January, except when the first Monday is January 1 or January 1 is a Sunday, in which case, the following Wednesday. Even year—The Legislature shall be in recess on August 31 until adjournment sine die on November 30.
Colorado	*Constitution:* The general assembly shall meet in regular session at 10 AM no later than the second Wednesday of January of each year.	*Constitution:* Regular sessions of the general assembly shall not exceed one hundred twenty calendar days.
Connecticut	*Constitution:* There shall be a regular session of the general assembly on the Wednesday following the first Monday of January in the odd-numbered years and on the Wednesday following the first Monday of February in the even-numbered years…	*Constitution:* The general assembly shall adjourn each regular session in the odd-numbered years not later than the first Wednesday after the first Monday in June and in the even-numbered years not later than the first Wednesday after the first Monday in May…

State	Convening Date	Limit on Session Length
Delaware	*Constitution:* The General Assembly shall convene on the second Tuesday of January of each calendar year.	*Constitution:* Each session shall not extend beyond the last day of June unless the session is recalled by the Governor or the mutual call of the presiding officers of both Houses.
Florida	*Constitution:* A regular session of the legislature shall convene on the first Tuesday after the first Monday in March of each odd-numbered year, and on the first Tuesday after the first Monday in March, or such other date as may be fixed by law, of each even-numbered year.	*Constitution:* A regular session of the legislature shall not exceed sixty consecutive days.
Georgia	*Constitution:* The General Assembly shall meet in regular session on the second Monday in January of each year, or otherwise as provided by law.	*Constitution:* The General Assembly may continue in session for a period of no longer than 40 legislative days in the aggregate each year.
Hawaii	*Constitution:* The legislature shall convene annually in regular session at 10:00 o'clock AM on the third Wednesday in January.	*Constitution:* Regular sessions shall be limited to a period of sixty legislative days. Any session may be extended a total of not more than fifteen days.
Idaho	*Statute:* At the hour of twelve o'clock PM on the Monday on or nearest the ninth day in January the regular session of the legislature shall be convened.	None.
Illinois	*Constitution:* The General Assembly shall convene each year on the second Wednesday of January.	None.
Indiana	*Statute:* The general assembly shall convene in session on the date fixed during the annual November organizational session, but no later than the second Monday in January.	*Statute:* Odd years—The first regular session of each term of the general assembly shall adjourn sine die not later than April 29 in any odd-numbered year. Even years—The second regular session of each term of the general assembly shall adjourn sine die not later than March 14 in any even-numbered year.
Iowa	*Constitution:* The general assembly shall meet in session on the second Monday of January of each year.	*Statute:* …each such member shall receive the sum of eighty-six dollars per day for expenses of office … the payments shall be made only for one hundred ten calendar days for the first session [odd year] and one hundred calendar days for the second session [even year].
Kansas	*Constitution:* The legislature shall meet in regular session annually commencing on the second Monday in January.	*Constitution:* Odd years—None. Even years—The duration of regular sessions held in even-numbered years shall not exceed ninety calendar days. Such sessions may be extended beyond ninety calendar days by an affirmative vote of two-thirds of the members elected to each house.
Kentucky	*Constitution:* Odd years—The General Assembly shall convene for the first part of the session on the first Tuesday after the first Monday in January in odd-numbered years. Even years—The General Assembly shall then adjourn until the first Tuesday after the first Monday in January of the following even-numbered years.	*Constitution:* Odd years—The General Assembly, in odd-numbered years, shall meet in regular session for a period not to exceed a total of thirty (30) legislative days; nor shall a session occurring in odd-numbered years extend beyond March 30. Even years—nor shall a session of the General Assembly continue beyond sixty legislative days nor shall it extend beyond April 15.

State	Convening Date	Limit on Session Length
Louisiana	*Constitution:* Odd years—All regular sessions convening in odd-numbered years shall convene at noon on the second Monday in April. [Scope of session is limited by constitution] Even year—All regular sessions convening in even-numbered years shall be general in nature and shall convene at noon on the second Monday in March. *Constitutional amendment adopted in 2010 will change convening dates effective in 2012.	*Constitution:* Odd years—The legislature shall meet in such a session for not more than forty-five legislative days during a period of sixty calendar days. Even years—The legislature shall meet in such session for not more than sixty legislative days during a period of eighty-five calendar days.
Maine	*Constitution:* The Legislature shall convene on the first Wednesday of December following the general election in what shall be designated the first regular session of the Legislature; and shall further convene on the first Wednesday after the first Tuesday of January in the subsequent even-numbered year in what shall be designated the second regular session of the Legislature.	*Statute:* The first regular session of the Legislature, after its convening, shall adjourn no later than the 3rd Wednesday in June [of the odd year] and the 2nd regular session of the Legislature shall adjourn no later than the 3rd Wednesday in April [of the even year].
Maryland	*Constitution:* The General Assembly shall meet on the second Wednesday of January, nineteen hundred and seventy-one, and on the same day in every year thereafter.	*Constitution:* The General Assembly may continue its session so long as in its judgment the public interest may require, for a period not longer than ninety calendar days in each year. The ninety days shall be consecutive unless otherwise provided by law. The General Assembly may extend its session beyond ninety days, but not exceeding an additional thirty days, by resolution concurred in by a three-fifths vote of the membership in each House.
Massachusetts	*Constitution:* the general court shall assemble every year on the said first Wednesday of January.	*Chamber rule:* All formal business of the first annual session of the General Court [odd year] shall be concluded no later than the third Wednesday in November of that calendar year and all formal business of the second annual session [even year] shall be concluded no later than the last day of July of that calendar year.
Michigan	*Constitution:* The legislature shall meet at the seat of government on the second Wednesday in January of each year at twelve o'clock noon.	None.
Minnesota	*Statute:* The legislature shall meet at the seat of government on the first Tuesday after the first Monday in January of each odd-numbered year. When the first Monday in January falls on January 1, it shall meet on the first Wednesday after the first Monday.	*Constitution:* The legislature shall meet at the seat of government in regular session in each biennium at the times prescribed by law for not exceeding a total of 120 legislative days. The legislature shall not meet in regular session, nor in any adjournment thereof, after the first Monday following the third Saturday in May of any year.

State	Convening Date	Limit on Session Length
Mississippi	*Constitution:* The Legislature shall meet at the seat of government in regular session on the Tuesday after the first Monday of January of the year AD 1970, and annually thereafter.	*Constitution:* such sessions shall be limited to a period of one hundred twenty-five (125) calendar days for regular 1972 session and every fourth year thereafter, but ninety (90) calendar days for every other regular session thereafter. Provided further that the House of Representatives, by resolution with the Senate concurring therein, and by a two-thirds vote of those present and voting in each house, may extend such limited session for a period of thirty (30) days with no limit on the number of extensions to each session.
Missouri	*Constitution:* The general assembly shall meet on the first Wednesday after the first Monday in January following each general election. The general assembly shall reconvene on the first Wednesday after the first Monday of January after adjournment at midnight on May thirtieth of the preceding year.	*Constitution:* The general assembly shall adjourn at midnight on May thirtieth until the first Wednesday after the first Monday of January of the following year, unless it has adjourned prior thereto.
Montana	*Statute:* The term of service shall begin on the first Monday of January next succeeding his election.	*Constitution:* The legislature shall meet each odd-numbered year in regular session of not more than 90 legislative days.
Nebraska	*Constitution:* Beginning with the year 1975, regular sessions of the Legislature shall be held annually, commencing at 10 AM on the first Wednesday after the first Monday in January of each year.	*Constitution:* The duration of regular sessions held shall not exceed ninety legislative days in odd-numbered years unless extended by a vote of four-fifths of all members elected to the Legislature, and shall not exceed sixty legislative days in even-numbered years unless extended by a vote of four-fifths of all members elected to the Legislature.
Nevada	*Constitution:* The sessions of the Legislature shall be biennial, and shall commence on the 1st Monday of February following the election of members of the Assembly.	*Constitution:* The Legislature shall adjourn sine die each regular session not later than midnight Pacific standard time 120 calendar days following its commencement.
New Hampshire	*Constitution:* …shall assemble annually on the first Wednesday following the first Tuesday in January.	*Constitution:* each member shall receive mileage for actual daily attendance on legislative days, but not after the legislature shall have been in session for 45 legislative days or after the first day of July following the annual assembly of the legislature, whichever occurs first.
New Jersey	*Constitution:* The legislative year shall commence at noon on the second Tuesday in January of each year.	None.
New Mexico	*Constitution:* Each regular session of the legislature shall begin annually at 12:00 noon on the third Tuesday of January.	*Constitution:* Every regular session of the legislature convening during an odd-numbered year shall remain in session not to exceed sixty (calendar) days, and every regular session of the legislature convening during an even-numbered year shall remain in session not to exceed thirty (calendar) days.
New York	*Constitution:* The legislature shall, every year, assemble on the first Wednesday after the first Monday in January.	None.

State	Convening Date	Limit on Session Length
North Carolina	*Statute:* Odd year—beginning at 12:00 noon on the third Wednesday after the second Monday in January. Even year—set by resolution.	None.
North Dakota	*Constitution*: twelve noon on the first Tuesday after the third day in January or at such other time as may be prescribed by law but not later than the eleventh day of January.	*Constitution:* No regular session of the legislative assembly may exceed eighty natural days during the biennium.
Ohio	*Constitution:* Each general assembly shall convene in first regular session on the first Monday of January in the odd-numbered year, or on the succeeding day if the first Monday of January is a legal holiday, and in second regular session on the same date of the following year.	None.
Oklahoma	*Constitution:* The Legislature shall meet in regular session at the seat of government at twelve o'clock noon on the first Monday in February of each year	*Constitution*: the regular session shall be finally adjourned sine die not later than five o'clock PM on the last Friday in May of each year.
Oregon	*Statute*: The regular sessions of the Legislative Assembly shall be held at the capital of the state and shall commence on the first day of February of each year, except that if the first day of February is a Thursday, Friday, Saturday or Sunday, the regular session shall commence on the following Monday.	Constitution: A session beginning in an odd-numbered year may not exceed 160 calendar days in duration; and (b) A session beginning in an even-numbered year may not exceed 35 calendar days in durations.
Pennsylvania	*Constitution:* It shall meet at twelve o'clock noon on the first Tuesday of January each year.	None.
Rhode Island	*Constitution:* There shall be a session of the general assembly at Providence commencing on the first Tuesday of January in each year.	None.
South Carolina	*Constitution:* The first session of the General Assembly elected under this Constitution shall convene in Columbia on the second Tuesday in January, in the year Eighteen hundred and Ninety-seven, and thereafter annually at the same time and place.	*Statute:* The regular annual session of the General Assembly shall adjourn sine die each year not later than 5:00 p.m. on the first Thursday in June. In any year that the House of Representatives fails to give third reading to the annual General Appropriation Bill by March thirty-first, the date of sine die adjournment is extended by one statewide day for each statewide day after March thirty-first that the House of Representatives fails to give the bill third reading. The session may also be extended by concurrent resolution adopted by a two-thirds vote of both the Senate and House of Representatives. During the time between 5:00 PM on the first Thursday in June and the extended sine die adjournment date, as set forth herein, no legislation or other business may be considered except the General Appropriation Bill and any matters approved for consideration by a concurrent resolution adopted by two-thirds vote in both houses.

State	Convening Date	Limit on Session Length
South Dakota	*Constitution:* The Legislature shall meet at the seat of government on the second Tuesday of January at 12 o'clock PM.	*Constitution amendment in 2008:* A regular session of the Legislature shall not exceed forty legislative days, excluding Sundays, holidays and legislative recess.
Tennessee	*Constitution:* the second Tuesday in January.	*Constitution:* However, no member shall be paid expenses, nor travel allowances for more than ninety Legislative days of a regular session, excluding the organizational session, nor for more than thirty Legislative days of any extraordinary session.
Texas	*Statute:* The legislature shall convene in regular session at 12 noon on the second Tuesday in January of each odd-numbered year.	*Constitution:* No Regular Session shall be of longer duration than one hundred and forty (140) (calendar) days.
Utah	*Constitution:* Annual general sessions of the Legislature shall be held at the seat of government and shall begin on the fourth Monday in January.	*Constitution:* No annual general session of the Legislature shall exceed 45 calendar days; federal holidays are excluded in the calculation of the 45-day limit on annual general sessions of the Legislature.
Vermont	*Constitution:* biennially on the first Wednesday next after the first Monday of January.	None.
Virginia	*Constitution:* The General Assembly shall meet once each year on the second Wednesday in January.	*Constitution:* no regular session of the General Assembly convened in an even-numbered year shall continue longer than sixty (calendar) days; no regular session of the General Assembly convened in an odd-numbered year shall continue longer than thirty (calendar) days; but with the concurrence of two-thirds of the members elected to each house, any regular session may be extended for a period not exceeding thirty days.
Washington	*Statute:* Regular sessions of the legislature shall be held annually, commencing on the second Monday of January.	*Constitution:* During each odd-numbered year, the regular session shall not be more than one hundred five consecutive days. During each even-numbered year, the regular session shall not be more than sixty consecutive days.
West Virginia	*Constitution:* Regular sessions of the Legislature shall commence on the second Wednesday of January of each year. Except in the year one thousand nine hundred seventy-three and every fourth year thereafter, the Legislature begins session on the second Wednesday of February.	*Constitution:* The regular session of the Legislature held in the year one thousand nine hundred seventy-three and every fourth year thereafter shall, in addition to the meeting days preceding the adjournment provided for in section eighteen of this article, not exceed sixty calendar days computed from and including the second Wednesday of February, and the regular session held in all other years shall not exceed sixty calendar days computed from and including the second Wednesday of January. Any regular session may be extended by a concurrent resolution adopted by a two-thirds vote of the members elected to each house determined by yeas and nays and entered on the journals.

State	Convening Date	Limit on Session Length
Wisconsin	*Statute:* The regular session of the legislature shall commence at 2 PM on the first Tuesday after the 8th day of January in each year unless otherwise provided.	None.
Wyoming	*Statute:* Odd year—The general and budget session of the Wyoming legislature shall commence on the second Tuesday of January of odd-numbered years. Even year—The budget session of the Wyoming legislature shall commence on the second Monday of February of even-numbered years.	*Constitution:* The legislature shall not meet for more than sixty (60) legislative working days excluding Sundays during the term for which members of the house of representatives are elected, except when called into special session. The legislature shall meet for no more than forty (40) legislative working days excluding Sundays in any (1) calendar year, except when called into special session. *Statute:* Odd year—The general and budget session of the Wyoming legislature shall commence on the second Tuesday of January of odd-numbered years and shall continue for an additional thirty-nine (39) legislative working days unless both houses agree to an earlier adjournment. Even year—The budget session of the Wyoming legislature shall commence on the second Monday of February of even-numbered years and shall continue for an additional number of legislative working days as agreed by both houses of the legislature or as limited by the Wyoming constitution.

Appendix C
Committee Procedures

Source: National Conference of State Legislatures

It is not possible for all legislative business to be conducted by the full membership; some division of labor is essential. Legislative committees are created to do the "homework" of the legislature. They act as the gatekeepers of information and provide citizens and interest groups with a formal opportunity for input into legislative decisions. To expedite the flow of legislation on the floor, legislatures have strengthened the role of standing committees in considering bills.

Committee actions and reports. The majority of legislative bodies give great flexibility to committees in setting their agendas, and the committee chair usually determines which—and when—bills will be heard (see tables 04-4.29 and 04-4.30). On the other hand, the committees in 22 chambers do not have discretion over which bills to hear—rather, they must hear all bills referred to them (see table 04-4.31).

Legislatures vest committees with a wide variety of powers to dispose of bills. The options range from reporting a bill with no changes to actually killing it (see table 04-4.32). For example, committees in 20 chambers may refer bills to an interim study. In 40 chambers, committees may carry bills over to the next session.

Eighteen legislative assemblies, however, require committees to report all bills referred to them (see table 04-4.33). Although this practice may increase the number of bills sent to the floor, it prevents committees from holding bills and gives the entire body an opportunity to consider all legislation.

When a committee completes its work upon a bill, it issues a committee report, "the official release of a bill or resolution from a committee." Legislative chambers usually require that committee reports contain specific information. Table 04-4.34 illustrates the items that must be included in (or attached to) a committee report. The items required most commonly are the committee's recommendation for action (by 96 chambers), all adopted amendments (by 89 chambers) and the signature of the chair (by 79 chambers).

Committee minutes. The ASLCS Glossary of Legislative and Computer Terms defines "minutes" as an "accurate record of the proceedings of a meeting in chronological order." Not all legislative assemblies require that their committees produce minutes (see table 04-4.35). Although 60 chambers require committee minutes, 17 legislative assemblies do not consider the minutes to be an official record of the body (see table 04-4.36).

Only three chambers—Connecticut Senate, Nebraska Senate and New Hampshire Senate—require that committees produce verbatim minutes for all meetings. In the Pennsylvania House, verbatim minutes are produced only for public hearings. In the Louisiana Senate, a verbatim transcript is prepared only when requested by majority vote of the committee members.

In the majority of legislative assemblies, the minutes are a summary of committee actions rather than a verbatim record. Tables 04-4.37 through 04-4.39 illustrate the items included in committee minutes.

Although the majority of legislative chambers require committee minutes to be produced, the deadlines for their completion vary greatly (see table 04-4.40). The requirements range from a very fast turnaround (by the end of the day on which the committee meeting was held) to one that is much more delayed (the end of the legislative biennium).

In 46 chambers, committee minutes must be approved (see table 04-4.41). Most commonly, the minutes are approved by either the committee members or the committee chair.

Table 04-4.42 illustrates the various formats in which minutes are distributed to committee members. Although this usually occurs via paper copy, postings to Intranet or Internet sites also are fairly common. In the Michigan and Ohio Senates, minutes may be sent by e-mail attachment.

Committee minutes usually are available to people outside the committee. Table 04-4.43 illustrates from where the minutes may be obtained.

KEY FOR TABLE 04-4.29
B = Both chambers
S = Senate
H = House or Assembly

NOTES:
1. The following chambers did not return a survey: American Samoa Senate and House, District of Columbia Council, Guam Senate, Northern Mariana Islands Senate and House, Puerto Rico Senate and Virgin Islands Senate.
2. Arizona. The House Rules state that, upon presentation of a petition containing the signatures of two-thirds or more of the committee members, a bill not on the committee agenda shall be scheduled for discussion at the next committee meeting.
3. California. In the Assembly, the Rules Committee may make this determination.
4. Connecticut. In the House, committee members also have input.
5. Florida. The House may refer a bill to committee by motion.
6. Illinois. In the Senate, the Rules Committee also may have input.
7. Maine. According to the Senate, the secretary of the Senate and clerk of the House suggest a committee reference, then the members of both chambers vote on the reference.
8. Maryland. In the House, the speaker's legislative staff and the majority leader refer bills to the appropriate committees.
9. Massachusetts. In the Senate, the clerks also have input.
10. Michigan. In the Senate, the Senate majority leader has input. Also, a bill must be heard upon written request of the majority of a committee's members.

Table 04-4.29, Who Determines Which Bills Will Be Heard

State	The presiding officer	The committee chair	The bill author(s)	Other
Alabama		B		
Alaska		B		
Arizona		S	H	2
Arkansas		S	H	
California		S	S	3
Colorado	S	H		
Connecticut		B		4
Delaware		B		
Florida	B	B		5
Georgia		B		
Hawaii		B		
Idaho		B		
Illinois	H	S		6
Indiana	H	S		
Iowa		B		
Kansas		B		
Kentucky		B		
Louisiana		B	S	
Maine	H	H		7
Maryland	H	S		8
Massachusetts	S	H		9
Michigan		B		10
Minnesota		B		
Mississippi		B		
Missouri		B		
Montana	B			
Nebraska				11
Nevada	H	S		12
New Hampshire	H			13
New Jersey	S	B		
New Meico		H	S	
New York		B	H	
North Carolina	H	B	S	14
North Dakota	B			
Ohio		S		15
Oklahoma		B		
Oregon		B		
Pennsylvania		B		
Rhode Island	H	B		16
South Carolina	H	B		
South Dakota	B			
Tennessee	S	H	H	17
Texas	S	B	S	
Utah	H	S		18
Vermont		B		19
Virginia		B		20
Washington		B		21
West Virginia	B	B		22

11. Nebraska. The reference committee (the Executive Board) has input.
12. Nevada. In the Senate, a majority of the committee membership may request that items be placed on the agenda.
13. New Hampshire. In the Senate, the Senate president determines in which committee a bill will be heard.
14. North Carolina. In the Senate, another leader and committee staff also have input.
15. Ohio. In the House, all bills must be heard at least once by a committee, unless the bill was introduced after May 15 of the second year of the General Assembly.
16. Rhode Island. In the House, another leader also has input.
17. Tennessee. In the Senate, the clerk offers advice and counsel.
18. Utah. In the House, the Rules Committee recommends to which committees that bills should be assigned. Speakers occasionally disregard the proposed assignments and refer bills to other committees.
19. Vermont. In the House, any member has input.
20. Virginia. In the House, the committee staff provide input.
21. Washington. In the House, leadership sometimes gives input.
22. West Virginia. In the House, any member has input

KEY FOR TABLE 04-4.30

B = Both chambers

S = Senate

H = House or Assembly

NOTES:

1. The following chambers did not return a survey: America Samoa Senate and House, District of Columbia Council, Guam Senate, Northern Mariana Islands Senate and House, Puerto Rico Senate and Virgin Islands Senate.
2. Arizona. The House Rules state that, upon presentation of a petition containing the signatures of two-thirds or more of the committee members, a bill not on the committee agenda shall be scheduled for discussion at the next committee meeting.
3. Arkansas. In the House, committees may set special orders of business to consider bills. Otherwise, the consideration follows a calendar based chronologically on when the bill was assigned to committee.
4. Connecticut. In the House, committee members also have input.
5. Michigan. In the Senate, the Senate majority leader has input. Also, a bill must be heard upon written request of the majority of a committee's members.
6. Nevada. In the Senate, a majority of the committee membership may request that items be placed on the agenda.
7. North Carolina. In the Senate, another leader and any member may give input.
8. Vermont. In the House, any member may give input.
9. Washington. In the House, leader occasionally gives input.

Table 04-4.30, Who Determines When A Bill Will Be Heard

State	The presiding officer	The committee chair	The bill author(s)	The committee staff	Other
Alabama		B			
Alaska		B			
Arizona	S	B			2
Arkansas		S			3
California		B			
Colorado		B			
Connecticut		B			4
Delaware		B			
Florida	B	B			
Georgia		B			
Hawaii		B			
Idaho		B			
Illinois	H	S	S		
Indiana		B			
Iowa		B			
Kansas		B			
Kentucky		B			
Louisiana		B	S		
Maine		B			
Maryland		B		H	
Massachusetts		B		B	
Michigan	s	H			5
Minnesota		B			
Mississippi		B			
Missouri		B			
Montana		B			
Nebraska		S			
Nevada		B			6
New Hampshire		B			
New Jersey	S	B			
New Meico		B			
New York	H		B		
North Carolina	H	B	S		7
North Dakota		B			
Ohio		B			
Oklahoma		B			
Oregon		B			
Pennsylvania		B			
Rhode Island	H	B			
South Carolina	H	B			
South Dakota		B			
Tennessee		B			
Texas		B		S	
Utah		B		S	
Vermont		B			8
Washington		B		H	
West Virginia	H	B			

Table 04-4.31, Requirements for Standing Committees to Hear All Bills

IN THE FOLLOWING CHAMBERS, STANDING COMMITTEES HEAR ALL BILLS THAT ARE REFERRED TO THEM.

- Colorado Senate and House New Mexico House
- Delaware House North Dakota Senate and House
- Kentucky Senate Ohio House (4)
- Maine Senate and House (3) South Dakota Senate and House
- Massachusetts Senate and House Tennessee Senate
- Montana Senate and House Utah House
- Nebraska Senate Vermont Senate
- New Hampshire Senate and House

IN THE FOLLOWING CHAMBERS, STANDING COMMITTEES DO NOT HEAR ALL BILLS THAT ARE REFERRED TO THEM.

- Alabama Senate and House Missouri Senate and House
- Alaska Senate and House (2) Nevada Senate and Assembly
- Arizona Senate and House New Jersey Senate and General Assembly
- Arkansas Senate and House New York Senate and Assembly
- California Senate and Assembly North Carolina Senate and House
- Connecticut Senate and House Ohio Senate
- Delaware Senate Oklahoma Senate and House
- Florida Senate and House Oregon Senate and House
- Georgia Senate and House Pennsylvania Senate and House
- Hawaii Senate and House Rhode Island Senate and House
- Illinois Senate and House Tennessee House
- Indiana Senate and House Texas Senate and House
- Iowa Senate and House Utah Senate
- Kansas Senate and House Vermont House
- Kentucky House Virginia Senate and House (5)
- Louisiana Senate and House Washington Senate and House
- Maryland Senate and House West Virginia Senate and House
- Michigan Senate and House Wisconsin Senate and Assembly
- Minnesota Senate and House Wyoming Senate and House
- Mississippi Senate and House Puerto Rico House

NOTES:

1. The following chambers did not return a survey: American Samoa Senate and House, District of Columbia Council, Guam Senate, Northern Mariana Islands Senate and House, Puerto Rico Senate and Virgin Islands Senate.
2. Alaska. The uniform rules for both chambers contain a requirement for committees to hear all bills that are referred to them but, in practice, the committees do not.
3. Maine. In the House, bills must be heard unless the public hearing rule is waived by the presiding officers or the sponsor requests withdrawal the bill and it receives an "ought not to pass" recommendation.
4. Ohio. In the House, all bills introduced before May 15 of the second year of the General Assembly must have at least one hearing.
5. Virginia. In the House, in practice, committees hear all bills.

Appendix D
Lobbyist Activity Report Requirements

Source: National Conference of State Legislatures

This table is intended to provide general information and does not necessarily address all aspects of this topic. Because the facts of each situation may vary, this information may need to be supplemented by consulting legal advisors. It reflects in summary form statues in effect as of December 31, 2009, or statutes that took effect shortly thereafter.

State	Who Must Report/Required Contents of Activity Reports
Alabama 36-25-19	Lobbyists, principals (Excludes public employees who are lobbyists)
	Cost of items given to legislators excluded from the definition of "thing of value" if the lobbyist spends more than $250 on them in one day. Include recipient, date. Nature, date of financial transactions between lobbyists and legislators worth more than $500. Direct business associations with legislators. Detailed statement showing exact amount of any loan given or promised to a public official, candidate, public official or candidate.
	Items excluded from the definition of "thing of value" are: campaign contributions; seasonal gifts worth less than $100; hospitality for the public official or members of his or her household; tickets to social or sporting events; transportation, food and beverages when the provider is present and lodging expenses in the continental U.S. and Alaska for educational or informational purposes; reimbursement for travel and subsistence in connection with an economic development research or trade mission; promotional items commonly distributed to the general public and food and beverage of nominal value.
	*Any person not otherwise deemed a lobbyist who negotiates or attempts to negotiate a contract, sells or attempts to sell goods or services, engages or attempts to engage in a financial transaction with a public official or public employee in their official capacity and who within a calendar day expends in excess of two hundred fifty dollars ($250) on such public employee, public official, and his or her respective household shall file a detailed quarterly report of the expenditure with the commission
Alaska 24.45.061	Lobbyists, Principals
	Lobbyists: Name, address, amount from each source of lobbying income including, but not limited to, salary, fees and reimbursements. Aggregate lobbying expenses of lobbyist and principal in these categories: food and beverage, living accommodations, travel. Date, nature and recipient of each gift worth more than $100 to a public official. Name, official position of any public official or member of public official's family with whom lobbyist has transacted more than $100 in money, goods or services. Include the nature, date and value of exchange. Name, address of business entities lobbyist has exchanged more than $100 in money, goods or services with in which the public official is a proprietor, partner, director, officer or manager, or has a controlling interest. Include the date, amount, and nature of the exchange.
	Principals: Statement verifying a contract for lobbying services with each lobbyist. Principal's name, address, phone. Identification of the principal's nature and interests. Name, date, amount, address of recipient of each payment made to influence legislative or administrative action. Date, nature and recipient of each gift valued at more than $100 to a public official. Description of legislative or administrative action principal seeks to influence. Names of employed lobbyists, as well as total amounts paid to each categorized as salary, fees, and reimbursement.

State	Who Must Report/Required Contents of Activity Reports
Arizona 41-1232.02 41-1232.03	Lobbyists for Compensation, Designated Lobbyist, Principals, Public Bodies, Designated Public Lobbyists, Authorized Public Lobbyists

Lobbyist for Compensation, Designated Lobbyist:
Designated/Authorized Public lobbyist: Aggregate amount of all expenditures less than $20 received by or benefiting a member of the legislature. Include aggregate of all expenditures of $20 or less that were received by or benefited a member of the legislature and that were made by an authorized public lobbyist. This subsection does not apply to an expenditure that was made by a public lobbyist or authorized public lobbyist and that was received by or benefited an employee of a public body, if the employee is not a member or employee of the legislature or a member of the household of a member or employee of the legislature. Shall list separately the aggregate of expenditures made on behalf of each public body and the aggregate not made on behalf of the public body. Itemized list of all expenditures, regardless of whether to lobby. Include date, amount, name of member of legislature benefiting, category of expenditure and name of public body the expenditure was made on behalf of. List separately all expenditures that benefit state employees.

Information pertaining to all of the above reports: "Categories" for these reports are: food or beverages, speaking engagement, travel and lodging, flowers, other. The following expenditures are not required to be disclosed: lobbyist's personal sustenance, office expenses, filing fees, legal fees, employees' compensation, lodging and travel. Items excluded from the definition of gift pursuant to section 41-1231, paragraph 9, subdivision (a), (c), (d), (f), (g), (h), (i), (j), (k) or (l). Special events for legislators must be reported, but expenses don't have to be allocated to individual legislators. Report a description, date, location, name of the legislative body invited and total cost. Lobbyists cannot give state officers and employees gifts worth more than $10 in a year or gifts that are designed to influence official conduct of a member or employee.

Itemized list of all single expenditures, regardless of whether or not made in the course of lobbying. These single expenditures shall be itemized separately, and each itemization shall include the date of the expenditure, the amount of the expenditure, the name of the state officer or employee receiving or benefiting from the expenditure, the category of the expenditure and the principal on whose behalf the expenditure was made. Aggregate amount of expenses of twenty dollars or less received by or benefiting a state officer or employee, whether or not the expenditures were made in the course of lobbying. The report shall list separately the aggregate of expenditures made on behalf of each principal and the aggregate not made on behalf of any principal.

Principals: Itemized list of all single expenditures, whether or not the expenditures were made in the course of lobbying. Shall be itemized separately, and each itemization shall include date, amount, name of state officer or employee receiving or benefiting from the expenditure, category of expenditure and name of lobbyist or other person who made the expenditure on behalf of the principal. Aggregate amount of all expenditures less than $20.

Public body: Itemized list of all single expenditures, whether or not the expenditures were made in the course of lobbying. Shall be itemized separately, include date, amount, name of member of legislature receiving or benefiting, category of expenditure and name of the designated public lobbyist or authorized public lobbyist who made the expenditure on behalf of the public body. Aggregate amount of all expenditures less than $20 benefiting a member of the legislature. All expenditures attributable to lobbying made for the personal sustenance, filing fee, legal fees, employees' compensation, meals, lodging and travel of the public lobbyist.

Arkansas 21-8-604	Lobbyists

Total of all expenditures made or incurred by the registered lobbyist on behalf of the registered lobbyist or by his or her employer or any officer, employee, or agent during the preceding period. Itemized list of expenditures, including those on behalf of the lobbyist's employer or employee. Itemize according to financial category, employers and clients, including food and refreshments, entertainment, living accommodations, advertising, printing, postage, travel, telephone, and other expenses or services. Personal living expenses not incurred directly for lobbying need not be disclosed. Itemized listing of each: gift to or on behalf of public servants; payment of more than $40 for food, travel or lodging on behalf of a public servant; other items worth at least $40 given to or on behalf of a public servant. Identify above items by date, value, name of individual benefiting and item description. (Special events need not be allocated by individual. Report the name, date and location of the event, as well as the group of public servants invited, the exact amount the lobbyist paid toward the expenditure, the name of the lobbyist's employer making the expenditure and the names of all other lobbyists or principals who contributed.) A detailed summary of money loaned or promised or line of credit established to a public servant or anyone on behalf of the public servant if more than $25 per individual. Details of business associations with lobbyists.

State	Who Must Report/Required Contents of Activity Reports

California
Gov't Code
86111-86115.5

Lobbyists, Lobbying firms, Lobbyist employers, People who spend more than $5,000 per quarter attempting to influence legislative or administrative action

Definitions: "Activity expense," under 86111, means any payment made or arranged to be made that benefits any elected state official, legislative official, agency official, state candidate or a member of the immediate family of any of the above. Activity expenses include gifts, honorariums, consulting fees, salaries and any other compensation except campaign contributions. Whenever activity expenses are reportable, include the date, amount or value of each, the full name and position of the beneficiary and the payee, if someone else.

Lobbyists: All activity expenses. All contributions of $100 or more made or delivered by the lobbyist to any elected state officer or state candidate. The lobbyist shall provide this report to his or her employer or firm as well.

Lobbying Firms: Name, address, phone. Name, address phone of each entity who contracted with the firm for lobbying services, description of the interests of the contracting entity, total payments including fees and reimbursements from the entity. Total payments received for lobbying services. Periodic reports by each lobbyist in the firm. Each activity expense incurred including those reimbursed by a person who contracts for services. If the firm subcontracts with another lobbying firm, include the name, address, phone of subcontractor; name of entity the subcontractor was retained to lobby; total amount of payments made to subcontractor. Date, amount, recipient of any contribution of $100 or more filer made to elected state official, state candidate, committee controlled by an elected state officer or candidate or committee primarily formed to support such officers or candidates. If the firm communicates directly with elected officials, and lobbying is its main purpose, the report must also contain the name and title of each partner, owner, officer and employee of the firm who, on at least 5 occasions during the period, engaged in direct communication with any elective state official, legislative official or state agency official for the purpose of influencing legislative or administrative action.

Lobbyist employers and anyone else who spends more than $5,000 per quarter attempting to influence legislative or administrative action: Name, business address, phone of lobbyist employer or other person filing the report. Total amount of payments to each lobbying firm. Total amount of payments to lobbyists employed by the filer. Description of specific lobbying interests of the filer. Periodic reports by each lobbyist employed. Each activity expense of the filer, as well as a total. Date, amount, recipient of any contribution of $100 or more filer made to elected state official, state candidate, committee controlled by an elected state officer or candidate or committee primarily formed to support such officers or candidates. Total of all other payments to influence legislative or administrative action, including overhead expenses and all payments to employees who spend at least 10 percent of their compensated time per month on activities related to influencing legislative or administrative action (unless payments are made to influence ratemaking or quasi-legislative proceedings before the Public Utilities Commission, in which case, other provisions apply.)

State and Local Agencies: Those required to file must also disclose on a separate form all payments, except for overhead expenses, of $250 or more during period toward: goods and services used by a lobbyist to support lobbying activity; payments of other expenses which wouldn't have been incurred but for lobbying activities; dues or other payments to organizations that spend at least 10 percent of their expenditures or $15,000 per quarter in lobbying activities. For all of the above, include the name, address of payee; total payments made during period; and cumulative amount paid for year.

Colorado
24-6-301-303.5

Professional lobbyists, Lobbyist firms, People who spend more than $200 in a calendar year on gifts or entertainment benefiting a public official, State officials and state employees engaged in lobbying

Professional Lobbyists and Lobbyist Firms: Gross income for lobbying since last statement; name, address of any source providing $100 or more. (Separate disclosure statements not required for sources named above.) Name of public officials to or for whom expenditures of $50+ have been made by or on behalf of the disclosing person for gifts or entertainment in connection with lobbying; include amount, date, and principal purpose of the gift or entertainment. (All amounts a professional lobbyist spends on a covered official for which the lobbyist is reimbursed, or the source of which is a contribution, shall be deemed to be for gift or entertainment purposes.) Sum of expenditures made by or on behalf of the disclosing person to covered officials (this term includes legislators) for gift or entertainment purposes in connection with lobbying which are not already stated. Cumulative reports must be filed annually. Annual reports should identify the source and amount of all income for lobbying. If any business is subcontracted, only the subcontractor needs to file reports. The firm that subcontracted must file an addendum stating the total amount of gross income that is being reported by another firm.

Persons who spend more than $200 in a calendar year on gifts or entertainment benefiting a public official: Expenses for personal needs, such as meals, travel, lodging, parking need not be reported. **Report:** name, address of persons contributing $100 or more to or for the disclosing person for lobbying during the calendar year; amount of contribution. Sum of contributions made to or for the disclosing person for lobbying since the last disclosure statement. Sum of contributions since last disclosure statement not required to be listed individually. Name of public officials to or for whom expenditures of $50+ have been made by or on behalf of the disclosing person for gifts or entertainment in connection with lobbying; include amount, date, and principal purpose of the gift or entertainment. (All amounts a professional lobbyist spends on a covered official for which the lobbyist is reimbursed, or the source of which is a contribution, shall be deemed to be for gift or entertainment purposes.) Sum of expenditures made by or on behalf of the disclosing person to covered officials (this term includes legislators) for gift or entertainment purposes in connection with lobbying which are not already stated.

State Official or State Employee Lobbyists: Legislation official or employee is lobbying on. Amount of each expenditure of public funds used for lobbying. Estimate of the time spent on lobbying or preparation thereof by any state official or employee of the department.

State	Who Must Report/Required Contents of Activity Reports
Connecticut Chapter 10, 1–96	Client lobbyists (persons on behalf of whom lobbying takes place, and who make expenditures for lobbying),Communicator lobbyists (those who communicate directly with public officials)
	Client Lobbyists: Expenditures made. Fundamental terms of contracts, agreements or promises to pay compensation or reimbursement or to make expenditures in furtherance of lobbying. Itemized statement of each expenditure of $10 or more per person for each occasion made by the registrant or a group of registrants for the benefit of a public official in the legislative or executive branch, a member of his staff or immediate family, itemized by date, beneficiary, amount and circumstances. Events where all members of the legislature or all members from a region of the state are invited need not be reported unless the price is more than $30 per person.

Communicator Lobbyists: Amounts of compensation, reimbursement from each client during the previous year. Fundamental terms of contracts, agreements or promises to pay or receive compensation or reimbursement or to make lobbying expenditures; categories of work to be performed; dollar value or compensation rate of contract at the time of registration. Any amendments to these fundamental contract terms, including any agreements to subcontract lobbying work. Any expenditures for the benefit of a public official in the legislative or executive branch or a member of the staff or immediate family of such official which are unreimbursed and required to be itemized. Such report shall not include the disclosure of food and beverage provided at a major life event, as defined by the commission, of the registrant.

Under 1-96e, any registrant who reimburses a public official more than $10 in necessary expenses connected with an article or speech in his or her official capacity shall file a separate disclosure statement within 30 days. |
Delaware 5835	Lobbyists
	Separate reports required for each employer represented. Each report must include the total expenditures during reporting period for all direct expenditures, costs or values, whichever is greater, provided for members of the General Assembly or for employees or members of any state agency for: food and refreshment; entertainment, including the cost of maintaining a hospitality room; lodging; fair value of travel exceeding 100 miles; recreation expenses; and gifts or contributions, excluding political contributions as defined in Chapter 80 of Title 15 provided to members of the General Assembly.
Florida 11.045 *(Accurate for legislative lobbyists only)*	Lobbyists
	Name of lobbyist, and principal (one per form.) Amounts of expenditures in the following categories: food and beverage, entertainment, research, communication, media advertising, publications, travel, lodging, special events, other. Only each principal's designated lobbyist reports expenditures paid directly by the principal. The following need not be reported: Lobbyists' and principals' salaries, office expenses, personal expenses for lodging, meals and travel, campaign contributions. Shall be filed through electronic filing system.
Georgia 21-5-73	Lobbyists
	A description of all expenditures or the value thereof made on behalf of or for the benefit of a public officer or on behalf of or for the benefit of a public employee for the purpose of influencing a public officer by the lobbyist or employees of the lobbyist or by any person on whose behalf the lobbyist is registered if the lobbyist has actual knowledge of such expenditure. For each expenditure, include: amount, date, description. Name, title of the benefiting public officer or, if simultaneously incurred for an identifiable group of public officers the individual identification of whom would be impractical, a general description of that group. If applicable, the number of the bill, resolution, ordinance, or regulation in support of or opposition to which each expenditure was made. List the aggregate expenditures on food, beverages, and registration at group events to which all members of an agency are invited. Entire legislative chambers or portions of them are considered agencies. List the aggregate expenditures on food, beverages or expenses afforded public officers, members of their immediate families, or others that are associated with normal and customary business or social functions or activities. Disclose the names of members of the immediate family of a public officer employed by or whose professional services are paid for by the lobbyist during the reporting period.
Hawaii 97-3	Lobbyists, People who spend more than $750 in 6 months lobbying, not counting travel expenses, People who pay for lobbying services.
	Name, address of each person with respect to whom lobbying expenditures worth $25 or more/day were made by the filer, amount or value of each expenditure. Name, address of each person with respect to whom total lobbying expenditures of $150 or more were made; amount or value of each expenditure. Sum of all lobbying expenditures made by filer during in excess of $750 during the statement period. Name, address of each person making contributions to filer for the purpose of lobbying in the total sum of $25 or more; amount of such contributions. Subject area of legislative and administrative action which was supported or opposed by the person filing the statement during the statement period.

State	Who Must Report/Required Contents of Activity Reports
Idaho 67-6619	Lobbyists
	Totals of all expenditures the lobbyist made or cause his or her employer to make (not including payments made directly to the lobbyist.) Segregate totals by category such as entertainment, food and refreshments; advertising, etc. (The lobbyist's reimbursed living and travel expenses need not be reported.) The name of any legislator or executive official to whom or for whose benefit on any one (1) occasion, an expenditure in excess of: seventy-five dollars ($75.00) per person from 2008 through December 31, 2010, and in excess of one hundred dollars ($100) per person on and after January 1, 2011, for the purpose of lobbying, is made or incurred and the date, name of payee, purpose and amount of such expenditure. Expenditures for the benefit of the members of the household of a legislator or executive official shall also be itemized if such expenditure exceeds the amount listed in this subsection. In the case of a lobbyist employed by more than one (1) employer, the proportionate amount of such expenditures in each category made or incurred on behalf of each of his employers. The subject matter of proposed legislation and the number of each senate or house bill, resolution, memorial or other legislative activity or any rule, ratemaking decision, procurement, contract, bid or bid process, financial services agreement or bond in which the lobbyist has been engaged in supporting or opposing during the reporting period; provided that in the case of appropriations bills, the lobbyist shall enumerate the specific section or sections which he supported or opposed.
Illinois 25 ILCS 170/6	Lobbyists or principals, depending on the situation
	Who Reports: Every lobbyist registered who is solely employed by a lobbying entity; any lobbyist who is not solely employed by a lobbying entity; every lobbying entity registered under this Act. If an individual is solely employed by another person to perform job related functions any part of which includes lobbying, the employer must report lobbying expenditures incurred on the employer's behalf as shall be identified by the lobbyist to the employer preceding such report (salary, compensation to lobbyist not included.) Persons who contract with another person to perform lobbying activities shall report all lobbying expenditures incurred on the employer's behalf. Any additional lobbying expenses incurred by the employer shall be reported by the employer. **Contents:** itemized individual expenditures or transactions, including the name of the official on whose behalf the expenditure was made, the name of the client or whose behalf the expenditure was made (if applicable), the total amount of the expenditure, a description of the expenditure, the address and location of the expenditure if the expenditure was for an intangible item such as lodging, the date on which the expenditure occurred and the subject matter of the lobbying activity, if any. Names and addresses of all clients who retained the lobbying entity together with an itemized description for each client of the following: lobbying regarding executive action, lobbying regarding legislative action, and lobbying regarding administrative action, including the agency lobbied and the subject matter. Expenditures attributable to lobbying officials shall be listed and reported according to the following categories: travel and lodging (including all travel and living accommodations made for or on behalf of officials in the state capital during legislative session), meals, beverages and other entertainment, gifts (indicating which were given on the basis of personal friendship), honoraria, any other thing or service of value not listed, setting forth a description of the expenditure. The category travel and lodging includes, but is not limited to, all travel and living accommodations made for or on behalf of State officials in the State capital during sessions of the General Assembly Expenditures incurred for hosting receptions, benefits and other gatherings held for purposes of goodwill or otherwise to influence executive, legislative or administrative action to which there are 25 or more State officials invited shall be reported listing only the amount of the expenditure, the date, and the estimated number of officials in attendance.
Indiana IC 2-7-3-3 IC 2-7-3-3.3, IC 2-7-3-3.5	Compensated lobbyists, Those who compensate lobbyists
	2-7-3 Separate report for each entity that pays the lobbyist for lobbying services. Total lobbying expenditures in at least these categories: compensation to others who perform lobbying services; reimbursement to others who perform lobbying services; receptions; entertainment, including meals (except functions all legislators are invited to); gifts made to a legislative person. A statement of each: expenditure for entertainment (including meals and drink); or gift that equals fifty dollars ($50) or more in one (1) day, or expenditures for entertainment (including meals or drink) or gifts that together total more than two hundred fifty dollars ($250) during the calendar year, if the expenditures are gifts made by the lobbyist or the lobbyist's agent to benefit a specific legislative person. A list of the general subject matter of each bill or resolution concerning which a lobbying effort was made within the registration period. The name of each member of the general assembly from whom the lobbyist has received an affidavit required under IC 2-2.1-3-3.5 (Expenses for office, personal sustenance, services of support staff that are not lobbyists need not be reported.) **2-7-3-3.3** A lobbyist shall file a written report whenever the lobbyist makes a gift with respect to a legislative person that is required to be included in a report under section 3(a)(3) of this chapter. This report must state the following: the name of the lobbyist making the gift; a description of the gift; the amount of the gift.

State	Who Must Report/Required Contents of Activity Reports

Indiana (continued)
IC 2-7-3-3
IC 2-7-3-3.3,
IC 2-7-3-3.5

Compensated lobbyists, Those who compensate lobbyists

2-7-3-3.5

If an expenditure for entertainment (including meals and drink) or a gift can clearly and reasonably be attributed to a particular legislative person, the expenditure must be reported with respect to that particular legislative person. A report of an expenditure with respect to a particular legislative person: must report actual amounts; may not allocate to the particular legislative person a prorated amount derived from an expense made with respect to several legislative persons; to the extent practicable. An activity report must report expenditures for a function or activity to which all the members of a legislative body are invited. Expenditures reported for a function or activity described in this subsection may not be allocated and reported with respect to a particular legislative person. If two (2) or more lobbyists contribute to an expenditure, each lobbyist shall report the actual amount the lobbyist contributed to the expenditure.

For purposes of determining whether the expenditure is reportable, the total amount per legislative person must be determined; not the amount each lobbyist contributed. Each lobbyists must report the actual amount contributed, even if the amount would not have been reportable if only one lobbyist made such an expenditure of that amount. Expenditures may not include any amount that the particular legislative person contributed. An activity report may not report expenditures or gifts relating to property or services received by a legislative person if the legislative person paid for the property or services the amount that would be charged to any purchaser of the property or services in the ordinary course of business. An activity report may not report expenditures or gifts made between close relatives unless the expenditure or gift is made in connection with a legislative action. An activity report may not report expenditures or gifts relating to the performance of a legislative person's official duties, including the legislative person's service as a member of any of the following: (1) The legislative council, (2) The budget committee, (3) A standing or other committee established by the rules of the house of representatives or the senate, (4) A study committee established by statute or by the legislative council. A statutory board or commission. An activity report may not report a contribution.

Iowa
68B.38
Senate Rule 6

Lobbyists

Per statute:
Client names. Amount and recipient of contributions made to candidates for state office during calendar months during the reporting period when the general assembly is not in session. The recipient of the campaign contributions. Expenditures made by the lobbyist in doing any of the activities that would require someone to register (examples include making expenditures over $1,000/year to communicate with public officials or receiving compensation to encourage the defeat or passage of legislation, rule or executive order).

Clients must provide all salaries, fees, retainers, and reimbursement of expenses paid or anticipated to be paid by the lobbyist's client to the lobbyist for lobbying purposes during the preceding year. The amount reported to the general assembly and the board shall include the total amount of all salaries, fees, retainers, and reimbursement of expenses paid to a lobbyist for lobbying both the legislative and executive branches.

Per Senate Rule:
Lobbyists must report on the following, but are not limited to: time spent at the state capitol building from the first day of session until the day of adjournment; time spent attending meetings or hearings which result in communication with members of the general assembly or legislative employees about current or proposed legislation; time spent researching and drafting proposed legislation with the intent to submit to a member of the general assembly or a legislative employee; time spent actually communicating with members of the general assembly and legislative employees about current or proposed legislation.

Kansas
46-269

Lobbyists

Name, address of each person who compensated or reimbursed the lobbyist. Aggregate value of lobbying expenditures over $100, except for office overhead, by the lobbyist or lobbyist's employer in these categories: food and beverages provided as hospitality to a state officer or employee or his or her spouse; entertainment, gifts, honoraria or payments; mass media communications; recreation provided as hospitality; communications for the purpose of influencing legislative or executive action; and all other reportable expenditures. Each lobbyist spending $100 or more for lobbying in any reporting period shall report any gift, entertainment or hospitality to members of the legislative and judicial branches. Include full name of the recipient and value. Several exemptions exist for meals and for individual expenditures of less than $2.

State	Who Must Report/Required Contents of Activity Reports
Kentucky 6.821, 6.824 *(Accurate for legislative lobbyists only)*	Legislative agents, Employers, Representatives of organized associations, coalitions, or public interest entities
	Legislative agents must file separate forms for each employer. Representatives or organized associations, coalitions or public interest entities must identify the source of the organization's financial resources. **All Filers:** For expenditures on behalf of legislators or members of their immediate family for food, beverages consumed on premises give name of legislator or family member, total expenditures, description and date. **Legislative Agents:** Total expenditures, regardless of whether they were reimbursed. Cumulative amounts, except personal expenses, spent on food, beverages, lodging, transportation, entertainment, and other lobbying expenses. Under 6.824, details of financial transactions for the benefit of members of the legislature, the governor, cabinet secretaries, or certain state employees. Include name of the official or employee; purpose, nature of transaction; date made or entered into. **Employers:** Total lobbying expenditures. Itemized list of amounts spent for receptions or other events, date, location, name of the group of public servants invited. Itemized list of other amounts spent for lobbying, including food and lodging, reimbursements to public officials; not including personal expenses. Cumulative compensation paid to legislative agents, prorated to reflect the time they were engaged in lobbying during the period. Under 6.824, details of financial transactions for the benefit of members of the legislature, the governor, cabinet secretaries, or certain state employees. Include name of the official or employee; purpose, nature of transaction; date made or entered into.
Louisiana 24:55	Lobbyists
	A listing of each subject matter lobbied during each reporting period. The total of all expenditures made during each reporting period; the aggregate total of expenditures attributable to an individual legislator or public servant, other than a legislator, in the legislative branch of state government during each reporting period, including the name of the legislator or other public servant. The aggregate total of expenditures attributable to the spouse or minor child of a legislator during each reporting period (the name of the spouse or minor child shall not be included). The aggregate total of such expenditures shall be reported as followed: "The aggregate total of expenditures attributable to the spouse of (insert name of legislator) was (insert aggregate total of expenditures). The aggregate total of expenditures attributable to the minor child or children of (insert name of legislator) was (insert aggregate total of expenditures)." The aggregate total of expenditures for all reporting periods in the same calendar year. The aggregate total of all expenditures attributable to an individual legislator or public servant (other than a legislator) in the legislative branch of state government for all reporting periods during the same calendar year, including the name of the legislator or other public servant. The aggregate total of all expenditures attributable to the spouse or minor child of a legislator for all reporting periods during the same calendar year. The name of the spouse or minor child shall not be included. The aggregate total of such expenditures shall be reported as follows: "The aggregate total of expenditures attributable to the spouse of (insert name of legislator) for all reporting periods during the year was (insert aggregate total of expenditures).The aggregate total of expenditures attributable to the minor child or children of (insert name of legislator) for all reporting periods during the year was (insert aggregate total of expenditures)." Each report shall include a statement of the expenditure for each reception, social gathering, or other function to which the entire legislature, either house, any standing committee, select committee, statutory committee, committee created by resolution of either house, subcommittee of any committee, recognized caucus, or any delegation thereof, is invited which amount is attributable to such invitation. Any report of such amount shall include the name of the group or groups invited and the date and location of the reception, social gathering, or other function. Any expenditure for any reception or social gathering sponsored in whole or in part by a lobbyist, individually or on behalf of a principal he represents, held in conjunction with a meeting of a national or regional organization of legislators or legislative staff shall be reported by including the name of the national or regional organization, the date and location of the reception or social gathering, a general description of persons associated with the organization invited to attend the reception or social gathering, and the amount of the expenditure. The provisions include without any limitation any expenditure for any of the following: a single activity, occasion, reception, meal, or meeting held during the same period and in the same general locale as a meeting of such an organization and to which some persons associated with the organization are invited; a single activity, occasion, reception, meal or meeting that is part of the scheduled activities of a meeting of such an organization and that is open to persons attending the meeting. Any expenditure for any meal or refreshment consumed by a legislator in connection with any out-of-state event shall be reported in accordance with the provisions of this Section. Any expenditures by a lobbyist's principal or employer made in the presence of the lobbyist shall be reported by the lobbyist as provided in this part.

State	Who Must Report/Required Contents of Activity Reports
Maine 317	**Lobbyists**
	Name, address of lobbyist, employer. Names of individuals who lobbied during the month. Amount of compensation received for lobbying activities during the month (the amount of compensation received for lobbying officials in the legislative branch, officials in the executive branch and constitutional officers must be reported separately). The amount of compensation received for preparation of documents and research for the primary purpose of influencing legislative action and to lobbying by the employee's regular rate of pay based on a 40-hour week. Amount of expenditures made or incurred by the lobbyist for purposes of lobbying for which the lobbyist has been or expects to be reimbursed (the amount of expenditures for lobbying officials in the legislative branch, officials in the executive branch and constitutional officers must be reported separately). When expenditures for the purposes of indirect lobbying exceed $15,000 during a month that is the subject of the report, the specific dollar amount of expenditures for indirect lobbying made or incurred during the month by a lobbyist, lobbyist associate or employer, with separate totals for expenditure categories as determined by the commission, the legislative actions that are the subject of the indirect lobbying and a general description of the intended recipients. Amount of expenditures by the lobbyist or the employer directly to or on behalf of one or more covered officials, including members of the official's immediate family. Name of official in the legislative branch or a member of that official's immediate family on whose behalf expenditures totaling $25 or more were made in any calendar month; date, amount, purpose. Date, description, cost and list of all officials of the legislative branch or administrative agency or members of an official's immediate family present for events that cost more than $250. Each legislative action by number or, if unknown, by topic, on which the lobbyist is lobbying. Identification of each legislative action for which the lobbyist was compensated or expects to be compensated or expended in excess of $1,000 for related lobbying activities, including all original sources of money received from employer. A list of all of the employer's original sources and a statement of the dollar amounts contributed or paid by the original sources to the employer. If the original source is a corporation, nonprofit corporation or limited partnership, the corporation, nonprofit organization or limited partnership, not the individual members or contributors, must be listed as the original source.
Maryland 15-704	**Lobbyists**
	Total executive or legislative lobbying expenditures in these categories:
	Total individual regulated lobbyist compensation, excluding reported expenses
	Office expenses of the regulated lobbyist
	Professional and technical research
	Publications that expressly encourage communication with one or more officials or employees
	Witnesses, including the name of each and the fees and expenses paid to each
	Meals, beverages for officials, employees, or members of their immediate families Except as provided in §15-708 (d) (2) of this subtitle, food, beverages, and incidental expenses for officials of the Legislative Branch for meals and receptions to which all members of any legislative unit were invited
	Food, beverages for members of the General Assembly at the respective times and geographic locations of meetings of legislative organizations
	Food, lodging, scheduled entertainment for officials and employees at meetings at which the officials and employees were scheduled speakers
	Tickets, free admission extended to legislators to attend charitable, cultural, and political events sponsored or conducted by the reporting entity and to each of which all members of a legislative unit were invited if this is at least the second occurrence and the cumulative value of the tickets is more than $100
	Other gifts worth more than $200 to or for officials, employees, or members of their immediate families; other expenses.
	Date, location, and total expense of the regulated lobbyist for each meal, reception, event, or meeting reported above.
	Name of each official, employee, or member of the immediate family of an official or employee who has benefited from one or more gifts with a cumulative value of $75 during the reporting period regardless of whether the gift was from more than one entity or was given in connection with lobbying activity. Certain receptions need not be allocated to individual recipients by name. Regulated lobbyists who are not individuals must also report the name and permanent address of each entity that provided at least 5% of the regulated lobbyist's total receipts during the preceding 12 months.

State	Who Must Report/Required Contents of Activity Reports
Massachusetts 3:43, 3:44, 3:47	Executive agents, legislative agents, Employers of executive or legislative agents, Groups that don't employ lobbyists, but that spend more than $250 a year lobbying

Executive agents, legislative agents: Itemized statement of campaign contributions, lobbying expenditures; all expenditures made for or on behalf of certain state officials including legislators if they total more than $35 a day. Itemize in categories including: meals, gifts, transportation, entertainment, advertising, public relations, printing, mailing and telephone; include names of the payees, amount paid to each; names of the candidate or political committee to whom or to which the contribution was made, and the amount and date of each contribution. For meals, entertainment or transportation, identify by date, place, amount, and the names of all persons in the group partaking. List of all bill numbers of legislation acting to influence in the course of his employment if the executive or legislative agent specifically referenced the bill number while acting to promote, oppose or influence legislation.

Employers of executive or legislative agents: Itemized list of all lobbying expenditures, including expenditures to or on behalf of public officials. Itemize in the following categories: specific expenditures for meals, gifts, transportation, entertainment, advertising, public relations, printing, mailing, and telephone; include names of the payees and the amount paid to each. Where such expenditure is for meals, entertainment or transportation, said expenditure shall be identified by the date, place, amount, and names of all persons in the group partaking. When such compensation is included as part of a regular salary or retainer, the statement shall specify the amount of the agent's salary or retainer allocable to his legislative duties. If no such apportionment is possible, the statement shall indicate such impossibility and disclose the full salary or retainer.

Groups that don't employ lobbyists, but that spend more than $250 a year lobbying: Names, addresses of the principals of such group. Purposes of the organization. Identification of state issues affecting the group's purposes. Total expenditures in connection with lobbying. Expenditures for or on behalf of certain public officials including legislators, itemized in at least these categories: meals, transportation, entertainment, advertising, public relations, printing, mailing and telephone; include names of the payees, amount paid to each. For meals, entertainment or transportation, identified by date, place, amount, names of those partaking. Itemized list of campaign contributions with the name of each candidate or committee, amount, date. Names, addresses of every person, group or organization contributing at least $15 or during the year for the objectives of the group.

State	
Michigan 4.418	Lobbyists, Lobbyist agents

Update of information required on registration form. Lobbying expenditures by category, listed for the reporting period and cumulative totals. Required categories are as follows: food and beverage for public officials that exceeds $25/day or $150/year (include recipient name and amount. for large receptions, list total amount, rather than prorated per attendee); advertising and mass mailings; other expenditures of more than $5. Date, nature, amount and parties to financial transactions worth at least $775 in goods or services between the reporting person or someone acting on his or her behalf and a public official or a member his or her immediate family, or a business with which the individual is associated. Date, nature, amount and parties to travel, lodging expenses of more than $500 paid for or reimbursed to a public in connection with public business by that public official in excess of $500.00. (Several exceptions apply to financial transaction disclosure requirements.) Brief description of lobbying activities for the period.

State	
Minnesota 10A.04	Lobbyists, Principals

Lobbyists: Total lobbying disbursements, separately listing those to influence: legislative action, administrative action, and actions of a metropolitan government. Breakdown into categories including but not limited to: publications and distribution; other printing; media, including the cost of production; postage; travel; fees, including allowances; entertainment; telephone; other. Amount, nature, name and address of recipient, date of each gift, item, or benefit, excluding contributions to a candidate, worth at least $5 to certain officials by the lobbyist or a lobbyist employer. Original source of money in excess of $500 in any year used for the purpose of lobbying. For each source, include, name, address, and employer, or, if self-employed, the occupation and principal place of business. General description of the subjects lobbied in the previous 12 months.

Principals: Report the total amount, rounded to the nearest $20,000, spent by the principal during the preceding calendar year to influence: legislative action, administrative action, and actions of a metropolitan government. Report a total amount that includes: all direct payments by the principal to lobbyists in this state, all expenditures for advertising, mailing, research, analysis, compilation and dissemination of information, and public relations campaigns related to: legislative action, administrative action and actions of a metropolitan government. Report all salaries and administrative expenses.

State	
Mississippi 5-8-9, 5-8-11	Lobbyists, Lobbyist clients

Lobbying expenditures in these categories: Payments to lobbyists, whether salary, fee, reimbursement, other expenses at request of lobbyist; payments for those portions of office rent, utilities, supplies, support personnel attributable to lobbying activities; payments incurred soliciting or urging others to communicate with officials when at the request of the client; purchase, payment, distribution, loan, forgiveness of a loan or payment of a loan by a third party, advance, deposit, transfer of funds, a promise to make a payment, or a gift of money or anything of value for any purpose. Name of giver and recipient, description, value, nature of item, place and date of transfer for each thing of value given to a public official. For events to which all legislators are invited, report the total cost of the reception and the number in attendance.

State	Who Must Report/Required Contents of Activity Reports
Missouri 105.473	Lobbyists (executive lobbyists, judicial lobbyists, legislative lobbyists, elected local government official lobbyists)
	Expenditures by lobbyist or principals made on behalf of all public officials, their staffs and employees, and their spouses and dependent children, separated into at least the following categories: printing and publication; media and advertising; travel; entertainment; honoraria; food and beverages; gifts. Itemized list of name of recipient, nature, amount of each expenditure by the lobbyist or principal, including a service or anything of value, for all expenditures paid or provided to or for a public official, such official's staff, employees, spouse or dependent children. Total expenditures by a lobbyist or principal for occasions, identity of group invited, the date, description of occasion, amount of expenditure for each occasion when any of the following are invited: all members of the senate, which may or may not include senate staff and employees under the direct supervision of a state senator; all members of the house of representatives, which may or may not include house staff and employees under the direct supervision of a state representative; all members of a joint committee of the general assembly or a standing committee of either the house of representatives or senate, which may or may not include joint and standing committee staff; all members of a caucus of the majority party of the house of representatives, minority party of the house of representatives, majority party of the senate, or minority party of the senate; all statewide officials, which may or may not include the staff and employees under the direct supervision of the statewide official. Expenditures made on behalf of a public official, the public official's staff, employees, spouse or dependent children, if such expenditure is solicited by such public official or above-named associated individual, name of such persons, except any expenditures made to any not-for-profit corporation, charitable, fraternal or civic organization or other association formed to provide for good in the order of benevolence and except for the provision on occasions listed above. Details of direct business relationships the lobbyist has with any public official. For all of the above, the portion spent on the lobbyist need not be reported
Montana 5-7-208 5-7-112	Principals who spends more than $2,150 on lobbying expenses per year
	If payments are made to influence any official action by a public official or made to influence other action and legislative action, report must include all payments in which the principal spent $5,000 or more. Itemized and identifying payee and beneficiary, in these categories: printing; advertising; postage; travel; salaries and fees, including allowances, rewards, and contingency fees; entertainment, including food and refreshment; telephone; other office expenses. Lobbying expenses worth at least $25 to benefit a public official. Lobbying expenses worth at least $100 to benefit more than one public official, but if an entire chamber is invited, list the beneficiary as such. Contributions, membership fees of $250 or more per year paid to the principal for lobbying purpose, with full address of each payer and issue area for which payment was earmarked. Official actions on which the principal or the principal's agents exerted a major effort, statement of principal's position.
Nebraska 49-1483, 49-1483.03	Lobbyists, Principals
	Lobbyists: Amounts spent on lobbying expenses, itemized, in these categories: miscellaneous expenses; entertainment, including expenses for food and drink, lodging, travel, lobbyist compensation, lobbyist expense reimbursement, admissions to a state-owned facility or a state-sponsored industry or event, and extraordinary office expenses directly related to the practice of lobbying. Amount, terms, recipient of any money loaned, promised, paid by a lobbyist, principal, or anyone acting on behalf of either to an official in the executive or legislative branch or member of such official's staff. Total spent on gifts, other than admissions to a state-owned facility or a state-sponsored industry or event, aggregated in these categories: legislators, executive branch officials. Aggregate expenses for entertainment, admissions, and gifts for each of the following categories of elected officials: legislators and officials in the executive branch of the state. When the nature of an event at which members of the Legislature or executive branch are entertained makes it impractical to determine the actual cost, the cost of entertainment shall be the average cost per person multiplied by the number of members of the Legislature or executive branch in attendance. Although these reports are required quarterly, a separate, additional report is required anytime a lobbyist or principal receives or spends more than $5,000 in one month for lobbying purposes.

Principals: All of the above, plus names, addresses of people who gave more than $100 in any one month for lobbying purposes. |
| Nevada 218H.400 | Lobbyists |
| | Total expenditures made on behalf of a legislator or organization whose primary purpose is to support legislators of a particular political party and house, including expenditures made by others on behalf of the registrant. Identity of each legislator and organization on whose behalf expenditures were made, itemized by legislator and organization (unless all legislators were invited). For expenditures over $50 made by or on behalf of a registrant, include a compilation of expenditures itemized in the following categories: entertainment; costs of events hosted by the organization represented by the registrant; gifts and loans to a legislator, to an organization whose primary purpose is to provide support for Legislators of a particular political party and house, or to any other person for the benefit of a Legislator or such an organization; other expenditures directly associated with legislative action, not including personal expenditures for food, lodging and travel expenses or membership dues. |

State	Who Must Report/Required Contents of Activity Reports
New Hampshire 15:6	**Lobbyists**
	All fees received from any lobbying client that are related, directly or indirectly, to lobbying, such as public advocacy, government relations, or public relations services including research, monitoring legislation, and related legal work. All expenditures made from lobbying fees, including by whom paid or whom charged. Any honorarium or expense reimbursement or political contribution made by the lobbyist in his or her professional capacity, on behalf of the lobbyist, the partnership, firm, or corporation or by the lobbyist on behalf of the client or employer or by a family member of the lobbyist. The name of the client on whose behalf the expense reimbursement or honorarium was made, the name of the person receiving, the value, and a brief description of the honorarium or expense reimbursement. For each political contribution made: name of the candidate, office the candidate is seeking, value of the contribution, and a brief description of the contribution if it is an in-kind contribution. For all expenditures for salaries, benefits, support staff, and office expenses, related directly or indirectly to lobbying, a statement of the total aggregate expenses shall satisfy the requirement that an itemized statement of these expenses be filed.
New Jersey 52:13C-22; 52:13C-22.1	Governmental affairs agents who spend or are paid more than $2,500 a year to lobby. (These agents are individual lobbyists), Lobbyists (in this state "lobbyist" has a meaning similar to "principal" or "lobbyist employer" in other states.)
	Quarterly reports: Description of the particular items of legislation, regulation, or governmental process and any general category or type of legislation, regulation or governmental process on which the governmental affairs agent lobbied, and any particular items or general types of legislation, regulation, or governmental processes which he actively promoted or opposed during the quarter.

Annual reports: Expenditures relating to communication with, or providing benefits to, a legislator, legislative staff, the Governor, the Governor's staff, an officer or staff member of the Executive Branch, or communication with the general public, in these categories: media, including advertising; entertainment; food and beverage; travel and lodging; honoraria; loans; gifts; and salary, fees, allowances or other compensation paid to an agent. Report in aggregate by category unless they exceed $25.00 per day on one person, in which case detail separately as to the name of the recipient, date and type of expenditure, amount and to whom paid. Where the aggregate expenditures for communication with or providing benefits to one official exceed $200.00 per year, detail the type of expenditures, name of the intended recipient, amount and to whom paid. Where the aggregate expenditures for communication with the general public are more than $100.00 for one occasion, include the date and type of expenditure, amount and to whom paid. Whether the governmental affairs agent serves on certain state or local authorities, boards or commissions; date upon which his term expires. |
New Mexico 2-11-6	**Lobbyists, Lobbyist employers**
	Cumulative total of the expenditures made or incurred, in categories that identify the total separate amounts spent on: meals and beverages; other entertainment expenditures; gifts; and other expenditures. Amount, date, name of recipient of each political contribution made. Names, addresses and occupations of other contributors and the amounts of their separate political contributions if the lobbyist or lobbyist's employer delivers directly or indirectly separate contributions from those contributors in excess of $500 in the aggregate for each election to a candidate, a campaign committee or anyone authorized by a candidate to receive funds on his behalf.
New York Legislative Law 32-1A-1-h, 32-1A-1i	Lobbyists, Public Corporations, Clients who spend more than $2,000 a year on lobbying
	Lobbyists: Lobbyist's name, address, phone number. Lobbyist's client's name, address, phone. General description of subjects lobbied on, as well as the legislative bill numbers of any bills and the rule, regulation, and ratemaking numbers on which the lobbyist has lobbied. Names of people, organizations, or legislative bodies before which the lobbyist has lobbied. Compensation paid or owed to the lobbyist, and any lobbying expenses, to be listed in the aggregate if $75 or less and individually if more than $75. For items listed individually, disclose the amount, recipient and purpose. Expenses not to include: personal sustenance; printing and mailing less than $500. Must report lobbying activities for grants, loans and other disbursements of public funds over $15,000.

Public Corporations: Public corporation's name, address, phone number. Names, addresses, phones of all lobbyists retained, employed or designated. Copies of all agreements relating to each such retainer, employment or designation, and if the agreement was oral, a statement of its substance. General description of subjects lobbied on, as well as the legislative bill numbers of any bills and the rule, regulation, and ratemaking numbers on which the lobbyist and the public corporation have lobbied. Names of people, organizations, or legislative bodies before which the public corporation or its lobbyists have lobbied. Compensation paid or owed to each lobbyist and any expenses whether directly for the benefit of public officials or through lobbyists. List expenses in the aggregate if $75 or less and individually if more than $75. For items listed individually, disclose the amount, recipient and purpose. Expenses not to include: personal sustenance; printing and mailing less than $500.

Clients who spend more than $2,000 a year lobbying must file semi-annual reports with similar information as above. (Lobbyists and public corporations must file bimonthly.) |

State	Who Must Report/Required Contents of Activity Reports
North Carolina Chapter 120C-402	Lobbyists, Principals
	Notarized reports are due quarterly, even is there were no "reportable expenditures." They must be filed by 10 days after the reporting period ends. Lobbyists and Principals must file additional reports when they make reportable expenditures during any month the General Assembly is in session. These reports must be filed within 10 days of the end of the month in which the reportable expenditure was made. **Reportable expenditures:** Lobbyists, principals and "solicitors" must also generally report expenditures of more than $3000 on "solicitation" of members of the general public to influence legislative or executive action. Failure to file required reports can void the registration of the lobbyist, principal and solicitor and bars re-registration until reports are filed. The Secretary of State can also levy civil fines of up to $5000 per violation related to the required reports. The Secretary of State's office prescribes the reporting forms. The reports must include (1) reportable expenditures made for the purpose of lobbying, (2) solicitations of others costing more than $3,000, (3) reportable expenditures reimbursed to a lobbyist by the lobbyist's principal, and (4) all reportable expenditures for gifts that are given under the exceptions to the gift ban set forth in G.S. 138A-32(e). Reportable expenditures are generally defined as contracts with designated individuals and their immediate family members and any expenditure of more than $10 in value per designated individual per calendar day. Lobbyists' principals are required to file quarterly reports that include the same information as lobbyists' reports as well as details of the compensation paid to lobbyists. Article 8 of Chapter 120 requires a person to report expenditures of more than $200 in a calendar quarter made to a designated individual for the purpose of lobbying, even if the person making the expenditures is not a lobbyist.
North Dakota 54-05.1-03 (2)	Lobbyists
	Each expenditure of $60 or more spent on any single occasion on any individual, including the spouse or other family member of a legislator or the governor. Include a description of the nature of the expenditure; the amount; the date; and the name of the recipient.
Ohio 101.73	Legislative agents, Employers
	Legislative agents must file separate reports for each employer. Total expenditures for reporting period (employers should not include lobbyist compensation). For each expenditure to, at the request of, for the benefit of, or on behalf of a member of the general assembly, a member of the controlling board, the governor, the director of a state department or a staff member of any of the above, list: name of person to whom, at whose request, for whose benefit, or on whose behalf the expenditures were made; total amount of expenditure; description; date; item of legislation for which the expenditure was made; name of client on whose behalf expenditure made. List expenditures as payment for meals and other food and beverages in a separate list. Include only those to public officials who have already received $50 worth of food and beverages from lobbyist this calendar year. Do not include those provided at an event where the legislator spoke or participated in a panel discussion, or those provided at a convention of a national organization to which state agencies pay dues. Legislative agents or employers who have had financial transactions with or for the benefit of certain public officials including legislators must list details such as: name of public official or employee, purpose and nature of transaction, date.
Oklahoma (Forms available at Oklahoma Ethics Commission)	Lobbyists
	Lobbyist's name. For each thing of value given to a state officer or employee or a member of his or her family that exceeds $50 in the aggregate during a 6-month period, list the name of the recipient, date given, nature of thing of value, amount of expenditure, name of lobbyist principal on whose behalf item given. Reports must be notarized.
Oregon 171.745, 171.750	Lobbyists, Lobbyist employers
	Lobbyists: Total amount of all moneys spent by the lobbyist for the purpose of lobbying for: food, refreshments and entertainment; printing, postage and telephone; advertising, public relations, education and research; and miscellaneous. Include the name of the official to whom or for whose benefit the expense was made for each expense more than $50 on one occasion, date, name of payee, purpose and amount. (Don't include money spent on the lobbyist's personal living and travel, office overhead or salaries for support staff and maintenance expenses. **Lobbyist employers:** Total amount of money spent for lobbying activities on the lobbyist's behalf, excluding living and travel expenses. Name of any legislative or executive official to whom or for whose benefit, on any one occasion, an expenditure in excess of $25 for the purpose of lobbying is made by the person, but not including expenses lobbyists reported on their expense reports; date, name of payee, purpose and amount of that expenditure.

State	Who Must Report/Required Contents of Activity Reports
Pennsylvania 65 Pa. C.S. Sec. 13A05	Principals, Lobbyists
	An expense report required under this section shall be filed when total expenses for lobbying exceed $2,500 for a registered principal in a reporting period. In a reporting period in which total expenses are $2,500 or less, a statement to that effect shall be filed.

Names and registration numbers (when available) of all lobbyists by whom lobbying is conducted on behalf of the principal and general subject matter or issue being lobbied. Total costs of all lobbying for period, including: office expenses, personnel expenses, expenditures related to gifts, hospitality, transportation and lodging to state officials or employees, and any other lobbying costs. Total amount shall be allocated in its entirety among the following categories: costs for gifts, hospitality, transportation, and lodging given to or provided to State officials or employees and their immediate families, costs for direct communication, costs for indirect communication. Identify, by name, position and each occurrence, a State official or employee who receives from a principal or lobbyist anything of value which must be included in the statement. Shall not include the cost of a reception which the State official or employee attends in connection with public office or employment. Shall not apply to anything of value received from immediate family when the circumstances make it clear that motivation for the action was the personal or family relationship. Report shall also include name, permanent business address and telephone number of any individual, association, corporation, partnership, business trust or other business entity which contributed more than 10% of the total resources received by the principal.

Whenever any person makes an expenditure for indirect communication under this chapter, for the purpose of disseminating or initiating a communication, such as a mailing, telephone bank, print or electronic media advertisement, billboard, publication or education campaign, the communication shall clearly and conspicuously state the name of the person who made or financed the expenditure for the communication. |
Rhode Island 22-10-09(A)	Lobbyists, Persons who engage lobbyists to act as lobbyists.
	Complete report of lobbying expenditures including advertising; compensation paid to the lobbyists; all campaign contributions in excess of $100 to state and municipal elected officials and state political action committees; expenditures, gifts, and honorariums to public officials of $25 or more for each occurrence; The report shall include the names of the individuals receiving or in whose behalf the expenditures have been made, and the reason, date, and place of the expenditures.
Tennessee T.C.A. 3-6-303	Lobbyist employers
	The required employer's disclosure has three parts. The first is the "aggregate total amount of lobbyist compensation paid by the employer." For compensation paid to a person who performs duties in addition to lobbying "and related activities," the compensation is to be apportioned "to reflect the lobbyist's time allocated for lobbying and related activities in [Tennessee]." There is no definition of "related activities." The report is to be in monetary ranges from less than $10,000 to $400,000 or more. T.C.A.§ 3-6-303(a)(1). The second part is the "aggregate total amount of employer expenditures incurred for the purpose of influencing legislative or administrative action through public opinion or grassroots action, excluding lobbyist compensation." The Act contains a list of activities that constitute "public opinion and grassroots action." There is a required apportionment for "multi-state effect," and the report is to be in ranges from less than $10,000 to $400,000 or more. T.C.A. § 3-6-303(a)(2). Third: the employer must report in the same filing the "aggregate total amount" of expenditures for events paid for by the employer to which the entire membership of the Tennessee General Assembly was invited. T.C.A. § 3-6-303(a)(3).
Texas 305.006	Those who spend or receive more than $200/quarter for lobbying
	Total expenditures made to communicate directly with a member of the legislative or executive branch to influence action and that are directly attributable, as that term is used in Section 305.0062(b), to a member of the legislative or executive branch or the immediate family of a member of the legislative or executive branch, in these categories: transportation and lodging; food and beverages; entertainment; gifts, other than awards and mementos; expenditures made for the attendance of members of the legislative or executive branch at political fund-raisers or charity events. List also total expenditures made by the registrant or by others on the registrant's behalf and with the registrant's consent or ratification for: broadcast or print advertisements, direct mailings, and other mass media communications. List of the specific categories of subject matters about which the registrant, any person the registrant retains or employs to appear on the registrant's behalf, or any other person appearing on the registrant's behalf communicated directly with a member of the legislative or executive branch. Include the number or other designation assigned to the administrative action, if known.

If a registrant, or someone on the registrant's behalf, makes an expenditure that's more than 60 percent of the legislative per diem for transportation or lodging, or food and beverage for a member of the legislative or executive branch, include a report detailing: name of public official, place and date, purpose. In the case of food and beverage, report if given to members of public official's family. |

State	Who Must Report/Required Contents of Activity Reports
Texas (continued) 305.006	Those who spend or receive more than $200/quarter for lobbying
	If a registrant, or someone on the registrant's behalf, makes an expenditure that's more than 60 percent of the legislative per diem for transportation or lodging, or food and beverage for a member of the legislative or executive branch, include a report detailing: name of public official, place and date, purpose. In the case of food and beverage, report if given to members of public official's family.
	If a registrant, or someone on the registrant's behalf, gives a gift, memento or award worth more than $50, give the name of recipient, a description of the gift, and amount.
	If a registrant, or someone on the registrant's behalf, makes expenditures for the attendance of a member of the legislative or executive branch at a political fund-raiser or charity event, give the name of the member of the legislative or executive branch in whose behalf the expenditure is made; name of the charity or the name of the candidate or officeholder for whom the political fund-raiser was held; and the date of the fund-raiser or event.
Utah 36-11-201	Lobbyists, Principals, Government officials who lobby
	Total amount of expenditures made to benefit public officials during the quarterly reporting period. Total amount of expenditures made, by the type of public official, during the quarterly reporting period. Total amount of expenditures made to benefit any public official and total amount of expenditures made, by the type of public official, during the last calendar year. Disclosure of each expenditure made during the quarterly reporting period to reimburse or pay for travel or lodging for a public official, including: each travel destination and each lodging location, the name of each public official who benefited from the expenditure on travel or lodging, the public official type of each public official named, for each public official named, a listing of the amount and purpose of each expenditure made for travel or lodging, and the total amount of expenditures listed. Disclosure of aggregate daily expenditures greater than $10 made during the quarterly reporting period including: date, purpose, and location of expenditure, name of any public official benefited, type of the public official benefited, and the total monetary worth of the benefit that the expenditure conferred on any public official. For each public official who was employed by the lobbyist, principal, or government officer, a list that provides: name of the public official, and nature of the employment with the public official. Each bill or resolution, by number and short title, on behalf which the lobbyist, principal, or government officer made an expenditure to a public official. Description of each executive action on behalf of which the lobbyist, principal, or government officer made an expenditure to a public official. General purposes, interests, and nature of the entities that the lobbyist, principal, or government officer filing report represents. For a lobbyist, a certification that the information provided in the report is true, accurate, and complete to the lobbyist's best knowledge and belief.
Vermont 2-11-264	Lobbyists, Lobbying Firm, Employers
	Total spent on lobbying, including advertising (TV, radio, print, electronic media), expenses for telemarketing or polling if intended to influence legislative or administrative action. Contractual agreements in excess of $100 per year or direct business relationships that are in existence or were entered into within the previous 12 months between the employer and a legislator or administrator, a legislator's or administrator's spouse or civil union partner, or a legislator's or administrator's dependent household member. Total compensation to lobbyists. Itemized lists of gifts, regardless of whether in connection with lobbying, worth more than $15 to public officials including the date, nature, value, identity of official who requested the gift; identity of recipient. Monetary gifts, other than political contributions, are prohibited.
Virginia 2.2-426	Lobbyists, Principals who spend more than $500 to employ multiple lobbyists
	Statement from principal including principal's name, business address, phone, list of executive and legislative actions lobbied on, description of activities conducted. Total expenditures in these categories: entertainment, gifts, office expenses, communications, personal living and travel, compensation of lobbyists, honoraria, registration costs, other. Lobbyist's name, business address, phone. Whether lobbyist is employed by the principal, retained by the principal or not compensated. List of other lobbyists who represent the same principal. If employed by principal, give job title. If not compensated, indicate why not. If compensated, give dollar amount of compensation for lobbying work. List members of your entity who furnished lobbying services to your principal. Total amount paid to your firm for services rendered. Itemization of single entertainment expenses of more than $50, with date, location, description of event, number of officials invited, number attending. Names of officials who attended if cost of event was more than $50 per person. Breakdown of other costs for event. Gifts worth more than $25, with date, description, name of recipient, cost. Other expenses. Signatures of lobbyist and principal.

State	Who Must Report/Required Contents of Activity Reports
Washington 42.17.170 42.17.180 42.17.190	Lobbyists, Lobbyist employers, State or local government agencies that spend public funds to lobby

Lobbyists: Total lobbying expenditures by the lobbyist or on the lobbyist's behalf, segregated according to lobbyist employer and financial categories including: compensation; food and refreshments; living accommodations; advertising; travel; contributions; and other expenses or services. For expenditures of more than $25, give date, place, amount, names of those partaking. (Unreimbursed personal living expenses, office expenses including rent and salaries for paid staff not required to be reported.) Itemized list of contributions of money or personal property to candidates, elected officials and state agency officials or employees with date, amount, name of recipient. Subject matter of legislative or rule-making activity the lobbyist is lobbying on. Listing of each gift or honorarium of more than $50 to a public official with date, recipient and value. Total expenditures for lobbying expenses including political advertising, public relations, telemarketing, polling, including amounts, to whom paid and brief description of activity.

Lobbyist employers: Names of public officials or their family members to whom a lobbyist employer has paid compensation more than $500 in the preceding calendar year for personal employment or professional services, amount of compensation paid. Names of state officials to whom the reporting party made expenditures, amount, purpose. Total lobbying expenditures, whether through a lobbyist or not. All contributions made to a candidate or political committee supporting or opposing a statewide ballot proposition. Names, addresses of lobbyists employed, and total expenditures by each. Names, offices sought, party affiliations of candidates for state offices supported or opposed by independent expenditures of the person reporting, amount. Identifying proposition number, brief description of any statewide ballot proposition supported or opposed by expenditures not reported under this subsection, amount of each such expenditure. Additional special reports are required if contributions over $100 to certain public officials made.

State or local agencies: Name of the agency filing the statement. Name, title, and job description and salary of each elected official, officer, or employee who lobbied. General description of the nature of the lobbying. Proportionate amount of time spent on the lobbying. Listing of expenditures incurred by the agency for lobbying including but not limited to travel, consultant or other special contractual services, and brochures and other publications, the principal purpose of which is to influence legislation.

All of the above: Certain grassroots lobbying campaign expenses must be reported, under 42.17.200.

West Virginia 6B-3-4	Lobbyists

Total amount of expenditures for lobbying made or incurred by the lobbyist, or on behalf of the lobbyist by the lobbyist's employer. Segregate by financial category, including meals and beverages; living accommodations; advertising; travel; contributions; gifts to public officials or employees or to members of the immediate family of a public official or employee; and other expenses or services. (Unreimbursed living expenses, office expenses, rent and salaries to support staff are not required to be reported.) If a lobbyist is employed by more than one employer, the report shall show the proportionate amount of expenditures in each category incurred on behalf of his or her employers and subject matter of the lobbying activities in which the lobbyist has been engaged. If, during the period covered by the report, the lobbyist made expenditures or expenditures were made or incurred on behalf of the lobbyist in the reporting categories of meals and beverages, living accommodations, travel, gifts or other expenditures, the lobbyist shall report the name of the public official or employee to whom or on whose behalf the expenditures were made, the total amount of the expenditures, and the subject matter of the lobbying activity, if any:

Provided, That a registered lobbyist who entertains more than one public official or public employee at a time with meals and beverages complies with the provisions of this section if he or she reports the names of the public officials or public employees entertained and the total amount expended for meals and beverages for all of the public officials or public employees entertained: Provided, however, That where several lobbyists join in entertaining one or more public officials or public employees at a time with meals and beverages, each lobbyist complies with the provisions of this section by reporting the names of the public officials or public employees entertained and his or her proportionate share of the total amount expended for meals and beverages for all of the public officials or public employees entertained. Under this subsection, no portion of the amount of an expenditure for a dinner, party or other function sponsored by a lobbyist's employer need be attributed to a particular public official or employee who attends the function if the sponsor has invited to the function all the members of: The Legislature; either house of the Legislature; a standing or select committee of either house; or a joint committee of the two houses of the Legislature. However, the amount spent for the function shall be added to other expenditures for the purpose of determining the total amount of expenditures. Provided further, That if the expenditure is for a function to which the entire membership of the Legislature has been invited, the lobbyist need only report that fact, the total amount of the expenditure and the subject matter of the lobbying activity. If any one expenditure for a public official, including honorariums, totals more than $25, report the recipient's name, the total amount and the subject matter of the lobbying activity, if any. Certain expenses for grassroots lobbying must be reported under 6B-3-5.

State	Who Must Report/Required Contents of Activity Reports
Wisconsin 13.68	**Principals**
	Aggregate total lobbying expenditures made by principal and all lobbyists employed, excluding expenses for clerical support. Include compensation and reimbursements to lobbyists. Include expenses incurred while preparing to perform lobbying services, if research conducted is less than 3 years old. Include, if over $500, advertising campaigns or costs of other efforts to urge the general public to attempt to influence legislative or administrative action. Names, addresses of lobbyists who made or incurred more than $200 in lobbying expenses during the period, amount. If lobbyist is an employee, officer or director of the principal, include expenses for office space, utilities and employees used in preparing lobbying communications. For each legislative or administrative action or subject the principal spends more than 10% of his or her time lobbying on, an estimate of the time spent lobbying on it. Daily itemized record of time spent lobbying, segregated by: meetings with officials; research and preparation. Names of principal employees who is not a lobbyist, but devoted time to lobbying communications. Names of officials to whom certain reimbursements were paid, amount and date. Expenses for personal travel and living expenses except for those of unpaid volunteers whose primary traveling purpose is other than lobbying.
Wyoming 28-7-201 *(Accurate for legislative lobbyists only)*	**Lobbyists, Principals**
	Funding sources providing more than $500. Each loan, gift, gratuity, special discount or hospitality given to or on behalf of any legislator, state elected official or state employee more than $50.00, date, amount, name of public official. Include special events costing more than $500 to which legislators, members of any committee or any regional legislative delegation have been invited with the total expense, the group of legislators invited. Funding provided by any person or on behalf of the employer of the person to defray the cost of a meeting of any national or regional legislative organization shall not be reported. Any loan, gift, gratuity, special discount or hospitality paid or given to a bona fide charity or to defray the cost of a bona fide charitable event shall not be reported

Appendix E
The Initiative Process

Source: National Conference of State Legislatures

Initiative and Referendum States

State	Statues		Constitution
	Initiative	Popular Referendum	Initiative
Alaska	I*	Yes	None
Arizona	D	Yes	D
Arkansas	D	Yes	D
California	D	Yes	D
Colorado	D	Yes	D
Florida	None	No	D
Idaho	D	Yes	None
Illinois	None	No	D
Maine	I	Yes	None
Maryland	None	Yes	None
Massachusetts	I	Yes	I
Michigan	I	Yes	D
Mississippi	None	No	I
Missouri	D	Yes	D
Montana	D	Yes	D
Nebraska	D	Yes	D
Nevada	I	Yes	D
New Mexico	None	Yes	None
North Dakota	D	Yes	D
Ohio	I	Yes	D
Oklahoma	D	Yes	D
Oregon	D	Yes	D
South Dakota	D	Yes	D
Utah	D & I	Yes	None
Washington	D & I	Yes	None
Wyoming	I*	Yes	None
US Virgin Is.	I	Yes	I

Initiative—a law and/or constitutional amendment introduced by the citizens either to the legislature or directly to the voters.

D—*Direct Initiative*; proposals that qualify go directly on the ballot

I—*Indirect Initiative*; proposals are submitted to the legislature, which has an opportunity to act on the proposed legislation. Depending on the state, the initiative question may go on the ballot if the legislature rejects it, submits a different proposal or takes no action.

I*—Alaska and Wyoming's initiative processes are usually considered indirect. However, instead of requiring that an initiative be submitted to the legislature for action, they only require that an initiative cannot be placed on the ballot until after a legislative session has convened and adjourned.

Referendum—a process by which voters may express their judgment on statutes and/or constitutional amendments enacted by the legislature.

Appendix F
Legislative Pay

Source: National Conference of State Legislatures

2010 State Legislator Compensation and Living Expense Allowances during Session

State	Base Salary (annual or daily rate)	Session Per Diem Rate
Alabama	$10/day (C)	$3,958/month plus $50/day for three days during each week that the legislature actually meets during any session (U).
Alaska	$50,400/year	$189 or $234 /day (depending on the time of year) tied to federal rate. Legislators who reside in the Capitol area receive 75% of the federal rate.
Arizona	$24,000/year	$35/day for the 1st 120 days of regular session and for special session and $10/day thereafter. Members residing outside Maricopa County receive an additional $25/day for the 1st 120 days of reg. session and for special session and an additional $10/day thereafter (V). Set by statute.
Arkansas	$15,362/year	$136/day (V) plus mileage tied to federal rate.
California	$95,291/year	$173.00 per day for each day they are in session.
Colorado	$30,000/year	$45/day for members living in the Denver metro area. $99/day for members living outside Denver (V). Set by the legislature.
Connecticut	$28,000/year	No per diem is paid.
Delaware	$41,680/year	$7,334 expense allowance annually.
Florida	$29,697/year	$133/day for House and $133 for Senate (V) tied to federal rate. Earned based on the number of days in session. Travel vouchers are filed to substantiate.
Georgia	$17,342/year	$173/day (U) set by the Legislative Services Committee.
Hawaii	$48,708/year	$150/day for members living outside Oahu during session; $120/day for members living outside Oahu during interim while conducting legislative business; $10/day for members living on Oahu during the interim while conducting official legislative business.
Idaho	$16,116/year	$122/day for members establishing second residence in Boise; $49/day if no second residence is established and up to $25/day travel (V) set by Compensation Commission.
Illinois	$67,836/year	$139/per session day.
Indiana	$22,616.46/year	$138/day (U) tied to federal rate.
Iowa	$25,000/year	$137/day (U). $102.75/day for Polk County legislators (U) set by the legislature to coincide with federal rate. State mileage rates apply.

State	Base Salary (annual or daily rate)	Session Per Diem Rate
Kansas	$88.66(C)	$116/day (U) tied to federal rate.
Kentucky	$186.73/day (C)	$119.90/day (U) tied to federal rate (110% Federal per diem rate).
Louisiana	$16,800/year + additional $6,000/year (U) expense allowance	$159/day (U) tied to federal rate (26 U.S.C. Section 162(h)(1)(B)(ii)).
Maine	$13,526/year for first regular session; $9,661/year for second regular session.	$38/day housing, or mileage and tolls in lieu of housing (at rate of $0.44/mile up to $38/day) plus $32/day for meals. Per diem limits are set by statute.
Maryland	$43,500/year	Lodging $96/day; meals $32/day (V) tied to federal rate and compensation commission. $225/day for out of state travel. Includes meals and lodging.
Massachusetts	$58,237.15 /year	From $10/day-$100/day, depending on distance from State House (V) set by the legislature.
Michigan	$79,650/year	$12,000 yearly expense allowance for session and interim (V) set by compensation commission.
Minnesota	$31,140.90/year	Senators receive $96/day and Representatives receive $77/legislative day (U) set by the legislature/Rules Committee.
Mississippi	$10,000/year	$116/day (U) tied to federal rate.
Missouri	$35,915/year	$103.20/day (U) tied to federal rate. Verification of per diem is by roll call.
Montana	$82.64/day (L)	103.69/day (U).
Nebraska	$12,000/year	$109/day outside 50-mile radius from Capitol; $39/day if member resides within 50 miles of Capitol (V) tied to federal rate.
Nevada	$146.90/day maximum of 60 days of session for holdover Senators, $146.29/day for all other legislators.	Federal rate for Capitol area (U). Legislators who live more than 50 miles from the capitol, if require lodging, will be paid Hud single-room rate for Carson City area for each month of session.
New Hampshire	$200/two-year term	No per diem is paid.
New Jersey	$49,000/year	No per diem is paid.
New Mexico	None	$159/day (V) tied to federal rate & the constitution.
New York	$79,500/year	Varies (V) tied to federal rate.
North Carolina	$13,951/year	$104/day (U) set by statute. $559.00/month expense allowance.
North Dakota	$141/day ($148/day effective 7/1/10) during legislative sessions (C)	Lodging reimbursement up to $1,040/month (V).
Ohio	$60,584/year	No per diem is paid.
Oklahoma	$38,400/year	$150/day (U) tied to federal rate.
Oregon	$21,612/year	$116/day (U) tied to federal rate.

State	Base Salary (annual or daily rate)	Session Per Diem Rate
Pennsylvania	$78,314.66/year	$154 GSA Method $163 IRS High/Low Method.
Rhode Island	$13,089.44/year	No per diem is paid.
South Carolina	$10,400/year	$131/day for meals and housing for each statewide session day and committee meeting tied to federal rate.
South Dakota	$12,000/two-year term	$110/legislative day (U) set by the legislature.
Tennessee	$19,009/year	$185/legislative day (U) tied to federal rate.
Texas	$7,200/year	$168/day (U) set by Ethics Commission.
Utah	$117/day (C)	$106/day (U) lodging allotment for each calendar day, tied to federal rate, $61/day meals (U).
Vermont	$636.62/week during session; $118 per day for special sessions or interim committee meetings	Federal per diem rate for Montpelier is $101/day for lodging and $61/day for meals for non-commuters; commuters receive $61/day for meals plus mileage.
Virginia	$18,000/year Senate, $17,640/year House	House - $135/day (U) tied to federal rate. Senate $169 (U) tied to federal rate.
Washington	$42,106/year	$90/day
West Virginia	$20,000/year	$131/day during session (U) set by compensation commission.
Wisconsin	$49,943/year	$88/day maximum (U) set by compensation commission (90% of federal rate). Per diem authorized under 13.123 (1), Wis. Statutes, and Leg. Joint Rule 85. 20.916(8) State Statutes and Joint Committee on Employment Relations (JCOER) establishes the max. amount according to the recommendations of the Director of the Office of State Employment Relations. The leadership of each house then determines, within that maximum, what amount to authorize for the session.
Wyoming	$150/day (L)	$109/day (V) set by the legislature, includes travel days for those outside of Cheyenne.

Index

reform, 87–91
reporters, 100
researching problems and solutions, 87–91
resolutions, 127–28
Ritter, Bill, 82
running for office, 137–39

S

samples: bill, 27–28; budget narrative, 126; budget organization, 125; budget summary chart, 125; e-mail, 57; fact sheet, 67, 68–69; fiscal note, 116, 117–119; letter, 60; media plan, 104; opposition tracker, 76; petition, 63; press release, 105; supporter tracker, 75; telephone scripts, 54; vote count, 108
SEBEC (strike everything below the enacting clause), 113
separation of powers, 87
severed amendments, 112
Shuyler, Ashley, 80
Skolnik, Michael, 80–83
Skolnik, Patty & David, 80–83
social media outlets, 34, 78, 134
specialty boards, 88
sponsors, of bills, 23, 91, 94, 95
state budgets, 123–24, 126
state government, 87–88, 141–42
statutes, 24–25
statutory citations, in bills, 26
strike everything below the enacting clause (SEBEC), 113
substitute amendments, 112
support: for bills, 97–98; coalition of supporters, 73–74; of issues, 29–31; public support, 99–103; sample tracker, 75
surveys, 78

T

telephoning: legislators, 17, 31, 53–54, 78; sample scripts, 54
television, 101
term limits, 4, 7
testifying, 37–39, 94
testimony, 17, 21, 37–39, 94

threats, 30, 50
Tochtrop, Lois, 82
town hall meetings, 50, 78, 133
Twitter, 34, 78

U

unintended consequences, 111

V

Vann, Greg, 135
voice votes, 46
volunteering, 50, 133
vote counting: on amendments, 113; on bills, 38, 94, 107–9; sample, 108
voting, citizens and, 134
voting records, of legislators, 142

W

Web broadcasts, of public proceedings, 22
witness-protection programs, 135–36
Wolfe, Christine, 135–36
Wolfe, Vivian, 135–36
writing: editors, 78; legislators, 31, 59

Y

youth, advocacy for, 79–80

Notes